Performative Intergenerational Dialogues of a Black Quartet

Performative Intergenerational Dialogues of a Black Quartet promotes the importance of intergenerational Black dialogue as a collaborative spirit-making across race, genders, sexualities, and cultures to bridge time and space.

The authors enter this dialogue in a crisis moment: a crisis moment at the confluence of a pandemic, the national political transition of leadership in the United States, the necessary rise of Black, Indigenous, and People of Color activism—in the face of the continued murders of unarmed Black and queer people by police. And as each author mourns the loss of loved ones who have left us through illness, the contiguity of time, or murder, we all hold tight to each other and to memory as an act of keeping them alive in our hearts and actions, remembrance as an act of resistance so that the circle will be unbroken. But they also come together in the spirit of hope, the hope that bleeds the borders between generations of Black teacher-artist-scholars, the hope that we find in each other's joy and laughter, and the hope that comes when we hear both stories of struggle and strife and stories of celebration and smile that lead to possibilities and potentialities of our collective being and becoming—as a people.

So, the authors offer stories of witness, resistance, and gettin' ovah, stories that serve as a road map from Black history and heritage to a Black futurity that is mythic and imagined but that can also be actualized and embodied, now. This book will be of interest to scholars, students, and activists in a wide range of disciplines across the social sciences and performance studies.

Bryant Keith Alexander is a professor and dean in the College of Communication and Fine Arts and an interim dean in the School of Film and Television at Loyola Marymount University, USA. He is coauthor of *Still Hanging: Using Performance Texts to Deconstruct Racism* and *Collaborative Spirit-Writing and Performance in Everyday Black Lives*.

Mary E. Weems is a poet, playwright, scholar, and author of 14 books, including *Blackeyed: Plays and Monologues* and five chapbooks. Weems was awarded a 2015 Cleveland Arts Prize for her full-length drama *MEAT* and has also been nominated for a Pushcart Prize. She is coauthor of *Still Hanging:*

Using Performance Texts to Deconstruct Racism and *Collaborative Spirit-Writing and Performance in Everyday Black Lives*. Weems may be reached at www. maryeweems.org.

Dominique C. Hill, PhD, is a creative and vulnerability guide whose scholarship interrogates Black embodiment with foci in Black girlhood, education, and performance. An artist-scholar, Hill is an assistant professor of Women's Studies at Colgate University and is the coauthor of *Who look at me?!: Shifting the Gaze of Education Through Blackness, Queerness, and the Body*.

Durell M. Callier, PhD, is an associate professor in the Department of Educational Leadership at Miami University. An artist-scholar, he researches and interrogates the lived experience of Black youth and the racialized queer dynamics of power within educative spaces. He is coauthor of *Who look at me?!: Shifting the Gaze of Education Through Blackness, Queerness, and the Body*.

ICQI Foundations and Futures in Qualitative Inquiry
Series Editors: Michael Giardina and Norman K. Denzin.

From autoethnography, observation, and arts-based research to poststructural, new materialist, and post-qualitative inquiry, interdisciplinary conversations about the practices, politics, and philosophies of qualitative inquiry have never been stronger or more dynamic. Edited by Michael D. Giardina and Norman K. Denzin and sponsored by the International Congress of Qualitative Inquiry (www.ICQI.org), the Foundations and Futures in Qualitative Inquiry series showcases works from the most experienced and field-defining qualitative researchers in the world. Engaging critical questions of epistemology, ontology, and axiology, the series is designed to provide cornerstone texts for different modes and methods in qualitative inquiry. Books in series will serve the growing number of students, academics, and researchers who utilize qualitative approaches to inquiry in university courses, research, and applied settings.

Volumes in this series:

Performative Intergenerational Dialogues of a Black Quartet
Qualitative Inquiries on Race, Gender, Sexualities, and Culture
Bryant Keith Alexander, Mary E. Weems, Dominique C. Hill and Durell M. Callier

Advances in Autoethnography and Narrative Inquiry
Reflections on the Legacy of Carolyn Ellis and Arthur Bochner
Edited by Tony E. Adams, Robin M. Boylorn and Lisa M. Tillmann

Wayfinding and Critical Autoethnography
Fetaui Iosefo, Stacy Holman Jones and Anne Harris

For a full list of titles in this series, please visit: www.routledge.com/International-Congress-of-Qualitative-Inquiry-ICQI-Foundations-and-Futures/book-series/ICQIFF

Performative Intergenerational Dialogues of a Black Quartet

Qualitative Inquiries on Race, Gender, Sexualities, and Culture

Bryant Keith Alexander,
Mary E. Weems, Dominique C. Hill,
and Durell M. Callier

Routledge
Taylor & Francis Group

LONDON AND NEW YORK

Cover image: The cover image designed by Jane Frances Tse, an undergraduate Studio Arts major at Loyola Marymount University, is intended to pay homage to the cover of the 1970 book *A Black Quartet* by Ben Caldwell, Ronald Milner, Ed Bullins, and Leroi Jones (Amiri Baraka). The authors of *Performative Intergenerational Dialogues of a Black Quartet* (Alexander, Weems, Hill and Callier) pay tribute and libation to the plays of Caldwell, Milner, Bullins and Jones in Section 1 of this book.

First published 2023
by Routledge
4 Park Square, Milton Park, Abingdon, Oxon OX14 4RN

and by Routledge
605 Third Avenue, New York, NY 10158

Routledge is an imprint of the Taylor & Francis Group, an informa business

© 2023 Bryant Keith Alexander, Mary E. Weems, Dominique C. Hill, and Durell M. Callier

The right of Bryant Keith Alexander, Mary E. Weems, Dominique C. Hill, and Durell M. Callier to be identified as authors of this work has been asserted in accordance with sections 77 and 78 of the Copyright, Designs and Patents Act 1988.

British Library Cataloguing-in-Publication Data
A catalogue record for this book is available from the British Library

Library of Congress Cataloging-in-Publication Data
A catalog record for this book has been requested

ISBN: 978-1-032-22816-7 (hbk)
ISBN: 978-1-032-22818-1 (pbk)
ISBN: 978-1-003-27431-5 (ebk)

DOI: 10.4324/9781003274315

Typeset in Bembo
by Apex CoVantage, LLC

Dedication

We come together as a Black Quartet, four Black persons with PhDs, in voice and volition, in writing and righting the past toward our collective futures. In doing so, we give thanks, honor, and praise to those who came before us—the famous Black and Brown authors, and the Black and Brown Queer authors, whose words and wisdom sparked our passion for writing and who historicized the Black and Brown experience in poetry and prose, in rhythm and rhyme, and in theory and praxis: the activists and athletes who gave resistance feet and put poetry into motion, the dancers and movement artists who choreographed for People of Color recognizing our distinct cultural movements and the travels of our bodies, Black politicians and politicos who enacted laws so we can be represented and be invited to vote, and the singers and performers who told the stories of our lives in song and character. And we thank those everyday heroes—the familial folks, those who are still living and those who have long pass; those who sacrificed and struggled; those who have influenced our lives through bondage, Bible, and blood, through wisdom and wit, through example and exposition; the old folks and the young folks who tie us together in communion bridging the generational gap.

Throughout this volume of interlocking stories, you are all recognized and remembered. Read yourselves throughout each page and know that we remember, as we are consistently re-membering ourselves to you—as we keep our collective legacy of survival moving forward.

Bryant, Mary, Dominique, Durell

Contents

Performative Intergenerational Dialogues

An Introduction

The Black Quartet

An Introduction

The 1970 book *A Black Quartet* is a collection of four emerging Black playwrights: Ben Caldwell, Ronald Milner, Ed Bullins, and LeRoi Jones. The subtitle of the book states: "A revolution is now taking place on stage." The book presented four new Black plays from the Black playwrights, including "Prayer Meeting or, The First Militant Minister"—A One-Act Play by Ben Caldwell, "The Warning—A Theme for Linda"—A One-Act Play in Four Scenes by Ronald Milner, "The Gentleman Caller"—A Parable in One Act by Ed Bullins, and "Great Goodness of Life"—A Coon Show by LeRoi Jones. The back cover of the book reads, in part, "*For the first time American black playwrights have found their own true voice—and are using it. With pride. With confidence. With defiance. With awesome power.*"

This current project signifies on the importance of the originating *Black Quartet* book, a collection of plays, as a hallmark of Black theater excellence—to extend the dialogue through the prisms and potentialities of four Black teacher-artist-scholars operating within the constructions of higher education and as public intellectuals. The teacher-artist-scholars presented here—Bryant Keith Alexander, Mary E. Weems, Dominique C. Hill, and Durell M. Callier—come together in dialogue. We come together in an intergenerational Black dialogue on issues of *race, gender, sexualities, and culture* while expressing and scrutinizing aspects of Black lived experience for both self and others.

Each teacher-artist-scholar enters this project with a passion to do the critical, intellectual, and academic work of our disciplines through a culturally political frame that resonates with both celebration and concern on the continued Black struggle in everyday life and in the academic environs of our labor, which are not separate; each mandates an accountability to/of the other. A mandate to attend to the struggle and vulnerability of Blackness and Black bodies from the streets to the ivory tower and back, always attending to the fragile strength of Black femininity, Black masculinity, Black queerness, and the importance of Black straight-gay alliances in the Black community, asking the question: What is our responsibility to each other?

DOI: 10.4324/9781003274315-1

One of the arguments of ***Performative Intergenerational Dialogues of a Black Quartet*** is a commentary on why we stay and why we leave academia and how we use our bodies to bridge the boundaries of our habits and habitus. Another argument is developed in direct address and performative resistance about the academic constrictions on thought/style/scholarship/writing/ expression and publication in ways that are both literal and figurative. Publication as both the strictures of scholarly/academic writing—and the performative aspects of being public intellectuals that use varying modalities to reach diverse audiences including *the souls of Black folks*. Each entry in this new Black diary offers a performative response to the questions it asks as we perform private resistance through embodied forms of writing, making both the joy and discontent of our lives public.

This project gives homage to the originating trope of ***A Black Quartet***, both in name and in reference; themes of Black liberation, Black resistance, and Black empowerment resound throughout the project through our intersectional identities—with each author spending time to reflect on one of the contributions from the originating *black quartet* as we build new texts that narrate Black experiences. The project is structured through a series of interactive and dialogical mo(ve)ments, both actual staged dialogues between the authors in varying configurations, as well as performative texts—poetry, narrative, and dramatic plays (all original to the authors)—that always speak to/with/in/at the broader dialogue of the interactive texts on Black expressive arts and Black excellence—but particularly with/to and through these very particular Black persons.

In this volume of creative, performative, and autoethnographic texts the authors claim and promote the importance of intergenerational Black dialogue as a *collaborative spirit-making*. In many ways, the authors enter this dialogue in a crisis moment: a crisis moment at the confluence of a pandemic; the slow and disproportionate rate of vaccinations to address the COVID-19 pandemic that is disproportionately impacting Black and Brown people; the national political transition of leadership in the United States; the necessary rise of Black, Indigenous, and People of Color (BIPOC) activism—especially that of the monumental inroads of the Black Lives Matter movement, which has catalyzed national discourse and action related to diversity, equity, inclusion, and antiracism initiatives around the United States; and yet the continued murders of unarmed Black people, oftentimes wrestling with mental health, by police. And as each author mourns the loss of loved ones who have left us through illness or murder, we all hold tight to each other and to memory—as an act of keeping them alive in our hearts and actions, of remembrance as an act of resistance so that *the circle will be unbroken*. But we also come together in the spirit of hope: the hope that bleeds the borders between generations of Black teacher-artist-scholars, the hope that we find in each other's joy and laughter, the hope that comes when we hear both stories of struggle and strife and stories of celebration and smile—that lead to possibilities and potentialities of our collective being and becoming—as a people. So, we tell stories not just of the struggled past, which is important, but stories of triumphant and stories of *gettin' ovah*, stories that serve as a road map for a Black futurity that is not only mythic or imagined but that can also be actualized and embodied now.

The project moves out of a mournfulness into an action of transmission, that which happens in the intergenerational dialogues between Black people through struggle and recognition of how far we have come. We re-member ourselves to those times and moments in which the elders narrated the history of Black struggle in America, the banality of everyday experiences of triumph and survival, as well as the close examination of the DNA of generational knowledge about heritage, about relations and relationality, about blood lines, about disorders and diseases, about psychologies of knowing the self through the history of "our people" and "your people." And conversely, the intergenerational dialogue in which the next generation, *the young, gifted and Black* move into the White Ivory Tower as a bridge to the Black community, lifting as they climb to give knowledge back and to bring knowledge forward to co-inform the evolving history of Black people on both sides; no longer crabs in a barrel, we stand on the shoulders of one and then reach back for another. And while this engagement is constructed as "intergenerational," with Bryant and Mary claiming a few years ahead of Dominique and Durell—time is blended and bent in our dialogues. Age, gender, and sexuality are foregrounded in our particularity and plurality as Black people to offer a broad view of community.

We open this project with the first dialogical performance piece of our Black quartet. The following piece was first performed on Saturday, May 22, 2021, at the International Congress of Qualitative Inquiry anchored at the University of Illinois–Champaign but delivered in the mandated virtual sphere due to the global pandemic. This collaborative performance converges at the meeting of our individual work that was brought together for a performance opportunity. But it also serves as a culmination of years of informal dialogue, years of citing and reciting each other's work in other realms, years of watching and witnessing each other as Black people with a body of scholarly and creative work that is both extensive and emerging: a body of work that is informing and enlightening; a body of work that teases and taunts social structures of Black lived experience in a white-dominating society; a body of work that speaks to and across issues of race, gender, sexuality, and culture through the pragmatics of pedagogy and through performance and performative writing as modalities of enculturation and communication, as embodied forms of resistance.

Black Quartet: A Performance Script

Performers in order of engagement: Mary E. Weems, Dominique C. Hill, Durell M. Callier, Bryant Keith Alexander.

We set the tone using sound, movement, and gestures, inviting the audience into an experience.

To embody the quartet, we build in transitions of lines, movements, gestures of synchronicity and flow. The aesthetics help conjoin the individual pieces, generate the intended energy, and steward a process and experience both for the performers and the audience.

Figure 1 Black Quartet in Performance

   The performance begins with Mary E. Weems soulfully humming, then a loose groove of choreographic movement by Dominique, a desirous and yet gasping breathing by Durell, and then a direct line delivered by Bryant that speaks to Black struggle. The same rhythmicity and synchronicity are simulated at the end with a found poem that blends and intersplices the text of each presenter in the text as an interactive dialogue within a Black quartet.

   All performers wear black attire, with Mary E. Weems and Dominique C. Hill wearing wraps on their heads.

   A patterned dark, black-and-white, kente cloth print is consistently used as background for each of the four Zoom room frames of the quartet. Relative to Zoom technology, the imagery of the black-and-white kente cloth print may vary in each space—as exclusive background or mapped onto the black attire of the performer or performers—suggesting an African-inspired kente attire on body and headdress.

   Each performer has a beverage of choice in a medium-sized Mason jar. The beverage is a practical refresh engaged with at differing times in the performance, often at the beginning of speaking parts and transitions. The Mason jar is a Black colloquialism that the performers share as aspects of practical Black experiences—in which Mason jars signify traditions of homemade preserves and jams, everyday tableware, and drinking receptacles, along with jelly jars. To engage such use of the Mason jars is to signify a shared aspect of performative blackness.

Preamble

Mary symbolically enters: Humming sequence completed with a clap.

   Dominique enters: (after Mary's first clap—swaying and continues through humming sequence.)

Durell enters: (after Mary's second clap—breathing out loud at desired pace).

Bryant enters: (after Mary's third clap, he states aloud): Everyday something has tried to kill me and has failed.

(Mary completes humming sequence, and after she offers a double clap, all performers freeze.)

All performers speak the following line in a staggered sequence activating on duty:

Dominique:	It is our **duty** to fight for our freedom / It is our duty to win / We must love eachother and support each other / We have nothing to lose but our chains.
Bryant:	It is our **duty** to fight for our freedom / It is our duty to win / We must love each other and support each other / We have nothing to lose but our chains.
Durell:	It is our **duty** to fight for our freedom / It is our duty to win / We must love each other and support each other / We have nothing to lose but our chains.
Mary:	It is our duty to fight for our freedom / It is our duty to win / We must love each other and support each other / We have nothing to lose but our chains. *(As Mary's delivery of the line ends, Dominique begins.)*
Bryant:	Everyday something has tried to kill me and has failed.

Dominique ("Tough Skin")[1]

Like my grandma's swaying hips, I (re)membered to groove. On the way to write in the park, I made an impromptu left turn to play at the StoneQuarry Art Park. Somewhere between collecting dissertation data and learning my mother was diagnosed with stage four stomach cancer, between (re)membering that I'd spent time in juvenile detention and writing about it for the world to see, somewhere in and between the crevices of these moments, groove surfaced as an important tool. It stood in the gaps, an instead of settling, conforming.

Taking seriously Assata Shakur's insistence that "we have nothing to lose but our chains" and my mother's advice to acquire tough skin, groove[ing] is a form of living resistance. Non-prescriptive, fluid, embrace of the present, a process, a way forward, an invitation to attune to our visceral and guttural yearnings. Like a song on repeat, my mother's insistence, *you gone needta get some tough skin* is verse one of the unreleased but real song, "They don't want you to know your power." It is the story passed down from and through my mother into my body and called on while living in these repressive times.

Lesson: Your Freedom Will Require Tough Skin

If you want to make it in this world, you gone needta get some tough skin. This was my mother's insistence when I told her that my classmate, more specifically their mother, referred to me as a nigger. Gearing up for my sixth birthday

party, I wrote out invitations and passed them out in class. Anxiously awaiting RSVPs, I asked my classmates whether they planned to attend. The typi-
cal five-year-old questions came: Would I have games, and what kind? Will
there be food? Is so and so coming? Did they have to bring a gift? One of my
white classmates, let's call her Sarah, asked a grown-up question: What side of
William Street is the YMCA on? Is it closer to downtown or closer to Cheek-
towaga? Digging, I learned that Sarah had initially been given permission to
come to my party until her mom remembered the shifting demographic of this
street that cut across the city.

Sarah's mother wanted to know, did I live on the Black or white side of
the city? Was I Black or white? Perhaps Sarah's parent didn't want to expose
their child to an "adult" conversation, the pains of racism, their racial bias, or
some combination. Instead, Sarah was sent back to school to inquire, and my
responses determined that Sarah could not attend my party. Sarah did not likely
plan for the harm messengered in, the lesson my mother gave, or the tune
I hear on repeat in spaces soiled with isms and schisms for rendering me "the
other." And this was white fragility, racism, an example of how Black folk are
expected to be more mature, but that is not the point. The point being I went
back to my mother's "you gone needta get some tough skin" with new eyes,
experiences, and an older, Black body.

Instruction: Get Up and Go Live

Sitting on the porch, eyes filled with rivers and lips laying on my lap, my
mother offered guidance on the necessity of Blackgxrl (now Blackgxrlwomxn)
resistance. She demanded that I "get up," "wipe my eyes," and "go play." I don't
remember their order. As I look back, my mother was teaching me how to
resist. She gifted me the steps for living whole in a world that despises Blackness, a world I learned would also gawk at my audacity to be a Black lesbian
with "decolonial sensibilities."

The darkest sister of four and the darkest in our family 'til I arrived, my
mother, also referred to as Brown Bomber, developed some tough skin of her
own. She be a practitioner of the area. Growing tough skin lives in her garden.
Each time I revisit this moment, I see it vividly, looking up at her and saying
"no" multiple times before she urged, "If you want to make it in this world,
you gone needta get some tough skin." The specific questions she asked never
come back to me; I presume them inconsequential to her message. Essential,
however, is that making it in this world in this body requires a certain skill
set—crafting armor and recovering and medicine—play. To have tough skin
is to be able to withstand pervasive and invasive things like racism, sexism,
homophobia, racial-sexual oppression. To have tough skin is to have the capacity and audacity to stand face-to-face with unfavorable gazes and see yourself
beyond the limits of their imagination. To *make it* requires a groundedness and
a willingness to fight, to live life on our own terms. To make it is to traverse life
with deliberateness, mindfulness, and rhythm.

I thought my mother insensitive, mean, and all the things you say about a woman with tough but not-so-tough skin. I now understand my mother's insistence, to *keep on moving*, as an invitation to move out of my sorrows and into something that gave me joy. Although not by name, my mother was introducing me to groove(ing). Her instructions were clear: *You gone needta get some tough skin.* Living and worrying about what folk think cannot coexist. Which will you choose?

So, I went to play in the dirt. And this time, I didn't go alone. As I ran through the open fields into what was marked as "the secret garden," looking back to bat an eye, smile, and connect with my partner, I opened. Next to and inside of art pieces, I started to move my body, undulating, releasing, breathing. I wanted to discover the shapes we could make together while unbothered about who was witnessing. I danced to the tune of nature and with the sun's help and my commitment to groove(ing), my skin darkened, our love deepened, and I (re)membered my mother's, my great-grandma's, my family's garden—love and tough skin grow there.

Durell: Everyday something has tried to kill me and has failed.

Bryant (Black Notes): I Have Been Thinking a Lot About "Black Notes"[2]

Black notes scribbled on the walls of "The Door of No Return" in the African slave trade leading across the Middle Passage, messages written in words, scratches, tears, shit, piss, and wails that trigger and reverberate the Black notes of our existence.

Like the Shroud of Turin, Black notes leave a negative image of the scourged and crucified history of our people, produced by the alchemy of (white) man's inhumanity to (Black) wo/man, biochemical residue from body oils and intense spiritual energy activated on the tapestry of our lives create the ghosting image of African slave bodies in the bowels of ships—seamlessly pressed against each other, against the wooden surfaces of their captivity, melding and melting on the chains of their restraint. The lashing belts and whips to their backs creating a dirge of pain, and *the tracks of their tears* (think Smokey Robinson):

> Refrain of the lash followed by the verse of pain.
> Refrain of the lash followed by the verse of pain.
> Refrain of the lash followed by the verse of pain, with a *haunting musicality*.

All striking a chord of inhumanity pressed against the will to survive.

These are documentations, remembrances, and reminders, tortured discordant Black notes that resonate dissonance over distance, echoing over time to the present—like the cries of our brother Eric Garner:

> "I Can't Breathe!"
> "I Can't Breathe!"
> "I Can't Breathe!"

"I Can't Breathe!"
"I Can't Breathe!"
"I Can't Breathe!"
"I Can't Breathe!"
"I Can't Breathe!"
"I Can't Breathe!"
"I Can't Breathe!"

Eleven times before losing consciousness and dying. (July 17, 2014, Eric Garner murdered)

★★★★★★

I Have Been Thinking a Lot About "Black notes."

Dancing Black notes on a social grid with a lot of white space.

I am thinking about "Black Notes," the Black American jazz ensemble, and so many other Black ensembles remembered by *people of a certain age* like *The Temptations, Earth Wind and Fire, The Isley Brothers, The Whispers. . .* just to name a few.

These were coordinated and choreographed Black notes that embodied and promoted the culture with style and grace but not without having to traverse the borderlines of race that penetrated every aspect of their musical journeys as Black people in America.

Yet they persisted as storytellers of the Black experience through Black notes and expressive arts. And I am also thinking about those Black gospel voices that twisted and trailed Black notes with vocal trills, tremolos, and trivolettes that twist and turn and sustained notes with natural vibratos: people like *Mahalia Jackson, Sissy Houston, The Mighty Clouds of Joy, The Dixie Hummingbirds,* the original *Five Blind Boys of Alabama. . .* —all *holding God in their throat.*[1]

I have been thinking about the power in Black musical traditions, trumpeting and wailing tones from *voices as instruments* and *instruments as voices,* amplifying the Black experience in this country: spirituals, jazz, blues, hip-hop, rhythm and blues, rap, reggae . . . sounds and words and expressions that make the soul leap, the spirit weep, and the body sway.

Sway in such a way that the polyrhythms of our ancestral bodies illustrate a communicative musicality that is ancient, flowing from rich places beyond the cognitive and deep within the blood lines that we can trace back, back to the places from which we were snatched.

★★★★★★

I have been thinking a lot about "Black notes" in the collaborative spirit writing with our ancestors and between Mary and me and Dominique and Durell in our particularity and plurality.

I have been thinking about the ways in which Black notes are necessarily different from white notes—one is necessarily seen, sometimes considered conspicuous, under surveillance, behind bars, hanging on bars, and considered unruly.

Black notes, as related to Black people, are sometime considered loud, very loud, too loud, and hence uncivil to the Western or European canon—even when we are crying for help in everyday life through our music.

Not to be reductive, but the opposite of Black notes is *white noise*: "a colloquialism to describe a backdrop of ambient sound, creating an indistinct commotion, seamless in such way no specific sounds composing it as a continuum can be isolated as a veritable" (*google "White Noise"*).

. . .

★★★★★★

I have been thinking a lot about Black notes like love letters to Black people: the kind of notes written in secret code that only Black people can read, the kind of notes that you slip in the school locker of your secret crush, or the kind of notes that you secretly pass around announcing the meeting behind the barn at midnight but also the loud stereophonic Black notes that you deliver in the music blasting out of your car—that makes white folks turn their heads but make other Black folks say, "Yeah you're right!"

Black notes that say, "I see my blackness. I see your blackness."

And then authorizing yourself, your brothers, and your sisters (and those who live in between) to join with James Brown and sing, *"Say It Loud—I'm Black and I'm Proud"*—without apology.

Mary: Everyday something has tried to kill me and has failed.

Durell (Feelin' Real / Unbroken)[3]

I. Blackqueer like me

(Cue "Mother to Son" recited by Martin Luther King Jr [begins at 18:40 and plays in background, begin to recite after "profundity," adjust volume low].)[4]

Nobody ever told me Langston Hughes was queer, queer akin to the definition offered in *Black Like Us*. Edited by Carbado, McBride, and Weise (2002), *Black Like Us* was the first collection to amass a century of lesbian, gay, and bisexual African American fiction. The editors, in their preface, defined *queer* as signifying "identity and ideological nonconformity—not a particular sexual orientation," elaborating that the African American writers within were

> **queer** in terms of how they defined and embodied their racial identity, queer in terms of their conception and performance of their gender, **queer** in how they articulated and practiced politics, as well as **queer** in their intimate relationships and sense of sexual identity.
>
> (Carbado, McBride & Weise, 2002, p. xiv–xv)

When I first learned of *Black Like Us*, I was elated. My twenties were filled with coming into a sense of myself, my queerness, not just in terms of my sexual orientation but in all the ways I was queer and queered by normalizing institutions of power. Knowing that the collection existed, a history of evidence, of survival of a fuller view of our community and humanity was a gift.

The gift of meeting each of these authors, kin, was welcomed with excitement. *Black Like Us* opened up new registers of other beloved authors such as Langston Hughes, Hughes, whom I dressed up as for our annual Black History Month Celebration in third grade.

<pause>

The year is 1993. Black History Month was one of my favorite times of year, and I am teeming with excitement. All that excitement, however, was short-lived as the dread of forgetting my costume washed over me. In repeatedly practicing the poem that morning, I thought of little else.

Mrs. Jazz greeted class before the assembly, checking in with each of us, going over lines, our order in the program and costumes. A hush came over the jam-packed auditorium as the assembly began.

<increase volume of audio>

Reciting *Mother to Son*, resonated deeply with me, a single mother as I imagined like mine, encouraging her son (me) to persevere because she had despite the odds. Now, reflecting on all of what we learned about Black people and our accomplishments at my mostly Black elementary school, I wish somebody had told me Langston was queer. Back before I understood my own sexuality. Back before I understood how schools' queer Black kids like me, single family households with an extended network of care also helping to raise my sister and I. Back before I endured the taunts of "gay" and "faggy," seeking to discipline my softness. I don't think my favorite third-grade teacher Mrs. Jazz knew that Langston was queer. I don't think she purposefully withheld that information from me, from us. But I wonder what difference knowing would have made?

II. Remember

<Cue "Will the Circle Be Unbroken" (Bernice Johnson Reagon; lines are delivered at will as music fades after first stanza is sung).>

In his keynote address for OutWrite 92, Melvin Dixon leaves us an admonishment and responsibility as he says:

> You, then, are charged by the possibility of your good health, by the broadness of your vision, to remember us.
>
> (Dixon, 2000, p. 83)

I am 7 years old; I do not know Melvin Dixon yet or of the many brothers, (queer) fairy godfathers, butch queens, *<snap>* snap! queens, gay black ancestors I will need someday (Hemphill 1991, 1992; Riggs 1991). Those who had already dreamed me here, possible, healthy, alive, and free. At 7, I do not know Sweet Honey and the Rock. I do know this sound.

<pause, increase volume>

The meter and tone, Sunday morning Black Baptist. Yes, Bernice, the circle will be unbroken. The younger you in black-and-white celluloid, flat tongue, wide mouthed, surefooted, you greet me. Asking, as the title of the song suggests, "will the circle be unbroken," a memorialization, dirge, (re)membering of those who have died and of those who might risk their lives in the fight towards freedom.[5] I wonder now, how do you remember those you do not know?[6] How does the circle persist even when you aren't aware of those who came before you? Of those who have gone on, now?

III. black atlantics/queer atlantics
<*Cue "You Make Me Feel (Mighty Real)" by Sylvester; music plays in background as lines are delivered, increasing in volume as lines are finished*>
What if we thought of the forced voyage of enslaved human cargo as a very *queer* thing? The feeling with and for one another not in the I want to love up on you but rather another affect—another loving—willing to nurture in the hold. To survive together in the hold. A hold(ing) is present in his voice.

> i am now in my 20s
> reaching with and for
> across other Black and Queer Atlantics
> circles unbroken not by time or space
> not by disease
> the HIV/AIDS epidemic
> not by this pandemic
> calls to physically distance

Sylvester meets me for the very first time, sonically traversing time and space, singing my song:

> *I feel real when you touch me*
> *I feel real when you kiss me*
> *I feel real when you want me*
> *I feel real when you . . .*

Isn't it marvelous how we are made real in each other's image? In each other's remembrance? Embrace? But we can't touch or kiss or want or <*breathe*>
breathe.
<*pause and sip*>

> IV. won't you
>   i am still reaching
>   with and for
>   all I know now that i did not know then
>   forforforforforfor
>   Sylvester
>   You

Melvin Dixon
    You and you
Sweet Honey and the Rock
    Black notes
    And you and you and you
    And

Lucille Clifton
who reminds me that
    "everyday something has tried to kill me and has failed"
won't you come celebrate with me
this unbroken circle

Dominique: Everyday something has tried to kill me and has failed.

Mary (Black, Black Notes)[7]

<Opens by humming no particular song, like Granny used to on the vibe, and delivers lines at will.>

Bryant Keith Alexander gets me—we connect, our spirits, conjoining, ebbing and flowing like the Nile River . . . the kind of in-spirit collaborative connection you can't construct, contrive, or make up. You can't plan it, wish for it, dream about it. If it's going to happen, it does, and while I've collaborated at some level over the years with other folks, ours is a once in a lifetime pairing, one I know I won't have again with anyone else.

When I read his new piece "Black Notes" inspired by my performance text/play about the Black experience, I immediately wrote him to share how much I love it. . . . We have a rhythm of engagement in spirit-writing—this to the point that our two recent books, *Collaborative Spirit-Writing and Performance in Everyday Black Lives* and *Still Hanging: Using Performance Texts to Deconstruct Racism* dovetailed each other "in press."

Then, as I was returning home from a dentist's appointment this afternoon, some of the lines in the work grabbed me, and as I soon as I got home, I printed the piece off, grabbed a yellow highlighter, and started spiritually vibing on lines I divided into separate sections, one per page, resulting in a textual quintet. The only lines I added to this "found poem" were the lines of song for Mahalia Jackson and Aretha Franklin. And to make the sections of the quintet fit, I occasionally altered the word, for example, from *laughing* to *laughs*.

I titled this piece "Black, black Notes" because the first Black represents Black people and the second black musical notes.

    I.

I have been thinking about "Black Notes"
    Negro Spirituals

                    Black keys on a piano
                    Slave ships.
One Black body   a history of Black bodies motion
                              in loco motion
place a spread of kente cloth   African experiencesssssssss
                    the root center of world
Black telling stories of Black
Black notes *Motherless Chile Grace* a longing for return
                    and departure
Black female body speaking   un-orchestrated groans shouts
                    Laughs
                    Cries
                    com-inggggggggg
through the spirit.

II.

I have been thinking about "Black Notes"

Scribbled on the walls of The Door   in the African slave trade
Messages written   scratches, tears, shit, piss, crucified history

Produced by the (white) man residue from body oils
intense spiritual energy   tapestry African slave bodies
pressed against each

wooden surfaces
chains, lashing belts, backs, pain, *the track of their tears*
(thank you Smokey Robinson)

Refrain pain
Refrain verse
Refrain lash
the will to survive

Remembrances   and   Reminders   Black notes
dissonance

Echoing Eric Garner:

"I can't Breathe!
I
Can't
I Can't
I Can't

I Can't
Bre
athe!!!!!!!!!!!!
Dying"

III.

I am thinking "Black Notes"

Black American jazz
remembered
people age
like *The Temptations*
coordinated and choreographed

Black notes embodied and promoted culture
with style and grace

borderlines of race
musical journeys in America

Storytellers   Black notes
expressive arts

Black Gospel twisted Black notes
trills   tremolos and trivolettes
sustained notes

Mahalia Jackson "*Precious Lord, take my hand, lead me on
      let me stand*"
Aretha Franklin "*when my soul was in the lost and found
you came along to claim it*"
hold God in their throats
their voices breathing from the souls
of Black folks.

Spirituals, jazz, blues, hip hop, rhythm and blues, rap, reggae
Expressions that make the soul weep
Body sway   ancient   rich   blood lines
We can trace to the places we were snatched.

welcome dance in the South
catch the notes in the air
bring beats back to the ground
body parts notes   rhythms
dangling new notes felt

Blood and bodies remember.

IV.

I have been thinking "Black notes"

Black notes different from white notes
in collaborative auto/ethnography
one is seen
considered conspicuous
under surveillance
behind bars hanging
and unruly musical
uncivil to Europeans
even crying everyday
through our music
the opposite of Black notes is *white noise*
a backdrop of ambient sound
indistinct commotion
a continuum

persistent promotion of white privilege
erases the nature of itself
becoming an unsound
ssssssssssssssssssssssssssssssssssssssilence

White noise is so common in the lives of Black people it fades
with no meaning   lingers
a curious non-sense   like elevator music you hate

but hum until you have to either shoot yourself
or put on some real funk
getting you on the right track of your own
Blackness.

V.

I have been thinking about Black

Love letters to Black people
notes written in secret code   only Black people can read

notes that you slip in the school locker of your secret crush notes
you secretly pass around

announcing the meeting behind the barn at midnight.

Loud stereophonic Black notes   in the music blasting out of your car
that makes white folks turn

but makes other Black folks say "Yeah!"

Black notes you play from vinyl records   albums   and 45s
when Black people come to your crib

authentic labors of love
the message the meaning of the moment

Love letters like kneeling at protest marches
raising a fist
wearing your favorite **Black Lives Matter** t-shirt to your white
workplace

Black notes that sing—h-o-p-e
Black notes that say I see your Blackness
Brothers and sisters

Say it Loud—I'm Black and I'm Proud
Without
apology.

[A Black Chorus]

Bryant:	I have been thinking a lot about "Black notes."
Mary:	I have been thinking a lot about "Black **Black** notes."
Dominique:	I have been thinking a lot about "Black notes **and Groove.**"
Durell:	I have been thinking a lot about a Black Quartet, of **straight/gay singers and poets, and artists as ancestors, black notes in an unbroken circle.**
Bryant:	Black notes scribbled on the walls of "The Door of No Return" messages written in words, scratches, tears, shit, piss, and wails that reverberate the Black notes of our existence.
Mary:	Like the Shroud of Turin, Black notes leave a negative image of the scourged and crucified history of our people, produced by the (white) man's inhumanity, residue from body oils and spiritual energy on the tapestry of our lives create the ghosting image of African slave bodies.

Durell and Dominique:	Black notes like the sound of lashing belts and whips creating pain, and *the tracks of their tears. (Sing this line.)*
Bryant:	**I am thinking about "Black Notes,"** the Black American jazz ensemble, and so many other Black ensembles remembered by *people of a certain age* like *The Temptations, Earth Wind and Fire, The Isley Brothers, The Whispers . . . (Trail off here.)*
Mary:	These were choreographed Black notes that embodied and promoted the culture with style and grace.
Durell and Dominique:	They persisted as storytellers of the Black experience.
Mary:	I have been thinking about "Black Notes" Negro Spirituals Black keys on a piano.
Durell:	Blacks telling stories of Blacks.
Dominique:	Black notes *Motherless Chile Grace* a longing for return and departure.
Mary:	Black female bod[ies] speaking groans shouts Laughs Cries com-inggggggggg.
Bryant:	I have been thinking about the ways Black notes are different from white notes in a Black quartet
Dominique:	One is seen, considered conspicuous, under surveillance, behind bars, hanging on bars, and unruly. . . . uncivil to the Western European canon—even when we are crying for help every day.
Bryant:	The opposite of Black notes is *white noise*: Noise.
Mary:	White noise so common and every day in the lives of Black people, that it fades, a repetition of the same line, musical trope with no meaning, or lingers in the memory as a curious non-sense, like elevator music you hate—
Durell:	Like elevator music you hate!
Mary:	But find yourself humming until you have to either shoot yourself or put on *Sly and Family Stones.*
Dominique:	To get some real funk (or some **GROOVE**) back into your head, getting on the right track of your blackness, not the version that is nulli-fied in white noise.

Bryant:	I have been thinking a lot about Black notes like love letters to Black people.
Durell:	The kind of notes written in secret code only Black people can read. The kind you secretly pass around announcing the meeting behind the barn at midnight. *Nobody ever told me Langston Hughes was queer.*
Bryant:	Yeah, Durell, but also the loud Black notes you deliver in the music blasting out of your car— that makes white folks turn their heads but makes other Black folks say,
Bryant and Durell:	"Yeah you're right!"
Mary:	**I have been thinking a lot about Black notes:**
	Remembrances Reminders Black notes dissonance
	Echoing Eric Garner:
Bryant:	"I Can't Breathe!
Dominique:	"I Can't . . ."
Durell:	"I Can't . . ."
Mary:	"I Can't . . ."
	"I Can't. . .
	Bre
	athe!!!!!!!!!!!
All Together:	*<Delivered like an overlapping echo>*: **Black notes from our ancestors read:**
Durell:	"Don't forget."
Bryant:	"We are with you always."
Dominique:	"We are in you, always."
Mary:	"Soul strong and spirit proud."

The End

Post-Performance Script (For the Reader)

Bryant:	In the collating of the performance script, the collaborative negotiation of staging performance in a Zoom-based environment necessitated by pandemic conditions, the actual embodied performance, and the writing of this post-performance script (p-ps)—I deepened my love and respect for Dominique, Mary, and Durell. Oh, how damn smart they are. Oh, how beautifully brilliant they are in appearance, in knowledge, in generosity of spirit, and in critical creativity. And oh, how they are always and already so familiar to

me—like family. But also, in the ways in which their performance of blackness resists the monolithic construction that is so often imposed on Black peoples. Each, Dominique, Mary, and Durell, present their personhood in ways that are both particular and plural, signifying a part of the diversity of Black people anchored in the history of our collective struggles, always pushing at the false borders that inhibit our possibility.

Mary: Beginning with our first Zoom meeting about our "Quartet" panel, I felt like the lyrics to Pharrell Williams song "Happy:"
It might seem crazy what I'm about to say.
Sunshine she's here, you can take a break
I'm a hot air balloon that can go to space.
With the air, like I don't care baby by the way.
The wonderful, taste-like-mo **craziness** of working with three other Black folks I admire, first constructing then performing what we really wanted to say, unfiltered through the lens of what will white folks think or feel as they bear witness in a conference setting, concentrating instead on the goal of our ad hoc collective to share what it means to be Black, beautiful, complex and in synch. Looking back at the image of us in our quadrant, my eyes see the squares as intersecting circles, our stories traveling on an ancestral continuum, our voices in the moment with our words, doing things we hadn't practiced, keeping Bryant's reminder to stay in the moment, in mind. The **sunshine** or light resulting from taking a break between parts to bathe in the knowledge my sista and brothas were sharing, following along with the script, anxious to jump in at my turn. The intergenerational learning from each other. Listening to the banter between Bryant and Durell, always started by Bryant reminding me of an older brother messin' with his baby brother in ways that both tease and love, like floating in **air**—our ability to create together the closest I've come to flying, Dominique's movement adding rhythm, taking me back to a youth of doing modern dance and wishing I'd kept it up.

Dominique: There. I was inside my box, inside our performance box—a quartet communicating the textures of Black notes and seeing each other, of questioning why we learned (Blackqueer) things so late, and how to stay alive, while Black, in repressive and troubled times. Though on a screen in a box, we couldn't stay in our corners. When Bryant uh huh'd, leaned in grace-filled (as if asking for more), or took a drink from his mason jar after someone's line, the visual division marked by individual boxes melted away. "We" became "A." Or when Mary's hearty laugh met a word or hip sway I offered, we became a phrase. Sometimes I got lost in the emphatic soundtrack of Durell's Blackqueer eulogy. Got lost in Mary's (re)memory of how it feels to create out of the experience of being seen (by Bryant). Got lost in the Black notes built from the process and particularity of us. One's pause made room for another's affirmation. One's shoulder shimmy invited a remixed line or two. While we all had (still have) distinct ways of being, performing, and telling it like it is, we made and became sound, the opposite of noise.

Durell: What is there to say? All of what was felt, nearly escapes words. Because this was a culmination of generations of Black scholars, of Black auto/ethnographers, of Blackity Black Black goodness, manifesting. Because this was soul-filled Black notes, filling the airwaves, creating resonances, syncopating our heartbeats to one chorus, to a collective rhythm. Because this was reunion. It was (re)connecting. Connecting. That thing we so desperately seek as *homo performans*, so desperately as we continue to grapple with the ravages of dis/ease, political unrest, and the very real fights for our very lives, for breath, for clean water, air, a living with it all. And where might living with it all begin if not in and on the Black notes, the keys between, creating sharps and flats, liner notes to this collective 45 record we cut from nothing, CliffsNotes to histories of marginalization and triumph, histories of greatness in spite of the interruption of colonization, imperialism, the peculiar institution, loss to HIV/AIDS, the war on drugs, the war on crime, and so on. Didn't you hear it in Mary's hum, all of that? That initial invite, hand clap, beckoning us on, conjuring up alladat? Didn't you see it in Dominique's sway, her levitation, undulating on screen. Didn't you feel it in Bryant's Cheshire smile, in his responsiveness to each of us, his mmm-hmmms, and punctuated joy turned laughter, turned pride, turned love. Didn't you? I did.

Collectively: We enter *Performative Intergenerational Dialogues of a Black Quartet: Qualitative Inquiries on Race, Gender, Sexualities, and Culture* as collaborative partners writing and singing in a quartet; a group of four defined and divinely beautiful performing Black persons with PhDs, engaged in a composition of meaning with critical and creative intent. Each of us singing our parts sometime baritone, alto, soprano, tenor, sometime shifting voices and blending tones to create both harmony and discordance. Always knowing that the musical tropes of Black lives exist in the in-betweenness of harmony and discord—utilizing all the notes, and especially the black notes on the piano. Each of us speaking/writing/performing to narrate the story of our lives in joy and sorrow, in doubt and determination, and in celebration and resistance toward collective communal futures.

Overview of Book

What follows are six sections of the book structured around critical themes of our engagement: **Section I: Tribute and Libation to *A Black Quartet:*** In this section, each of the four authors of this new collaborative Black quartet take the time to offer a performative response as tribute to the original pieces in *A Black Quartet*: " 'The Warning—A Theme for Linda'—A One-Act Play in Four Scenes" by Ronald Milner, " 'The Gentleman Caller'—A Parable in One Act" by Ed Bullins, " 'Prayer Meeting or, The First Militant Minister'— A One-Act Play" by Ben Caldwell, and "Great Goodness of Life—A Coon Show" by LeRoi Jones. Here, the authors do not try to offer an exclusively academic critique or reading, we offer a sense of the soul-filled significance of the work as it continues to make contributions and commentaries on Black culture. We write in a voice and style of our own heart and spirit as we each read one of the plays and then allow the resonate traces of experience and encounter with the text—to translate onto paper in ways that might both reveal and revel in the cultural impact of knowing, maybe filtered through aspects of our own Black lived experience to render the emergent response. Each signify on content and intent—and thus these pieces read as both tribute and libation, offering performative responses to performance texts.

Section II: Motha/Sista and Fatha/Brotha Wit: Listening to the Lessons: The entries in this section are both collaborative and individual but always dialogical; the authors speak to our experiences and encounters with differing notions of "motha wit" and "fatha wit"—the wisdom of Black elders at times teasing through the pleasures and pains, what was told and what was not told—celebrating and mourning the connections and gaps in our lives. And while the pieces speak to the cultural experience of this phenomena as passed from generations of mothas and grandmothas/fathas and grandfathas there is always an unspoken question: Will we (will I) ever be considered worthy enough of offering motha wit or fatha wit, which is really a question of yearning that asks—will others see me (us) worthy of dispensing such knowledge from our lived experiences—to be valued and sought out by others as well as we remembered? The question is really a challenge that we present to ourselves as we celebrate, to some degree, our own experiences—and claim the authority to share wit and wisdom.

Section III: Letters to Those Who Mattered: The letters that we present in this section are not evidence of nonfictive conjurings or fanciful tales. These are letters of first-person direct address. Letters that our souls have longed to write to those who mattered in our lives; only halted in time relative to our coming of age or coming of knowing the import of those past relationships and now missed opportunities. Letters *to those who mattered*: those of importance, consequence, note, weight, significance in our lives—in the immediate past and lingering presence. Those for whom our words of respect and gratitude, or maybe even words of remorse, regret, or disdain, may have fallen short in the passage of time or never uttered at all. Only now have we been able to write the direct discourse of our care or concern across time, across generations, and across lived circumstances to bridge the gaps of our loss or distance.

Section IV: Monuments of Memory and Remorse: In this section, we are interested in the monuments of memory and remorse that we build as psychologies of knowing ourselves in relation to an absented other or local/communal/national monuments that emerge as historical landmarks or immediate response to trauma; like roadside memorials that sprout as immediate public mourning, remembrance, and riot, some of which are signified by flowers, balloons, photographs, stuffed animals, and other artifacts that connect the living to the dead at the time of the dying, some of which are renewed and refreshed in continued grieving or the active process of sustaining of anger and outrage. Often becoming more formal monuments to memory—statues, murals, T-shirts, tattoos, and posters as anthems, as a political *activist affect* of those who choose to remember and then act on the happening as object lesson and grievance.

Section V: B(l)ack Talk: The construction of "B(l)ack" is a two-sided co-informing of meaning that signifies for us a doubling effect. The immediacy of seeing "Black" signifies the subject of focus: Black people and the essence of and/or the performativity of blackness, not as monolithic, reductive, or restrictive but maybe as a cosmological configuration of being. An acknowledged being with a groundedness in African roots filtered and tainted by the American experience, forged through the caldrons of slavery, struggle, and survival—(re)cognized. Within the construction of "B(l)ack," the reference to "back" is not coincidence. It is a charge of remembrance—to look backward to (re)member the self in history (the past), in community (to the present), with a forward thinking toward our collective futures. The doubling recognitions of positionality and action demands the triple stages of seeing as a thrice relational orientation that includes the subject of experience and being, the moment of reengagement of histories, and the reorientation to knowing of that experience through a critical memorialization of the self as active agent. Hence, "Black talk" is quintessential to Black people, as both colloquial and stylistic, as well as a focus on issues that matter to Black people. The pieces in this section bleed the borders and boundaries of all other sections to address the issues, the Black issues that are most pertinent to these four Black persons engaged in this dialogue—in the moment of writing. Sometime the issues are addressed directly and other times—they are addressed indirectly—through play, parody or parable that is also a part of the Black cultural dialect.

Section VI: Voting Rights and Writing Volition: The section begins with the question, "Why did Black people vote for Trump? And we find ourselves asking ourselves about "voting rights"—which in many ways are being challenged again in this country, again, suppressing the voting rights of People of

Color. Gerrymandering practices are still popular as intentional redesigns to redistrict voting zones to establish knowingly unfair political advantages for one political party over another by manipulating the binds, borders, bounds, and boundaries of electoral districts—most often used to control the Black vote/the colored vote, to suppress the Black vote/colored vote, to keep suppressed People of Color and our voice through our vote in the determination of local, state, and national elections. And then it makes us begin thinking about *writing as an act of voting, writing as volition*, writing as a means of righting ourselves in history, writing as a means in which we practice our power and will, to assert our will on determining the direction of our individual and collective futures.

Notes

1 Dominique's primary contribution to "A Black Quartet" is drawn from her essay: Hill, D. C. (2021, March). "Assata's (Groove[ing]) Daughter: An embodied lyrical autoethnography of resistance." *International Review of Qualitative Research.* doi:10.1177/1940844720978749.

2 Bryant Keith Alexander's contribution of "Black Notes" is drawn from Alexander, B. K. & Weems, M. E. (2021). *Collaborative spirit-writing: Performative in everyday struggle.* New York: Routledge, but originated in this performance.

3 Durell M. Callier's contribution to "A Black Quartet" is drawn from his essay: Callier, D. M. (2020, November). "Feelin' real/unbroken: Imagining blackqueer education through autopoetic inquiry." *International Review of Qualitative Research.* doi:10.1177/1940844720974104.

4 Dr. King closes his 1967 speech to students at Barratt Junior High School in Philadelphia, PA by reciting Langston Hughes' poem, "*Mother to Son.*"

5 Bernice Johnson Reagon was a founding member of the SNCC (Student Non-Violent Coordinating Committee) Freedom Singers. The group was formed in 1962 by SNCC field secretary Cordell H. Reagon and was a part of the arts and cultural leg—the cultural work that SNCC coupled with its political organizing (Bernice Johnson Reagon).

6 See Dillard, C. (2011). *Learning to remember the things we've learned to forget.* New York: Peter Lang Press.

7 Mary E. Weems's contribution of "Black, black notes" is drawn from Alexander, B. K. & Weems, M. E. (2021). *Collaborative spirit-writing: Performative in everyday struggle.* New York: Routledge, but originated in this performance.

Section I

Tributes and Libation to *A Black Quartet*

We often give **tribute** as acts, gestures, statements, written words, or gifts that are intended to show gratitude, respect, or admiration, extolling the virtues of an individual, entity, deity, or an accomplishment with effects or presence that linger as motivation or inspiration. In the performance of a tribute, like eulogies, tributes also work to reknit a community torn asunder by a departure or show how the offerings of the celebrated are woven into the cultural cosmologies (or fabric) of the community—as actor or agent, as stimulus or soldier, as scribe or sage—maybe as remembrance, reminder, remorse, or reflection on who we are or could be as a people. The one offering the tribute seeks to match or mimic the majesty of the celebrated, trying on words or deeds to invoke presence or importance using tropes of grandeur in relation to the literal and figurative artifact of relation, offering a reading or rendition, a sign or signification of that which is elevated and celebrated, if not exalted, and in the process, showing how the source of inspiration lives as both memory and memorial.

This section is intended as a tribute to the 1970 book *A Black Quartet* and the work of the four Black playwrights: Ben Caldwell, Ronald Milner, Ed Bullins, and LeRoi Jones, who made up this literary dramaturgical force. As noted in the introduction, the subtitle of the book states: "A revolution is now taking place on stage"—as it moves to present four plays written by Black playwrights, for Black audiences, featuring Black characters and experiences, both the literal and the figurative, as well as the imagined, remorse-filled, and aspirational aspects of everyday Black life as call-and-response. In this section, each of the four authors of this new collaborative Black Quartet takes the time to offer a performative response as a tribute to the original pieces in *A Black Quartet*: "'The Warning—A Theme for Linda'—A One-Act Play in Four Scenes" by Ronald Milner, "'The Gentleman Caller'—A Parable in One Act" by Ed Bullins, "'Prayer Meeting or, The First Militant Minister'—A One-Act Play" by Ben Caldwell, and "Great Goodness of Life—A Coon Show" by LeRoi Jones. Here, the authors write in a voice and style of our own heart and spirit, as we each read one of the plays and then allow the resonate traces of experience and encounter with the text—to translate onto paper in ways that might both reveal

DOI: 10.4324/9781003274315-2

and revel the cultural impact of knowing, maybe filtered through aspects of our own Black lived experience to render the emergent response. Each signifies on content and intent—and thus, these pieces read as both tribute and libation, offering performative responses to performance texts.

In many ways, a tribute is a **libation**, a ritual pouring of a liquid as an offering to a god or spirit or in memory of those who have died and what resonates of their present/absence. The act of giving libation is one of the most sacred of covenants between the material and the spiritual worlds. In many African cultures, as practiced in the Black motherland or reimagined as rescue and reminder in contemporary African American cultures, libation is common as a ritual practice at the beginning of Black (African/African American) cultural ceremonies and celebrations. Hence, the importance of libation at the beginning of this new book project. Libation as tribute is an *offering by and on behalf of all humanity, those living and those yet-to-be-born, to ancestors, to the Creator, to other divinities, and to the environment. Through this ritual, Afrikans affirm and reestablish Ma'at: cosmic harmony, balance, interconnection, and interdependence within, between and among humans, the environment, the spirit world, and the Creator.*[1] Like the very nature of this new project, libation is a generational and intergenerational connectivity of life, an articulate performative act that serves as a commitment to the contiguity and a continuation of Black being—within and for community. The ceremony and company of libation are a collective commitment to culture and the circle of life, which shall be unbroken.

For Whom or What Do YOU Pay Tribute or Pour Libation?

The pieces in this section stand alone, but they can and should accompany the reading of the original plays in the 1970 book *A Black Quartet* **and the work of the four Black playwrights: Ben Caldwell, Ronald Milner, Ed Bullins, and LeRoi Jones. What the reader of each set will discover is an intergenerational dialogue that continues a conversation about race, gender, sexualities, and culture as critical components of the Black experience then, now, and always.**

BKA

Note

1 Drawn from Nehusi, K. (2015). *Libation: An African ritual of heritage in the circle of life.* Kuala Lumpur, Malaysia: Upa Press. Also see: Libation https://powerfulblackstories. net/2016/10/11/the-african-origin-of-libation.

1 Generational Drama/ Intergenerational Trauma

Bryant Keith Alexander

(A performative commentary on the play: "The Warning—A Theme for Linda" by Ronald Milner).

> *"They all is sweet and gone do something good for everybody—while they talkin', courtin'. But when they get the goose and it's time to build a table—then the pot always come up with a hole it. Now you see if it don't."*
>
> From "The Warning—A Theme for Linda" by Ronald Milner

Every generation has its own dramas. The challenges of everyday life in which the answers to the who, what, where, by what means, why, how, when questions establish conflict in a confluence of circumstances that leaves a residue of effect in living.[1] Whether these dramas are caused by broader national and world conditions with local effects or cultural conditions that circulate in the cosmologies of local communities (or families)—dramas demand audiences. And separate from the actuality of the happening through a scientific reasoning of effects—perspective taking occurs in dramas that always establishes a *grammar of motives* for both action or blame.[2] If that generational drama offers empowering templates for living, maybe there are constructive lessons for learning and preventing the lingering effects of the happening.

Generational dramas travel. They travel on the tongue in "the telling of the told" as people narrate their experience as processes of healing or of keeping the old wounds open in the perceived unforgettability and unforgiveability of a happening.[3] They tell of experience sometimes as a curse to those who would not heed their warning. They also tell and retell the story as an object lesson to be learned from knowing (or not knowing) that the telling provides a template of despised sociality to which they do not want repeated, although the intrigue in the told becomes a desire for a firsthand experience—not for the drama per se but for the flight of living that energized the telling of the told. In such cases, when listened to and acted on, generational dramas become intergenerational traumas, the repetition of patterns that are shame and challenge-filled. But somehow interpreted and inevitably reenacted as if the telling was linked with

DOI: 10.4324/9781003274315-3

a complicity in the blood, like an inherited disease or disorder that preordains the reenactment—with each generation bartering and brokering between the voices of mothers and fathers, between powerful cultural institutions, and collective identity formations that become fomented "between the telling and the told."[4]

Between the telling and the told, there exists a tension, maybe an *interstitial space* between remembering and articulating experience and the reasonability of what was told to what happened and what was heard in the told.[5] Each stirring passions of possibility in the telephone-game transmittal of lived experience and rumor—in which details are lost in translation and transmittal. What did the listener cue into, and how does that inform action? I am interested in the scripts of re-reenactment crafted from the told that often are tainted or tortured and how the questions of *who, what, where, by what means, why, how, when* are not fully defined—creating a recipe of disaster when one tries to cook up the same concoction of experience.

A quintessential sharing of generational drama occurs between mothers, daughters, and granddaughters—and easily happens between fathers, sons, and grandsons in that way we have in culture—to pass on lessons of our trials and tribulations, of our travels and triumphs along a spectrum of reasons and regrets. Such stories are sometimes relegated to genres of experience—particularly "how to be a woman" or "the how to be a man" stories—often bartering on issues of performative gender and sexuality but usually in an exclusively assumed heteronormative framework that parallels the progenitive intentions or complications of having sex, all of which (intentionally or otherwise) marginalize gender possibilities as it perpetuates a hierarchy of normalcy and its presumed opposite. In either case, such storying about performative gender and sexuality pathologize the chaste and the most discerning, those who time their desire (and the directionality of that desire) in a psychological assessment of need and readiness.

The keen listener and observer of generational dramas, freely shared as object lessons or social dramas unfolding as family narratives, should not have to decode the messaging of these *aharmonic or disharmonic social conflict situations that erupt from the surface of ongoing social life.*[6] The keen listener of the telling of told should be able to understand the lesson—if it, in fact, is told to disrupt patterns of pain. While I am interested in the generational dramas that come with warnings, like a medication we take to dull pain or curb desire or the theme or the subject of a talk that we use as argument or caution. I am also interested in the generational narratives that we could share that are empowering to new possibilities, not stories that instill intergenerational traumas but stories of hopeful possibilities, stories like rhetoric that provide *the ability, in each case, to see all the available means of persuasion*[7] and tools and tips for success are offered for wish-filled change taking:

Stories that say:

> Love is love whether with a man or woman, or between those who see and respect the realities and possibilities of "the other"—in their being and becoming.

Stories that say:

> Before you give yourself to someone body and soul, invest and respect in the possibilities of you.

Stories that say:

> Sex is not a tool of subversion or a weapon of conquest but a negotiation of intimacies for mutual desire, pleasure, and planned outcomes.

Stories that say:

> Don't let anyone touch you without your permission, and should it happen—tell someone and don't suffer in silence only to play and replay your regrets and traumas as fantasy or nightmare.

Stories that say:

> You are a beloved child of God, made in the image of the divine, born in the fullness of glory and possibility—as you are—and as you will become.

Stories that say:

> Ask all the questions you need and seek the answers *by any means necessary*, as an *activist affect* for your own good.[8]

Stories that say:

> Love can exist and can be what you need and want it to be—in a mutuality of motivations, with all appropriate cares and cautions; don't compromise.

Stories that say:

> Sex can exist and can be what you need and want it to be—in a mutuality of motivations, with all appropriate cares and cautions; don't compromise for him, for her, for they, or them.

Stories that say:

> Know the difference between love and sex in a mutuality of motives, with all appropriate cares and cautions; and know the difference between what you need and what you want.

And we all need (and needed) to hear stories that empower(ed) us to say (as Linda in "A Warning"):

> "I mean, are you going to be a man? A real man? A strong man? [Are you going to be a _____ (*fill in the blank*)]. Because I'm going to be a real strong woman. [Because I am going to be a real strong _____ (*fill in the blank*)]. And I can't be bothered with anything else. . . . You understand don't you? I don't mean just . . . in bed. Just that. Just there. I mean—be that, be there, everywhere. You understand?"

These are some of the lessons from generational dramas that help break patterns and perpetuating intergenerational traumas.

These are some of the directives to and of our desire that must be articulated and boldly voiced to people of our collective possibility.

These are some of the questions that we must ask and answer before we can move forward in our new generational quest.

So, if we want to do the work of culture building and culture proliferation, let's get on with sharing issues and experiences grounded in the practices of critical cultural *information, formation, and transformation.*[9] Telling stories and lessons that provide information for living, that help the next generation deepen their formation of belief and take a progressive stand for their own well-being and then work toward transforming self, culture, and society. This should be at the core of any real intergenerational dialogue—working to bridge the past and present to better prepare for our collective futures—as a people.

Notes

1 See the Dramatistic Pentad: < https://en.wikipedia.org/wiki/Dramatistic_pentad>.
2 See Burke, K. (1969). *A grammar of motives.* Berkeley, CA: University of California Press.
3 Pollock, D. (1990). "Telling the told: Performing like a family." *The Oral History Review*, 18.2, 1–36. www.jstor.org/stable/4495291. Accessed May 30, 2021.
4 See Villenas, S. (2005). "Between the telling and the told: Latina mothers negotiating education in new borderlands." In J. Phillion, M. F. He, & F. M. Connelly (Eds.), *Narrative & experience in multicultural education.* SAGE Publications, Inc., 71–92. www.doi.org/10.4135/9781452204376.n5.
5 Villenas, S. (2005). Invokes Pérez' use of the term, *interstitial space, 87*; Pérez, E. (1999). *The decolonial imaginary: Writing Chicanas into history.* Bloomington: Indiana University Press.
6 Turner, V. (1974). *Dramas, fields, and metaphors: Symbolic action in human society.* Ithaca, NY: Cornell University Press, 37; Turner, V. (1985). *On the edge of the bush: Anthropology as experience.* Tuscon, AZ: The University of Arizona Press, 180, 196.

7 See Aristotle.
8 Here I am invoking the powerful aphorism of "by any means necessary" often attributed to Malcolm X but also linked to Frantz Fanon [Malcolm X *(1992). By Any Means Necessary (Malcolm X Speeches & Writings). New York: Pathfinder Press*; *Fanon, F. (2018). Alienation and Freedom. London: Bloomsbury.]* and rightfully linking it to Harris and Holman Jones' discussion on "activist affect." Harris, A. & Jones, S. H. (2019). "Activist affect." *Qualitative Inquiry*, 25.6, 563–565. doi:10.1177/1077800418800753.
9 I consistently draw the triplet of "information, formation, and transformation" from a contemporary interpretation of the Loyola Marymount University mission statement that speaks to "the education of the whole person." https://mission.lmu.edu/mission/missionstatement/.

2 When You Hear It From Her

Dominique C. Hill

(A performative commentary on the play "The Gentleman Caller" by Ed Bullins)
(She hangs up. Kock at the door sounds again and the MAID cross stage to door. She is in the classic image of how a negro maid is thought to look—large, heavy, black, sometimes though seldom smiling, mostly fussying to herself, but always in her place, as least for the moment.)
From "The Gentleman Caller," Ed Bullins

Scene: From Inside a Corner of Her Gut

(sounds heard of rumblings, bubble bursts, growling, and grinding teeth, stunted digestion, as if trying to break down something too gritty to pass cleanly and too slimy to chew thoroughly like a handful of chia seeds followed by runny tapioca pudding, like a bold-faced lie)

Nia:

And the love and respect I showed you. And the devotion and loyalty and gratitude you have for me.[1] (she smirks then laughs). These were the words Mrs. Mann the so-called Madame my great-great-grandma worked for thought would keep her put. Contained. In servitude. The nerve. Mrs. Mann didn't have the courage to love herself nor maRock. Though she did love to act, I'm told. To put on a show they called it. To sidestep blame, my great grandma would insist.

(looks down at her stomach and rubs her belly as if to soothe. The rumblings increase in volume and action)

She was full of shit. And these days, some gender studies scholars might say she was an oppressed subject regurgitating patriarchy. While some critical race scholars would interpret her moves erratic, reflective of the white imaginary. I offer no theories. No need. My motha told me bout dat woman. She was informed by her grandma, who learned about Mrs. Manns from maLegacy, maRock's daughter, that Mrs. Mann was a wannabe. Her story and character an interlude to the real story. She was summed up in a sentence and sound: She thought she was but we knew otherwise (toilet flush). Then Ma would get down to the business, the heart of the matter.

DOI: 10.4324/9781003274315-4

My granny, ma's motha refused to activate the incantations buried beneath her skin and died trying to stand up.[2] What great grandma got from her mother that she passed down to my ma helped her survive being pushed down a flight of steps and living through a miscarriage incited by her once husband. It helped ma walk away from a job at the plant and start her cookbook business.[3] And well, maRock murdered Mrs. Mann, bathed in rose petals under moonlight, adorned herself in wild orange and bergamot, and assumed her position on the throne of her life. This sacred wisdom, she, we all carry is that we got spells in our bones and insurgent blood in our veins. We manifest things by caressing our skin.

(Nia stands in a dimly lit hallway, across from a framed painting of a woman with wild loose hair, caramel skin like hers, and purple lipstick. With her back to the painting as if about to become encased within it, she uses her left hand to peruse the right side of her face as if recalling care)

I know what love looks like. Can even smell it on hands that think about touching me. Ma told me love wasn't about words that sounded good but actions and words that give language to things done. Things about to be done or being thought about didn't matter.

MaRock didn't laugh when Mrs. Mann pretended to be in distress about her quitting because she knew the difference between comedic relief and urgent matters. And besides, she had made up her mind about quitting, about killing, about shape-shifting, and about beginning her career as a traveling gentlewoman who cared for her community and the spirits, hearts, and bodies of women.

Generations of Manns referred to my great-great-grandma as Mamie. Popular media and people who mis/used her (and others like her) describe her as nameless, "large, heavy, black, sometimes though seldom smiling."[4] The history books don't bother mentioning her.

No one in their right mind petitions their enemy for compliments nor opinion. Those insisting on her nonexistence were immaterial to her living. She knew her name and her power, Ma told me. And that was what we all needed to know and remember. Whenever it seems like I've forgotten, I slowly caress every inch of me to welcome in the reminder.

(Nia walks into the bathroom, stands before the mirror, and starts to undress. She turns to face the tub filled full of pink-colored water from the rose petals. A vile of wild orange and bergamot sits on the sink counter. Completely disrobed, she walks to the tub and submerges herself in the petals and water. The rumblings decrease to a hum of knowing. She emerges from underwater, places one hand on her heart and one on her belly, talking to herself, her body)

And the love and respect I show you often. And the devotion and loyalty and gratitude you have for me always is what keeps me able to hear Her despite the white noise.

Notes

1 Ed Bullins's 1970 "The Gentleman Caller" (p. 128).
2 In reference to June Jordan's narration of her mother's death by suicide in Jordan, J. (2002). "Many rivers to cross." In *Some of us did not die: New and selected essays of June Jordan*. New York: Basic Books, 235.
3 These moments of resistance, deliberate pivoting, and survival have buried within them, sewn into their sleeves violences less known and committed, nonetheless, violences known that bubbled up while reflecting on Black life and art, "The Gentleman Caller," and what gets swept under the rug in the name of some larger cause.
4 These same words appear in the description of the maid from Ed Bullins's 1970 "The Gentleman Caller" (p. 117) and are used here to emphasize that reverence can be felt in chosen descriptions of people.

3 "I Wish Cotton Was a Monkey"

Mary E. Weems

(A performative commentary on the play on Great Goodness of Live (A Coon Show) by LeRoi Jones (Amiri Baraka)).

Amiri Baraka's short play reads like a series of professional, rapid combinations to the face in the boxing ring of Black life, his genius with words causing me more than once to pause and sit in the tragic irony of what he described.

One of the greatest to come out of the Black Arts Movement and one of the creators of "Black Theater," which the collection *A Black Quartet*, where this play was first published heralds on its back cover as "Something's Happening—And You'd Better Know What it Is." *Great Goodness of Life (A Coon Show)* is described on the first page under the title "RIGHT ON!" as "[a] scalpel-like dissection of the soul of the Black Bourgeoisie." In it, the lead character, Court Royal, on trial for murder, although he hasn't literally killed anyone, unbeknownst to him has actually killed himself by killing his soul, is willing to do anything to be accepted by white folks, including killing his own son by shooting him in the face. This results in the white "Voice" declaring, "Case dismissed, Court Royal . . . you are free," and almost ending with Court Royal approaching his son's dead body, saying, "My soul is as white as snow, [my] soul is as white as snow. White as snow. I'm free. I'm free. My life is a beautiful thing" (p. 158). In a way, the last line of the play is the most cold-blooded. After Royal declares his life "a beautiful thing," Baraka writes in the actor's cue: "*He mopes slowly toward the edge of the stage, then suddenly a brighter mood strikes him. Raising his hand as if calling someone.*" Court Royal says, "Hey, Louise, have you seen my bowling bag? I'm going down the alley for a minute," his happy demeanor reminding me of the white folks who, after lynching a Black man, remove hair or some small body part for a souvenir, after getting their pictures taken for postcards to friends and family, and take the time to enjoy a picnic together to have some fun.

I was a little girl in the mid-'50s when *Brown vs. Board of Education 1* and *2* (the money to pay for school desegregation) became law but lived in all-Black neighborhoods until I was thirteen and almost finished with the sixth grade. Back then, the only Black people we saw on television, with rare exceptions, were maids, butlers, and actors willing to play coon roles depicting Black

DOI: 10.4324/9781003274315-5

people as lazy, shiftless, and stupid like Step N Fetchit. I just watched a short documentary about Hattie McDaniel, who turned Mammy into an infamous art form. She was the first Black woman to earn an Oscar for her role as the part-man, part-woman Mammy in *Gone with the Wind*. But since segregation was the law, Beaver couldn't sit among the white folks there to honor the awardees but rather had a special table set up in the back of the room. It hurts me to know that, and while I understand why she went, I wish to God, she'd told them to kiss her, (paraphrasing Della Reese) "entire Black ass." In the documentary, something I'd heard about her was confirmed when she was quoted as saying, "I'd rather play a maid than be one." Maybe so, Ms. Beaver, but those of us who are still living with and under the Mammy stereotype (think the two Trump-supporting sisters Diamond and Silk, Tyler Perry as Madea, etc.) today wish something else could have been possible, even though we realize other than "not" being an actor—there wasn't. Fast-forward to 2001 and the film *The Help*, which brought Beaver's Mammy persona to mind, about a small group of Black maids who rebel against their mistreatment by their white bosses by doing shit like shitting in their food and then miraculously ends with one of them going off, with no education or background in writing, to write and publish a book about being a maid. She later returned to her hometown as a successful writer, one of the final scenes in the movie at her church, where instead of holding the Bible, everyone held a hardback copy of the book. The film had a 25-millon-dollar budget but grossed 216-plus million at the box office, speaking to the ongoing popularity of movies that feature Black people in subservient positions, especially if there's a feel-good element—in this case, the revenge of crap in the food and fact that in spite of the odds, she pursued her dream and made it come true.

While being able to discern its entertainment value for some Black folks and the general audience, I hated everything about the movie, beginning with the fact that the author of the novel the film based on was inspired to write it because of her relationship with a former nanny (read Mammy) who took care of her when she was a child. Months after the film was released to high praise and good reviews, I read an article in a magazine I can't remember in this moment. In it, the Black actors, which included Viola Davis and Octavia Spencer, talked about the fact that while these roles were demeaning, they were glad to get the work in a Hollywood, which continues to privilege white men first and then not-too-old white women.

Our representation in film and television programming back then was so bad that we watched everything and anything available not only without critical reflection, but we also laughed our heads off as inferior-to-white stereotypes were reinforced. *The Jack Benny Show* comes to mind. In it, Eddie "Rochester" Anderson played Benny's butler, the pairing designed to mimic the White Master and Uncle Tom characters that were an integral part of the Black minstrelsy Rochester cut his teeth on as a young boy on the Vaudeville circuit. Back then, our televisions were only turned on for special programs, and *The Jack Benny Show* was a weekly event in our house. Kids on the floor adults on the couch, all of us watching intently, barely notice Benny. True to the minstrel tradition, Rochester's role was to play the coon to Benny's Massa, and while like slaves he did his job, he also tricked him whenever he could and talked about him behind his back. Anderson's signature line "What's that Boss?" indicating his difficulty understanding what Benny meant, even though he always completely understood. I also recall the Tarzan film series and Johnny Weissmuller, the white male star, the "only" person I can name from the films. All the Blacks in the first film and its sequels are portrayed as wild, running, shouting savages, in awe of Tarzan with his chimpanzee and Jane, who ruled a jungle filled with Black folks who knew a helluva a lot more about it than he did, yet he was the *Lord of the Jungle*. But when I read *Great Goodness of Life*, the one show that kept coming to mind was producer Hal Roach's *The Little Rascals*, a series of short, comedic shows about a group of poor children both Black and white, which was unheard of at the time, and their antics together in their neighborhood. Me and my family loved that show. We were poor, so we could relate to the setting and their day-to-day challenges, and none of us had ever been around any white folks, poor or otherwise, and it gave us a feeling of connection (not that any of us articulated this at the time) and let us know that white folks struggle too. I remember all the main characters: white Spanky, Alfalfa, Butch, Darla, and Froggy and Black: Buckwheat, Stymie, and Cotton. Each time we watched, they made us laugh, root for them when Spanky was coming up with ideas for them to make a few pennies, start a club, try to get Darla to like one or more of the white boys.

Even after I was long grown, I thought of the show fondly, for some reason the "I wish Cotton was a Monkey," repeating in memory at odd times like when I'm not even thinking about Black stereotypes—a tribute to the power of words. The "meanings" of a number of the elements of the shows never occurred to me until I watched an episode or two "after" I'd become aware of the power of stereotypes and how and why they remain prevalent today—unconscious/conscious reminders of what white's power consider our place in American society then and now—inferior to white people with the exception of our ability to sing, dance, and otherwise entertain them.

Watching *The Little Rascals*, I realized that there were stark and intentional differences between the kids. The white kids wore better clothes and shoes, spoke a more standard form of English, always came up with the ideas, and repeatedly poked fun at the Black children at some point. This morning I typed "I wish Cotton was a Monkey," into a search line, and before I could think about it, the original film appeared on the Vimeo website. The short was made in **1932** (more than two decades before I was born); the clip was called "A Lad An' A Lamp" and featured Spanky as a just-learning-to-talk little boy and the older Stymie, wearing his signature black bowler hat, and Cotton. Since it was only 1 minute 13 seconds long, I transcribed the dialogue:

(*Clip opens with a close-up of Spanky, a little older than a toddler, wearing a white knit tam and light-colored top and shorts. He's rubbing an old-fashioned kerosene lamp, the kind railroad and construction men and others used to provide light.*)

Spanky: I wish I had a monkey. I wish had a monkey. I wish Cotton was a monkey.

Cotton: Okay.

Stymie: Hey, be careful what you wishin' for, that lamp might work.
(Spanky barely audible)

Spanky: All he needs is a tail.
(Sitting with Cotton, a short distance from Spanky, Stymie is rubbing his own kerosene lamp)

Stymie: I wish my pappy was out of jail, I wish'd I had some chicken. I wish'd I had a big watermelon. I wish I had a big watermelon.
(Cut to Spanky, repeating his chant)

Spanky: I wish Cotton was a Monkey. I wish Cotton was a Monkey. I wish Cotton was a Monkey.
(Cut to Cotton eating watermelon then chimpanzee dressed like a boy, takes a seat over Cotton's head. Then cut to Spanky)

Spanky: I wish you was a Monkey, Cotton.
(Chimp throws firecracker and scares Cotton, who runs off, leaving Spanky and the chimpanzee)
(Cut to Stymie who's sitting holding an eaten watermelon slice and then running over to the Chimp, he turns to Spanky)

Stymie: Now look what you've done.
(In silent response, Spanky shapes his mouth like an "Oh")
[https://vimeo.com/47630104] accessed 7–3–2001

The End

Beginning with the title, everything about this clip is coded against the equalness of Blackness and toward the superiority of whiteness. The short actually has three "lads" in it, but the title, "A Lad an' a Lamp," makes it clear by omission that Stymie and Cotton are "not" boys/human. That the only other thing worth mentioning in this short film is the lamp. Their character names are instructive: Stymie, meaning to obstruct or thwart. Originating in golf, a stymie is when the opponent's ball lies between the other player's and the hole or goal of the game. In other words, Stymie's an obstruction, his role is to thwart the desires of his white playmates; in this case, he's blocking Spanky's "hole" or wish for Cotton to become a Monkey. Cotton, on the other hand, is the name of a major crop Black slaves were forced to plant, grow, harvest, and, in some cases, turn into fabric for the Massa's purposes:

Cotton

For: Willie Bonner

My friend leaves
me a picked
piece of cotton
I hold like our friendship.

A single boll encased
in plastic for protection
perfect fit.

Plastic cover
is a time machine
a quick look back
at a field uncovered
by hands so dark
they are magic
bodies bent from can't see
to can't see
talk in shorthand

there is no protection
sun like the whip
has its way
between rows
picked clean
of everything else
that can be sold

irony thick as sweat
fills my hands
and four brown
leaves cupping
the white
are me and him
holding on.

Neither of these Black boys is a person; they're objects at the mercy of Spanky. When Stymie wishes for a daddy not in jail or some chicken and a big watermelon, he reduces the wishes or desires of all Black folks down to two major stereotypes, all Black boys want their fathers to be released from jail, where they obviously belong, and we only eat two things—chicken and watermelon. Also, I note that Stymie, who's just watched Cotton be scared by the chimpanzee and run off, doesn't question what he sees a few moments later, giving full credit to Spanky when he says, "Now look what you've done." Last, we're never even given a reason why Spanky wants Cotton to be a Monkey bad enough to wish for it—implying that a "reason" beyond this white boy's desire isn't necessary.

At its heart, "A Lad An' a Lamp' is a coon show about white domination over Blacks, reinforcing the three-fifths-human stereotype and pointing out that according to Spanky/white males all a Black boy needs to be a full Monkey—is a tail/tale.

4 "And the Protest Goes On . . ."

Durell M. Callier

(A performative commentary on the play "Prayer Meeting or, The First Militant Minister" by Ben Caldwell)
Characters

    Minister
    Protester

The scene: The time is immediately following the deaths of Freddie Grey, Mya Hall, and Korryn Gaines at the hands of police officers in Baltimore City and County. The scene is set in an ornate, comfortable yet homey living room. The Minister is sitting in a reclined chair watching the 6 o'clock news. The room is dark, with the only true light coming from the TV screen at the opening. Before speaking a montage of protest images and sounds flood the space. Gil Scott-Heron's *Whitey on the Moon* is prominent throughout the montage, with the following lines played before the Minister speaks.[1]

> *I can't pay no doctor bill.*
> *(but Whitey's on the moon)*
> *Ten years from now I'll be payin' still.*
> *(while Whitey's on the moon)*
>
> *The man jus' upped my rent las' night.*
> *('cause Whitey's on the moon)*
> *No hot water, no toilets, no lights.*
> *(but Whitey's on the moon)*
>
> *. . .*
>
> *Was all that money I made las' year*
> *(for Whitey on the moon?)*
> *How come there ain't no money here?*
> *(Hm! Whitey's on the moon)*
> *Y'know I jus' 'bout had my fill*

DOI: 10.4324/9781003274315-6

(of Whitey on the moon)
I think I'll sen' these doctor bills,
Airmail special
(to Whitey on the moon)

<Springing up from the chair in a hurry>

Minister: Where is it? Where is it?
<The minister pauses as a flashback plays across their mind, hearing the words>
"And if you don't get justice you'll raise hell . . ." *<pause>* "He told me to tell
you that the time has come to put an end to this murder, suffering, oppression, exploitation to which the white man subjects us."[2]
*<the lines echo in the background as light fades up, with the Minister franti-
cally looking around their room for something>*
Minister: Now where is it. . .
<pauses>
I see I got mo work to do. Another lamb to the slaughter.
*<as the Minister flutters around the room the TV volume increases, causing the Minister
to stop looking for the item>*

<The Minister is seen turning between WJZ, local Baltimore news, & CNN news, taking seat in reclining chair>

<lines overlap and are background to Ministers lines>
Voiceover 1: "Tension turned to tragedy on Sulky Court in Randallstown"
We Just fired one round at her

Just one round, look at him the Po-lease chief <mimicking> just one round

And she fired back at us
10 minutes and hearing voices out in the hall, police got a key

<sitting up> Now can somebody splain to me how serving a warrant turns out to be a Battle at Jericho, more like a shooting at the O.K. Corral.

I opened the door slightly

I remember when you said to me Lor, shoot back, I knew then you meant armed resistance

Police say Gaines was pointing a shot gun at them and had a 5-year-old boy in her arm. . .[3]

And I'm still shooting back in all the ways I know how
But . . . but I'm starting to run out of bullets or is it faith that a change is gonna come or is it resolve or is it I'm just sick and tired of being sick and tired of being roped up, held back, held down, shot down— armed—unarmed—resisting to save our lives or running to save our lives or compliant, face down to save our lives
TO SAVE OUR LIVES
I still be out there Lor
<Scene cuts to Protest and the Minister takes up sign that says, "Not one More," marching and participating fully in the protest>

Minister: Say her name, say her name, say her name

\<listening intently\>

\<Voice-over of news reporter\> Voice-over 2: About 30 demonstrators held a rally at McKeldin Square in Baltimore's Inner Harbor on Saturday afternoon protesting police brutality in the wake of the killing of Korryn Gaines during a standoff with Baltimore County police.

Shouting, "Say her name" and "We won't stop until all the killer cops are in cell blocks," the group was led by the People's Power Assembly and a cousin of Gaines.

"It should be mandated that all police officers should do everything they can to save a life rather than take a life," Gaines's cousin Creo Brady told the crowd through a megaphone. "Put some value on human life."[4]

Minister: Put some value on human life. Weren't we just saying the same thing a few months back when they had that boy . . . Freddie . . . you know his name. Freddie Gray

\<*series of voice-over and news reports regarding Freddie Gray and the subsequent Baltimore Uprising are played in the background, the stage fades to black as images of Baltimore Uprising flash across the screen*\>

Minister: I was there at them protests. The Baltimore Uprisings they call em. Righteous retribution I say. Give em hell. If they can't do right by us. If we can't live. Can't have no right to life, liberty, and the pursuit of happiness, have a good education that lets us see ourselves wholly, beautiful, and divinely made.

If we can't have good-looking, well-kept neighborhoods, and continue to live in em once some developer comes along. If we can't be safe in our own backyards, protected from being swindled, robbing Paul to pay Peter all while owing some fat cat for a penny-anty pay-day loan. If we are no more than a neck under a knee—breath strangled out from our exasperated body—no more than a whimpering cry for help, our mama, your mercy, anybody. Seen no more than being out of place, out of time, wrong place,

Voice-over 3: Thousands of people descended on Baltimore from around the US on Saturday to voice their anger about Gray's death. Protesters marched peacefully from the site of Gray's arrest on Presbury Street to the western district police headquarters and on to City Hall for a downtown rally. They chanted, sang and carried placards with slogans such as 26-year-old Felicia Thomas's "BPD IS BREAKIN' OUR NECKS."[5]

Voice-over 4: \<*call-and-response*\> No justiceeeee, no peace. No justiceeeee, no peace. No justiceeee, no peace. \<*changes to singsong*\> No justice, no peace, No racist ass police, No justice, no peace, no racist ass police!

Voice-over 5: "Speaking at a late evening press conference alongside Mayor Stephanie Rawlings-Blake, Gray's twin sister Fredericka urged calm. 'Freddie Gray would not want this,' she said. 'Freddie's father and mother do not want any violence. Violence does not get justice.'"[6]

(*Continued*)

(Continued)

wrong time, shifty, the always suspect,
bitchy, too mad, too angry, too Black,
not the right Black, worth only sorry
sorry sad excuses, half apologies, that we
can't do nothin with, offered settlement
after settlement, after settlement but no
reparations, no equity, no change, no
justice. THEN BURN IT ALL BABY.
BURN IT ALL THE HELL DOWN.
<*Imagery and sound from Freddie Gray's funeral
play in the background and fade up and then
down as the Minister begins to deliver lines*>

I was there at that boy's funeral. Line long as
ever to view the body. . . . Baltimore was
mourning. We was mourning <*Minister hums
along and then begins to sing "I Surrender All"*>
I surrender all, I surrender all, All to thee my
precious savior, I surrender all.

And I was there for the aftermath. We have
got to tell our own stories. Right? Lor,
ain't that also how we continue to fight
back. To fight the man.

<*Hammond B3 organ plays in the background,
I surrender all, with the Minister humming along*>

Voice-over 6: "And as I thought about the
cameras I wondered did anybody recognize
Freddie when he was alive. Did you see
em, did you see em, did you see him."[7]

Voice-over 7:
In the seven years I've called Baltimore home,
I have never seen a more widespread
outpouring of love and support than I've
witnessed this week. Thousands of people
came out of their homes on Tuesday
morning to clean, to green, to feed. They
crossed boundaries and danced together,
sang together, prayed together, protested
together. Rather than wait for some official
call to action, as my friend Mary so accurately
described in her piece in the *CS Monitor*,
"Baltimore just did it." Many who live in and
love our city declared, "THIS is the Baltimore
I know," or "This is the REAL Baltimore," in
contrast to Monday night, which was not the
Baltimore they knew, and either explicitly or
implicitly, not the "real" Baltimore.
Coming together to clean up, or play music,
or peacefully march IS Baltimore. And it
is beautiful. It is another reason I love this
city. But Monday night was Baltimore too.
Creative people collaborating to express
their frustration, sadness and hope through
public art and musical performances?
That's Baltimore. Young people
expressing justifiable rage and anger
against persistent police brutality, poverty,
community disinvestment and political
disfranchisement? That is Baltimore too.

Neighbors sitting on stoops, faith communities uniting to meet citywide needs, young people organizing a movement for change that is, as my friend Laura describes hopefully, "smart, unapologetic and strategic"? That is Baltimore. But the criminalization of black children, and the systematic use of brute police force on Monday night to set them up instead of embrace and engage? That was Baltimore too.

To declare that the anger, frustration, and rage of young people in neighborhoods like Sandtown is "not Baltimore," is to once again deny, turn away from, and discount the lives and lived experiences of so many who also call Baltimore home.

Baltimore is my city, a city I love, which has embraced me as a relative newcomer. My husband and I are raising three kids here and sleep easy knowing they will be safe, engaged, inspired, educated, and loved. But just down the street, another parent fears her own child may "be the next Freddie Gray." Baltimore is that mother's city, too.

Maybe living in Baltimore has never meant wanting to throw a rock at a police officer, or smash a store window. Maybe you've never felt crushed by living in a neighborhood where more fathers, sons, and brothers than any other in a wealthy state are sent to prison. Maybe you could never imagine destroying your own block, because yours is a neighborhood of choice, not one you feel you must burn down in order to escape. But that doesn't make it not Baltimore. And if that is not your experience in Baltimore, as it is certainly not mine, our response cannot solely be to create more of what YOU love about Baltimore (but please, keep doing that too). If you did not recognize the anger and rage expressed in the streets of our city Monday night, ask yourself why? And then, how—how to better know this city we love, all the parts of it. We cannot simply cut and paste the parts of Baltimore we like and call the edited version, "real."

Right now many are wishing for peace in Baltimore. But for Baltimore to become a city that is Tuesday morning for all, not Monday night for many, we need justice, we need justice.[8]

<The mood of the scene shifts; we are taken from the comfort of the living room to a more present day rather than flashback of moments. We are on the street, in the area within Baltimore known as the "Meat Market," which is also where sex work takes place and where Black trans sex workers are known to frequent. The small crowd that is gathered can be heard saying, "Black Lives Matter, Black Lives Matter, Black Lives Matter," and other city sounds and protest sounds can be heard in the background.>

<Minister is seen, walking gingerly with cane to the crowd assembled, hanging just on the outskirts of the crowd a conversation ensues>

Protester: Hey hey, can I help you a bit.

<Minister looks around, and nods.>

Say, why you out here anyway?

<Somewhat taken aback>

Don't nobody care bout us no way. Not unless they a John, the popo, or another one of the girls.

Look over there, another new person moving into the neighborhood, to make it better. But does anybody round here know about my girl Mya. About that smile she had, how she was a jokester, how she was herself. I remember how she use to like getting all dressed up. Loved wearing skirts, was just real sweet you know realllllllll sweet *<pauses as if remembering something>*

You know one time. . . . Actually more than once she would let me or other girls stay with her whenever she could get a room at the motel. A little space of safety fo us. And, and, and, Mya, fo as sweet as she might be, she didn't take no shit neither, I mean, what choices do we have anyway, when all we trying to do is survive. I won't forget her kindness though, the way she use to always kid with me, Buttacup, Esha, and Shannen.

<The crowd starts moving to March the Old Goucher block, to take up space and be more visible in an ever-increasing type of invisibility that gentrification mixed with racism, transphobia, misgynoir and classism brings for girls like Mya. It is noticeable that the Minister is struggling to keep up with the crowd given their limited mobility.>

Voice-over 8: "For years, this spot at North Charles and 22nd Streets, near the main train station, has been the hub of Baltimore's transgender prostitution scene, a nightly choreography of cliches—heels too high, shorts too short, shirts too tight, wigs too big, makeup too heavy. Now, one of their friends is gone, and another is injured."[9]

Voice-over 9: "Mya, on the streets since 2009. . . . Officials identified them by their legal names Death, they say, comes too often, too young and too easy to a transgender population marginalized by a society that they say forces some to resort to prostitution, or what they call becoming 'survivor sex workers.'

'They are being driven to their deaths,' Bryanna A. Jenkins, 26, who runs a transgender advocacy group, said while on a tour of the neighborhood. 'Out here, you can be attacked. You can be raped. You can be arrested for being trans.'"[10]

Protester: You out here, bout the last one in this march, with a big ol cross round your neck, figured you was somebody deep in the church and for a moment I didn't know if you came here to bash us or love us, but I figured wouldn't nobody who wanted to hate on us, be bringing up the rear, with one good leg, and a tattered ol sign like yours in one hand a cane in the other.

Minister: Haven't you ever made the wrong turn somewhere? Turned the wrong way? Almost went down a one way? Been at the wrong place at the wrong time? I know I have. That's why I'm here. Still here.

<turning towards the audience and away from the Protester and march delivers the following lines as Peter Cottontale's "Breathe My Name" plays softly in the background> Still marching. Still screaming. Still here, just like I said I would be fightin. Fightin with every breath, I still got. . . . Because they call out to me, the nameless, the forgotten, the ones we won't show up for in the light, make room for in the rooms they can't even get to, might not know exists. Some of their names evade me I been out here so long, But I've got a promise to keep justiceeeeee or hell, justice or hell!

<Minister prepares to rejoin the audience, leaves sign planted at the makeshift memorial that has started to take place in remembrance of Mya and others lost whether to police brutality, transphobia, homophobia, or other systems of oppression>

<images of Black people harmed or killed by police, flash across the scene from the early 60s to present day, including images such as Arthur Miller, Clifford Glover, Move 9, Sandra Bland, George Floyd, Rekia Boyd, Breonna Taylor, Atatiana Jefferson, Philando Castille, Eric Garner, Mya Hall, Korryn Gaines, Freddie Gray, Tamir Rice, Tanisha Anderson, Oscar Grant. Chants of "Black Lives Matter," "Say Her Name," "No Justice No Peace," "We Remember" are heard in a cacophonous crescendo, ending with Sweet Honey & The Rock's "Ella's Song.">

Voice-over 10: "While the deaths of black men like Mike Brown, Eric Garner, and Freddie Gray have outraged people on social media platforms and on streets, little or no attention has been given to Hall's death. She and her friend have been written off as trouble. Hall's name is missing from Reddit, an online platform usually supportive of transgender victims of violence and black victims of police brutality.

While protests like those in Baltimore remind us that #BlackLivesMatter, the lives of fallen black women tend to matter less when it comes to summoning public outrage over their deaths. "When black men are killed, slogans like "hands up, don't shoot" or "I can't breathe" echo across the country. When black girls and women like Boyd are killed, there is comparative silence," writes Darnell Moore."[11]

Notes

1 A note on the script. It is written using Blended Scripting (Callier & Hill 2019), a methodology that places multiple and, at times, competing narratives into direct juxtaposition asking the audience to hold the weight of "official narratives" and those embodied, lived, culturally centered "unofficial" narratives that often humanize those who would otherwise experience another death and other acts of rhetorical violence in the ways they are narrativized and remembered.

2 Excerpts from Ben Caldwell's "Prayer Meeting Or, The First Militant Minister."

3 Taken from McClaughlin, M. & Almasy, L. (2016). *Woman killed in standoff with Baltimore County police was live-streaming.* CNN Report. https://www.cnn.com/2016/08/02/us/baltimor-shooting-randallstown-woman-likker/index.html.

4 Excerpts from Justin George (2016). "Small group protests Korryn Gaines death." *Baltimore Sun.*

5 Taken from Jon Swaine (2015). "Baltimore Freddie Gray protests turn violent as police and crowds clash." *The Guardian.*

6 Excerpt taken from Jon Swaine (2015). "Baltimore Freddie Gray protests turn violent as police and crowds clash." *The Guardian.*

7 Excerpt taken from Ruptly, T. V. (2015, April 27). "LIVE: Baltimore holds funeral for Freddie Gray." www.youtube.com/watch?v=TVzGSHHf5uk.

8 Excerpt is from, Kennedy, E. J. "Monday night was Baltimore, too." In *Preserve the Baltimore uprising: Your stories. Your pictures. Your stuff. Your history*. https://baltimoreuprising2015.org/items/show/10512 Accessed August 16, 2021.

9 Excerpt from Hermann, P. (2015). "Baltimore's transgender community mourns one of their own, slain by police." *Washington Post*, article.

10 Excerpt from Hermann, P. (2015). "Baltimore's transgender community mourns one of their own, slain by police." *Washington Post*, article.

11 Excerpt taken from Vandita's, "Police brutality: Why is Baltimore not outraged at Mya hall's death?" https://anonhq.com/police-brutality-why-is-baltimore-not-outraged-at-mya-halls-death/.

Section II

Motha/Sista and Fatha/ Brotha Wit

Listening to the Lessons

In the Black communities of our engagement, there was always something called "motha wit" and the correlate of "fatha wit" that was the same and not the same. And while parents and grandparents can be funny, with a sense of wittiness that signals both personality and humor, the wit to which we refer is more linked with mental sharpness and inventiveness; with keen intelligence, sometimes an indigenous knowing and wisdom; with a cultural aptitude of continuing experience and advice whether with humor or not—mostly not. In each, motha wit and fatha wit spoke in different ways to a natural or earned ability to cope with everyday matters by hook or by crook and then to dispense commonsense or colloquial logic and advice to family and friends, offering a sense of knowing response to the vagaries of living and the sophisticated issues of surviving with a consistent flow.

Motha wit and fatha wit were bidirectional and sometimes gender-specific (or directive), sutured to lived experience and the wisdom of the elders passed on like sustenance through an umbilical cord. The wit of each flowed when seemingly needed, as a sensed spigot that turned on and yet sometimes always flowing whether you thought you needed it or not—washing over you like a tide. And in spite of the times you didn't know you needed it and the times that you fought from receiving it and the times when you resented hearing it—the resonant traces of what you heard lingered long enough that you would eventually return to understand it as an offering. And maybe it became a template of survival that you used as a battering ram or barometer to navigate daily living. Such knowledge also came from older sistas and brothas who rehearsed their roles in relation to those who were younger, trying, as possible, to help them not make the same mistakes they did.

In the following pieces, both collaborative and individual but always dialogical, the authors speak to our experiences and encounters with differing notions of "motha wit" and "father wit"—at times teasing through the pleasures and pains, what was told and what was not told—celebrating and mourning the connections and gaps in our lives. And while the pieces speak to the cultural experience of this phenomena as passed from generations of mothas and grand-mothas/fathas and grandfathas—there is always an unspoken question: Will we

DOI: 10.4324/9781003274315-7

(will I) ever be considered worthy enough of offering motha wit or fatha wit, which is really a question of yearning that asks—will others see me (us) worthy of dispensing such knowledge from our lived experiences—to be valued and sought out by others as well as we remembered? The question is really a challenge that we present to ourselves as we celebrate, to some degree, our own experiences. So, we take the chance and do it anyway.

One of the four of us has been a parent, has known the love and legacy of departing knowledge to a biological child; the remaining three have not had that experience—and because of the directionality of our immediate desire—may not know the parenting paradigm from the heterosexual couplings—although the desire to parent is not limited to the particularity of such coupling—where there is a will or wit, there is a way. And as teacher-artist-scholar-performers, we know the nature of our personal/professional/pedagogical practices as forms of instruction, illumination, motivation, and empowerment for diverse audiences. So maybe the question of presenting motha/fatha wit is less biological and more social, cultural, relational, and orientational to the motha/fatha associational gesture and genre. Maybe by the virtue of aging and maintaining an organic connection to culture and community, maybe by being someone of virtue, the possibilities of being sought out or the pleasure of sharing wit become a practice of cultural proliferation, the knowledge of living bestowed from the elders by those who want to learn from their travels. And in time, and with the Lord's blessings, maybe we all become elders—as we speak to communities of culture and faith—whether tied by blood or by fate.

By virtue of the work that we are currently engaging in this project—we are, in fact, imagining and intuiting ourselves into those roles—inviting others to critically reflect on the generational and intergenerational sharing of knowledge—through experience and through cultural knowing that makes critical and important the indigenous theorizing of our people in the community, all of which and none of which has little to do with academic learning but has everything to do with how we all navigate through the trials, tribulations, and triumphs of our personal journeys with the guides who assist us along the way.

So, we listen to the lessons, and we invite the reader to use these entries as generative and generational narratives to their own lived experiences with motha/fatha wit—both received and dispensed.

BKA

5   Motha Wit

Mary E. Weems and Dominique C. Hill

Wit: (n) 1. Intelligence, quick understanding. 2a. Unexpected combining or contrasting of ideas or expressions. *O.E.D., 1996 Ed.*

Mary: Mama got pregnant with me when she was just sixteen; back then a girl couldn't stay in school unless she gave up the name of the father, and since mama refused—she had to drop out in the tenth grade. She could have gone back after I was born, but instead, she married my stepfather and by the time she was twenty-one, she'd had all four of us and became a single parent a few years later.

Consequently, she was still growing up, she was still listening and not always paying attention to the "Motha Wit" shared with her by her mama and the other mothas in her life. Here, we use the word *motha* in the term, instead of the more traditional *mother* for two reasons. First, because as speakers of African American English (see: Smitherman, 1977)[1] or Black English, we often use language in culturally specific ways, especially in conversation with other Black folks. Second, because in addition to our mamas, most Black women I know have grandmothers, aunties, play aunties, play mamas, and so on who help raise us by sharing their time, talents, and motha wit in an attempt to help us become strong, resilient, able-to-take-care-of-ourselves Black women, and since they've lived through what we've yet to experience, what they share listened to and followed in that moment or not, is an invaluable part of our growing up.

Mama's motha, my late grandmother and namesake, Mary Isabel Lacy, one of eight sisters and three brothers was the main woman in my life to share hers with me. Beginning when I was thirteen, the five of us moved into a big, four-bedroom house my grandparents bought so we would have a stable, consistent place to live. Mama tried hard to provide for us, but with one low-wage-earning job after another, we were always moving from one tenement roach-infested apartment to the next. Granny, which was what we called her, was my best friend and confidant.

I talked to her every day several times a day during the six years I lived with her until I moved out at nineteen, and she never provided any motha wit that didn't turn out to be true. In this moment, I wish to God I'd listened to her all

DOI: 10.4324/9781003274315-8

the time but am also feeling blessed that I did sometimes and "always" remembered her advice.

For example, she used to say, "Cookie, nothing worth having comes easy. You have to make sacrifices for what you want." Motha wit I took completely to heart when it came to making sure I became a homeowner at twenty-one so I'd never have to worry about living in substandard housing or being evicted if times got hard and, many years later, when I decided to go back to school while I was raising my late daughter Michelle alone. Not only did money stay funny, to the point I applied what I learned from granny about shopping secondhand, clipping coupons, and still finding a way to save money for a rainy day. By then, Granny had joined Grandpa in heaven, but this saying echoed in my spirit and helped me stay focused many a day when I was feeling stressed out and considering quitting.

Granny was born in 1914 to a mother (also named Mary) whose doctor had told her not to have any more children because she wouldn't survive, after my uncle Jim, her first child, was born in 1905. Eleven single births later, she and my great-grandfather, James Owens, were doing just fine. My great-grandmother had the motha wit to decide for herself and thank God she did, or my grandmother would never have been born.

Before we moved in with my grandparents, we used to regularly spend the night. Mama was very protective of us and would usually leave my siblings at home alone with me when we lived on our own, but Granny and Grandpa's house was the only place we were allowed to spend the night other than my late cousin Roz's house. Granny taught me how to pray. She used to say, "Cookie, say your prayers and be thankful for what you have." Granny taught me that God will always love me just as I am. This wisdom has served me well all my life, and the first thing I do each morning is thank God for their presence in my life, for my husband, for my ability to share my gifts, and for having enough to live a good life.

My late father's wife, my late step-mama whom I spent way more time with than my dad ever did, used to tell me, "Always have your own everything." She never explained why and I never asked, but some motha wit you can pick up from observing Black women you love. In this case, I knew that my step-mama's mother signed for her to marry my father when she was just fifteen years old, that my father completely controlled the finances in the house and almost everything else about her life. She taught me to have my own checking account and savings separate from whomever I wound up marrying, to establish and keep good credit, and to own my own home and car so that I'd always be an independent woman.

All my aunties on mama's side were strong, independent women. Some were married and some were not, but they all had their own minds and didn't take no shit from anybody. Even though I'm a spiritual rather than a religious person, I come from a family of Christians on both sides, and all my great-grandmother Mary's children had biblical names. My auntie Ruth talked the most about God and Jesus and any time one of us would go to her with a problem, she'd always say, "Give it to God." This is one excellent piece of motha wit that I wish I'd been able to do much earlier in my life—it would have saved me a lot of worry and heartache, in my relationships, childrearing, and job situations. But I have always been stubborn and for the most part, determined to do things my own way. As Granny also used to say, "A hard head makes a soft behind (she never cussed)," and while it took me a long time to give the guidance of my life, including my troubles to God—it's made the difference between living a life stressed out and for the most part being happy on a daily basis.

Mama and me have always had a complex, challenging relationship. I know she loves me, but growing up, she wanted me to do what she said without question, and I always had questions and resisted resulting in a lot of ass whoopins and smacks in the mouth. Once she'd gotten old enough to have some motha wit, she gave me the benefit of it twice. She told me, "Cookie, don't miss the chance to be a mother," when I'd always said I didn't want any children, and I am so glad and blessed that I listened to her. She also told me "Cookie, please don't marry that nigga," and I married my late daughter's late father anyway. Other than the fact that I had Michelle, nine months after we were married, he was the worst mistake I've ever made in my life. Enough said.

Auntie Gladys was a Black Puerto Rican woman from Lorain, and she was married to Granny's brother, my uncle Jim, the oldest of the eleven. I didn't get a chance to go to Lorain very often, but since Auntie Gladys was Mama's favorite auntie, we went there more than we went to any of my other auntie's houses. I loved her. She cussed like a sailor and drank whenever she got ready and was also a "no-shit" taker. One time I was talking to her about my troubles in one of my two lousy marriages, and she said, "Cookie, I'll still love you if you fuck up your life." For some reason, it made me feel better to know that no matter what I did she wouldn't judge me, that her love for me was unconditional.

Even though Mama didn't raise us in the church, my auntie Ethel was determined to make certain that I was baptized in the name of Jesus. When she told me, she was going to ask Mama if it was okay to pick me up and take me to church the next time the pastor was going to perform baptisms, I told her I didn't believe in Jesus and didn't want to go. She said, "Cookie, this ain't about what you want; you too young to know what you're talking about—you need Jesus." The next thing I knew, she'd talked to Mama and Granny, picked me up from the house, took me to her church, and had the pastor baptize me. I remember being terrified when without explaining anything, I was dressed in a white sheet and dunked down in the ice-cold pool behind the pulpit while the pastor said some words I didn't understand because I was traumatized. I hadn't thought about this in years until I met a white woman at my Eastern medicine doctor's office and we got into a conversation about religion. At some point, she asked me if I'd been baptized, and I first told her "yes" and then shared that I wasn't a Christian, which didn't seem to matter to her—she was happy that I had been and ended our conversation with "Bless you."

Granny met my grandpa on Halloween night in 1936 when she attended a dance where he was playing guitar in the band and married him less than two months later on Christmas Day. Forty-two years later, I observed her teach me a lesson about love I'll never forget. Sitting beside her in his hospital room, watching him suffer from colon cancer, she released the hand she'd been holding all day, leaned over, and whispered "It's okay, Duffy. I know you're worried about me, but I'll be alright. It's okay to let go." Not long after that, my grandpa passed in October 1978. Ten years later in the same month, I lost my granny too, to breast cancer. For almost a year I refused to cry, because I felt like if I did it would make her death real. Several years ago, I was in the Grand Central train station having something I can't remember and out of nowhere the distinct smell of tangerines, her favorite fruit, filled the air. I took out a pad and pen and wrote:

Tangerines

    For: Granny

Bring her back, the juice
the sting of memory, her
blood, the way her hands held
together when she peeled.
Each layer careful as her love, each
section chewed and sucked through a face
I can't re-see.

At night, I peel my own skin
the edges of my palms orange,
my fingers change to her fingers strange
at the ends of arms forming a circle,
making a space to enter.

My eyes hurt from the smell
that's never her.

I don't know where I'd be today without the support, unconditional love, and motha wit my granny, mama, step-mama, aunties, and the other Black women I'm not remembering provided, but I know my life would be lacking in the critical foundation created by what each of them shared.

Nowadays when I encounter young Black women in person and/or in various forms of media, I'm often (not always, have definitely met exceptions too) struck by the obvious lack of self-esteem and the motha wit that's part of elder mentoring in their lives. When I hear them reference themselves as bitches and hoes in casual conversation, fight over a boy and pay more attention to their smartphones and video games than almost anything happening in the world, I stop to reflect on my own life. I remind myself of all the Black women, including me, doing our best to mentor every young'un we can—to share our motha wit, listen to what they have to say, and offer support, love, and encouragement.

Dominique: "*Don't take no wooden nickels!*"

BJ stated this sternly for the first time when I was about six years old. It would take almost two decades, however, to return to her advice and get clear on the nature of these nickels. It would require some solid reflection thereafter to come to terms with the ones I'd unknowingly carried around and unsuccessfully tried to cash in. My great-grandma had a way with words and knew no such thing as biting her tongue. BJ was known for tellin' it like it is, and if your feelings weren't spared in the process, it was okay because that wasn't the goal. Looking back, I understand her aim to be to save us from ourselves, to lessen any potential misery we might endure. But BJ didn't and wouldn't communicate that part. Her motha wit was sharp, unapologetic, and from the gut.

The first grandchild of our family with a grandma working multiple jobs and a mother on a quest to find love and unknowingly herself, BJ and I spent lots of time together. She was my great-granny and friend in a way. Like when she was diagnosed with diabetes, she'd try to convince me to sneak her some *real* soda instead of the *shit* (Weight Watchers) she had to drink. And as her granfriend, I'd occasionally give her half-and-half and more often top her cup off with *real* stuff. As the first grandchild, she didn't hold her tongue with me. I surmise she wanted to teach me lessons before there was ever a trace of potential consequence. For instance, I loveeed me some Bubblicious gum, and every time we went to the store, I would ask for some. On this one particular day, I did my usual ask and BJ replied, "You steady asking for shit. You needta make sure there's more going in your pocketbook than goin' out." Back then, I stood at attention, mostly concerned this might be a different articulation of no, but it wasn't. It was, however, her way of insisting that I collect more than I spend. I would later understand her statement as a critique of having to ask for things. BJ didn't ask for nothing, nor did she apologize. Sometimes her motha wit came as a nice slice of spice, like in the grocery store that day. Sometimes, it was marinated into her movement, the series of motions she made with her body or her cane before saying something (Hill & Callier, 2020). Sometimes it was just an ice-cold slap to the face.

"*You stayed out all night wit a nigga and wanna come in and ask me for twenty dollars.*

You's a po' ass ho."

BJ transitioned on my seventeenth birthday. I was not privy to such burning honesty, but my mom and aunties have told this story on multiple occasions. Each time, they recount my aunt's hurt feelings and BJ's radical truth telling—if you are spending time with someone, and likely giving away your body, coming home broke is unacceptable and unthinkable. I suspect BJ was unfamiliar with the analytics of "queer of color critique," "feminism," and "womanism," as they come into popular knowledge much later in her life. Still, I imagine her laughing or smirking at them and demanding that I keep those labels off her person. Yet BJ is womanism and lived Black feminism. She knew the gift of the Black woman's body, knew it to be a source of power. She engaged queer as a state of being, practice, and critique. She taught me the importance of nature, of keeping your word, and family. BJ migrated from Tennessee to Buffalo, New York, to create a better life for her and her children. She is a waymaker, a pathfinder all her own.

After BJ dropped that motha wit, my aunt stood in shock and eventually departed BJ's room in tears. I'm not sure how much longer after her exit, BJ called to her and gave Auntie the money she requested. I sense, however, it wasn't about the tears. BJ needed my aunt, and eventually all of us (at different times), to feel the weight of our living. She needed us to smell our shit, to sit with the wooden nickels we accepted. She wasn't about to pretend they were legit currency; wasn't about to cash them in for us.

The pleasure to watch BJ move and teach and be, was all mine. Looking back, she, like the motha wit she served up, was spells, recipes even on how to live on your own terms. And while I packed some of them away (they do not serve my work as a vulnerability guide), like the need to always be on yo' shit, I appreciate what she offered me/us—a pathway home to our family's garden where tough skin grows (Hill, 2021) and a plot all my own awaiting my tending.

Mary:
★Found Poem inspired by and constructed from Dominique's Piece

"Don't take no"

BJ stated sternly.
Return to her advice
Solid reflection
Come to terms
A way with words
Biting tongue
Tellin' it like it is
Save us from ourselves.

Her motha wit was sharp
and from the gut.

First grandchild
BJ and I spent lots of time.
Diagnosed with diabetes
As her granfriend
as the first grandchild
she didn't hold her tongue
wanted to teach me.

Every time we went to the store
I would ask
BJ replied *You needta make sure there's more going*
in your pocketbook than goin' out.

Sometimes motha wit was marinated into her movement
Series of motions made with her body
Or cane
Sometimes it was just an ice-cold slap to the face.

BJ transitioned on my seventeenth birthday.
She taught me the importance of nature
Keeping your word
Family garden
where tough skin grows.

Dominique:
*Found Poem inspired by and constructed from Mary's Piece

"God Lives in Motha"

she was still growing up
she never provided any motha wit
mama tried hard to provide for us—
not only did money stay funny

"give it to God."

granny never provided any motha wit that didn't turn out to be true
the motha wit to decide for herself
"Cookie, say your prayers and be thankful for what you have."
some motha wit you can pick up,
observing Black women you love
it would have saved me a lot of worry and heartache

"please don't marry that nigga,"
"I'll still love you if you fuck up your life."
"It's okay to let go."

I remind myself.

Motha wit is necessary, honest, and far from monotone. From critically reflecting on time spent with aunties, grans, and other women, we concretized the sound, feel, and faith of motha wit. To motha, as evinced in the stories and wit offered earlier is a distinct skill set. It is a way of living, communicating lessons, a stylized way of attempting to save daughters (and others) from rock bottoms and other times to comfort us while on bended knee. Unintentionally, our writing journey helped us see each other differently and afforded the opportunity to share the wit that guides our living. With these new openings, came the possibility to again recognize the labor of mothering, of communicating lessons, and the time and difference between the two. Two daughters, two poets, two hearts suturing cross generations, regions, and mothas, together.

Note

1 Smitherman, G. (1977). *Talkin and testify in: The language of black America*. Detroit, MI: Wayne State University Press.

6   Fatha Wit (or Brotha Wit)

Bryant Keith Alexander and Durell M. Callier

Listen: take notice of and act on what someone says, respond to advice; make an effort to hear something; be alert and ready to hear something. Google

Bryant: In the Black community there is often a reference to "motha wit," that lineage of cultural knowledge passed on from *maternal figures like mothers, grandmothers, multiple aunties, and other play mothers who gave us invaluable advice*—often spoken about by women of women. Sometimes that is woman to girl-child, but the most notable of boys also listened. We listened when talked to and we listened through observation. But we also listened sometimes sitting off in the distance when girl-talk or woman-talk was happening—cooking, sewing, quilting, doing hair, sitting on the porch, or at church. Sometimes we were admonished in our listening because of the directionality of intent when women talked to women or women talked to girls.

We listened.

We the boy-children with particular sensibilities learning about our own sexuality, sensuality, sensitivities.

We listened.

We listened because the wit passed on by those motha mouths seemed to speak to a part of our being that we had not yet named and had not yet been beaten out of us by lessons of compulsory masculinity.

We listened.

We listened with the desire to know more, to hear more—not about the intimacies of certain acts but the intimacies of knowing, of sensemaking, of negotiating feels and bodies and relationships; the intimacies of talking about feelings and desires and yearnings (with someone like us as we witnessed the intergenerational and intra-gendered moments of sharing between women), which we know, now, was always the same and not the same, as it related to our desire, but the sharing established the possibilities in being both particular and plural.

We listened.

We listened because whether we had fathas and brothas in the house—the wit of their talk was different. The fatha wit and brotha wit (especially straight Black fatha and straight Black brotha talk) was *instrumental*. Talk that was used *to fulfill a need, such as to obtain food or drink or comfort or satisfaction*. Fatha wit and brotha wit sometimes had a *regulatory function that controlled the behavior of others including persuading,*

DOI: 10.4324/9781003274315-9

commanding, or requesting—both the female and feminine—through and for performances of the masculine to maintain a sense of control of what is presumed
to be the natural order. And anything outside of the presumed natural order, like
boy-children with particular sensibilities learning about their own presumed-to-be
nonnormative sexuality, sensuality, sensitivities was regulated in punitive ways—
attempts to discipline and straighten up. As opposed to that motha wit that used
language that was more heuristic *as a means of exploring, learning, and acquiring knowledge about one's environment, typically through the use of questions* or language that was
more *personal, interactional, or imaginative* that sometimes fit the talk of our spirits.[1]

We listened.

We listened as a form of research, as a way of gaining knowledge that would
inform our own possibilities and potentialities of still being boys, soon-to-
become men, with options for living and being and seeing ourselves in the
world with wit and charm.

But that does not negate the importance Black fatha wit or Black brotha wit.
I am the fifth child of seven children, the fourth boy of five boys. Black fathas
and Black brothas offer that lineage of cultural knowledge passed on from
*paternal figures like father, grandfathers, multiple uncles, and other play daddies gave us
invaluable advice*—often spoken about by men to men. Sometime that is man to
boy-child. "Don't let any man get over on you." This was a lesson about not
being taken advantaged of—in one way or another, not to be bullied.

We listened when talked to and we listened through observation. But we also
listened sometimes sitting off in the distance when boy-talk or man-talk was
happening—in the barbershops, working on that old car, barbecuing, sitting
on the porch, behind the barn sneaking a smoke, at church, having a drink.
Sometimes we were admonished in our listening because of the directionality
of intent when men talked to other men about their conquests or secrets that
they didn't want the mama's boy to tell. But the admonishment was also an
invitation *to listen and learn, look, and know the ways of men.*

We listened.

We listened in the natural way in which boys become men, different types of
men, the ones we modeled ourselves on and against. The ones who taught us
about strength and survival, who taught us about "playing the dozens" not just
about *joking and joning, clowning or capping,* but strategies of subversion, resilience,
and the quick come-back—with a joke, with a critique, with a punch that is
as much about protest (protestation) as it was about play; a defensive rehearsal,
a rehearsal for self-defense; an "acuity and proficiency with words";[2] "a verbal
facility that is [a] criterion used to separate the men from the boys."[3] But when
words failed, they taught us to brace ourselves for the real punch, and then how
to hit back—not just to hurt the body but also to harm the dignity. And the old
men, who had made their rounds in the world, sat back to tell of choices made
and paths they wished they had taken. "I should have left that old girl alone"
(talking about getting a young girl pregnant or that "crazy girl" who became
a stalker). And the absent men—those who turned to drugs and crime or the
absent Black fathas and Black brothas whose chose paths away to other families,

early death, or prison; those who taught us different lessons about being a man, a particular type of Black man. Or the Black brothas and uncles that the family didn't talk about because he was *sweet*—a euphemism for gay, the ones who they celebrated for their creativity, kindness, and generosity but shunned from the domains of masculinity because they were not procreating in a biblical sense and the directionality of their desire was considered off target, a waste of seed. "Don't waste your seed." Sex is for procreation, not recreation, we were taught, a skewed biblical reference that was never quite manifested if the level of play that was associated with sexual conquest and the shit-talking between men.

We listened.

We listened to their words and deeds. We listened to what they said to us and what they did to us: the heavy hand, the not-so-soft touch, the inappropriate touch, no touch. We listened and learned then made choices regarding our own being and becoming.

Durell: Yes, we listened and said yes when you could not, where you could not, because you could not.

And in our listening, we crafted lives you only imagined were possible, some of them beyond the dreams you had for us, others your very wildest hopes.

We listened and observed and took what we could to fashion ourselves—to fashion a life made for living.

From the substrate of sweat, and tears, and musk, and fuss, and tenderness in your own ways, we grew. We grew and learned how to grow things.

The men in my family—some of them—no, all of them, grow things.

Cousin Chicken and his container garden. A country oasis of tomatoes, cucumbers, peppers, and green beans could be found in his modest 6-foot by 3-foot concrete slab backyard. Fenced off from the alleyway, over East (Baltimore). A rowhome of love, from cinnamon-touched yeast rolls—soft, high, just sweeeeeet enough—to handcrafted wooden items—crosses, doves, prayer hands all with inspiration scriptures, engraved hearts, and sitting/stepping stools.

Cousin Chicken knew how to grow things

Cousin Tony knows how to grow locs. A converted Jehovah witness now Rastafari. His crown now hanging on by thin threads, as long as his days are long.

Uncle Arthur, his father, also knew how to grow a garden. My country cousins, as I knew that side of the family, not because they lived in the country—in some rural space—but because they lived, not in the city like us. No concrete jungle. Land. Land they owned, tended to, tilled, made beautiful around them. His garden unlike Cousin Chicken's. No need for containers here; straight from the soil sprouted, string beans, and strawberries, watermelon, and peppers, and cucumbers.

The men in my family know how to grow things.

Uncle Mikey could cuss a curse word out! Invented grammar rules on how to cuss a motha★ucka out, show a motha★ucka how much you care, encourage a motha★ucka to be their best self, leave a (sorry-a★★) motha★ucka alone, and love the hell out of em. He understood—taught me—that sometimes you used curse words like punctuation as period, comma-pause, question mark, exclamation mark, and at other times as the subject, verb, adjective to communicate with others. He grew in us a fanciful language alongside an imagination to know our history. And more than anything he knew how to grow a laugh. The punchline, the setup, the crazy cross-eyed, bug-eyed comical face that started in your belly and radiated out in seismic thunder. Through the flying fucccckkkk and sheeeeeit as he'd say them, you might find yourself bowled over in laughter. Cheeks rosy, stomach so full of laughs it hurt. Gran, his mother, in the background saying, "Boyee staph that." Laughter all in the car ride to and from school, in our house for unexpectedly visiting with McDonald's and a check-in, in his house through wafts of nag champa and Mary Jane, for my haircuts, and a careful eye when my sister and I needed a babysitter. He would make us laugh in serious and sad moments, in just because moments, when you shouldn't moments but needed to like at boring and hard things like church and funerals. Any moment he/we could.

Joy.

The men in my family know how to grow things. And I find myself, a man—whatever that may mean now, to you, in this time. Me, a brotha, uncle, partner, lover, friend, homegirl, great grandson of Florence and Herman, who begat Silvine, who begat Silvine, who begat me.

Me. I find I want to grow things, too, more than this lush indoor house plant garden.

I want to grow things from the soil

nourishing
    colorful
fruitful

lifesaving
    loving
    beautiful

joyous things
    in this same legacy.
    I come from people who are cultivators of soil and soul.
    The men, too, in my family know how to grow things.
    Which must me, so do I.

Found in Between

Bryant Keith Alexander

*A found poem from our interaction,

Yes, we listened,
and we witnessed,
and we experienced.

And in our being and becoming we stole,
we borrowed,
we inherited,
and we mimicked the pieces that made us whole in our
imagined-to-be-selves.
For some of us, boy-children with particular sensibilities, we strive to
regain and retain in our
own personhood—the power of "yes" to the "female" within as we strive
to be the person of
of desire.[4]

We grow things by our hands;
in the soil,
on our heads.
and on our faces that resembled
the men *with wit* who also played a part in our birth
and in our breathing, brothering, and becoming.

We learned to craft language like a cuss,
like a curse,
to cuss a curse,
or like a theory that did the work of informing and enlivening the real
in the everyday.

We come from people who are cultivators of soil and soul and spirit.
The men in our families know how to grow things,
the organic nature of man in nature,
as nature;
as father,
as brother,
as uncle;
as partner,
as lover,
as friend,
and the descendants of greatness who begat and begot, us.

Their examples beckon us to also plant and grow things, in one way in and the other.

Notes

1 Halliday, M. A. K. (1975). "Learning how to mean." In E. H. Lenneberg & E. Lenneberg (Eds.), *Foundations of language development: A multidisciplinary approach.* Academic Press, 239–265.
2 Dozens: <https://en.wikipedia.org/wiki/Dozens_(game)#cite_note-lefever-1>
3 Lefever, H. (1981, Spring). "Playing the dozens: A mechanism for social control." *Phylon,* 42.1, 73–85.
4 Spillers, H. (1987). "Mama's baby, papa's maybe: An American grammar book." *Diacritics,* 17.2, 80. doi:10.2307/464747.

7   I Affirm

Bryant Keith Alexander and Dominique C. Hill

She begins her emails to members of this Black Quartet always with, "I affirm . . ."

Always followed by a particular reference to the moment, the sun, the moon, or the universe.

I wait for those moments.

I wait for those moments because they seem to come at the right time when I need to be "affirmed"; when I need "affirmation" as a man, as a Blackman, as a Blackgayman, as a Blackgayman-teacher-scholar-administrator; someone who is making-it-by-the hardest, with some struggle to both finda-way for himself, and to help others to find their way.

I love the fact she uses the word *affirm* and not *declare*, as in "I declare," like putting forth a proclamation or in some parody of a delicate white southern bell who is astonished by the vagaries of everyday living that she has been privileged above; thus, pronouncing that she "attests" in some way to the realness of living a life of struggle that is not hers. But that she contributes to—that white woman, that is saying, "I do declare."—As if as a performative putting something to action in the world that benefits her desires and her needs; usually that others, maybe Black others, must activate and make real to her satisfaction.

She answers: This business of being Black and queer and youth and spirit-filled with style can be/has been messy. I akin my stylization to my insistence on existing in this space called academe on my own terms. I insist on being me.

Black like me comes from being raised as the third generation in the house and with that comes minding your manners, keeping your word, and knowing the value of language. Like whether someone was getting cursed out, chastised, or celebrated, the words were real. The words slapped and punched, almost as if making sure the person on the receiving end of the sentence was alive. I write, emails even, affirming life. I write emails to our Black Quartet with a spiritual sense that we are alive and make space for the contours of that living as the moment my message is received.

There is a messiness, ya know? A portion of me still unmade. I like it that way. Love it, in fact because this part of me, I imagine, is where my refusal lives. Like, yes, I know these are people I respect and yes this is MY university, and sure we are working on professional stuff, but these are also my people and they raised and they befriended me, and yes, my home training came with knowing the difference between precedent and purpose.

(Continued)

DOI: 10.4324/9781003274315-10

(*Continued*)

I love the fact that she is affirming Black people in the health and wealth of our being; in our continued struggle and survival; in our continued climbing or inching toward the possible; against all odds, alone—but hopefully together with other affirmed Black folks, affirming other Black folks.

I love the fact that when I receive that message,

when I receive her messages,

regardless of what follows the salutation—

it welcomes me into a conversation of being valued.

I wonder what the impulse is, and the origin is, of her repeated affirmations.

Something inside me itches to crawl into the cave of me. To be unseen? Like rewind, backtrack, redo.

I love that words have weight, like Black posteriors, like Black hands, like Black bodies making home. "I affirm" is, I feel, the weight of home. Like a meal with extended family. Like Black notes played during the repass. Like possibility.

I turned in my religious card over a decade ago and I still pray. These days my prayers look like dancing, like conversation by candlelight, like performing a poem, like the salutation, I affirm. It is seeing in spaciousness. Love with room to grow. Like waiting for a Black person to cross your path so you can pay them the most heartfelt compliment. I affirm you are being the element that helps you feel most Black and free today.

8 "Reading *(to/for)* Daddee"[1]

Bryant Keith Alexander

A Performative Address for First Generation College Students as an Activist Critical
Performative Pedagogy

While critical performative pedagogy (CPP) *is both a theoretical lens and a methodological practice located within the converging traditions of critical pedagogy, educational poet-
ics, and the embodied epistemologies of Performance Studie*s, and while CPP is evolving
to encourage *a deep kinesthetic and multi-dimensional process that incorporates questions
of systemic inequity, cultural hegemony, and unequal access into teacher education*—I am
thinking about an activist CPP that incite students to action.[2] For me, CPP can
also seek to stimulate an engaged participatory charge for/in/with student learning, a charge that is not just funneled through teachers teaching (and how) but
an encouragement in which students are required to bring the fullness of their
cultural knowledge and lived experience to bare upon and challenge their own
educational experience, thereby liberating themselves. For me, now, CPP invites
students to both demand and take authority of their learning in ways that are
not divorced from their cultural cosmologies and material bodies but fuses all the
available means of knowing past, current, and future selves in relation to diverse
sources of knowledge. My current engagement with the precepts of CPP converges with and through my work with critical autoethnography as a performative and pedagogical method of deconstructing my own painful experiences as a
student. This through a performative praxis that charges students *to construct meaning in their own learning that lives in their cultural body, felt in their bones, and situated
within the larger body politic* of their learning experience, whether that is spurred
on or invited by their teacher or not; a radical and renegade critical performative
pedagogy in which students reclaim their own learning—*by any means necessary*
and at times, includes, and is undergirded by, the use of performance autoethnography as embodied praxis for students to critically tell their truth.

★★★★★★

Writing critical autoethnography takes many turns, especially when it meets
at the intersections of the personal/pedagogical/professional and the scholarly

DOI: 10.4324/9781003274315-11

dimensions of our academic lives with a focus on societal injustice and the struggle for equity—this *theoretical lens and methodological practice* is consonant with CPP.[3] Allow me to offer you a sense of the triple turns in this current project: At first, what follows was *just* a deeply personal reflexive process of a son reflecting on his father—relative to the triggers of memory that force such critical rememberings—in which I explore deep-seeded issues of race, gender, and the sociocultural politics of education. Second, while finishing the piece, I was invited to offer the keynote address for the first-generation "First-to-Go" to college program at Loyola Marymount University (LMU). The complexity of such an invitation also meets at the nexus of occasion, ceremonial tropes of expectation, and the audience—in both their particularity and plurality. And the more I reflected on the invitation to do the keynote, the more I realized that it was not just an invitation to do a presentation or a performance but also to engage in a pedagogical moment. And being a first-generation student myself, I thought about having the initial project of a Black son with a PhD reflecting on his Black father with a fourth-grade education—to inform the First-to-Go address audience. And third, I was then reminded of this invitation to participate in these *critical performative pedagogical encounters*, and the piece that I was working on began to meet at yet another convergence of what my colleague Elyse Pineau speaks to as "the sedimented performativity of educational systems and subversive performances of classroom praxis" that now, I add, that students must demand an excavation, an unearthing of staid systems of educational encounters to open news spaces of possibility for their diverse learning and their diverse cosmologies of knowing in the classroom and the university at large.[4] And if the system does not do it, then the students must demand it. Thus, opening spaces not only for them to know and learn differently but also ways for us all to learn from them, differently, bridging that us/them binary that is both fact and fiction. The piece that follows is an autoethnographic confrontation of educational experience as a CPP, a call to arms, an approach that motivates students to claim their cultural experience as an essential component of their learning.

So, today I offer you a piece that speaks to the evolution of my personal reflection on my father as it met the politics of addressing first-generation students and how this becomes the evidence of a form of CPP that dynamizes my own scholarship and administrative life. In my presentation today—I recast you as both "first-to-go" students and for those of you, who are first to encounter the elastic potentials and possibilities of CPP, to witness how such an approach can manifest as a performative act of public scholarship. For some of you, my recasting of you in this way will be an easy role to play. For others, I invite you to lean into the experience of *the other*. This is what I presented to those First-to-Go students and now, to you.[5]

Reading *(to/for)* Daddee[6]

It is an absolute pleasure to welcome you all to LMU and into the First-to-Go Program.

Congratulations!

There are many ways that I could engage you today, today at this important moment, this important juncture as you poise and pose at a port of entrance into your college experience, and as you serve as a first point of contact and guide for your families into higher education.

I want to offer you a very particular approach of welcome that is fitting to the moment, because it is also fitting to my own reflections on being a first-to-go student.

I invite you follow me and see if you can read my intent as I share with you a recently written piece; one that I read out loud for the first time; for you, today—on this occasion.

I call it, "Reading *(to/for)* Daddee." Daddee is how I refer to my father, who passed away nearly 20 years ago but who is ever present with me.

It begins in this way:

I have written often about my father having a fourth-grade education in relation to my PhD. Ultimately those past references were not to *read* him, as in to demonize him, or even less so—it had nothing to do with elevating myself above him. But it had everything to do with lessening the presumed gap in our joint humanity and my deep love for him, through the socially constructed and misplaced perceptions on intelligence linked with academic accomplishment. The nature of this presumed gap came into sharp relief for me recently when a colleague (a Black woman of my generation who works on this campus), spoke about listening to the audiotape version of the book *Caste: The Origins of Our Discontent* by Isabel Wilkerson.[7] Have you read it? You should.

My colleague stated how she reveled in both the insights of the book, the historical truisms of Black struggle and subjugation in a caste system designed to keep people of African descent down at the lowest rung of society—in a caste system of our discontent. She also said how she reveled in the male voice that narrated the book. In her reveling, she reflected on how her father would read to her as a child, commenting on the depth of his care and the performativity of his reading to make the experience of her listening dynamic to the worlds and words he narrated, to make her act of listening both entertaining and informative. All of that came back to her in the experience of listening to the narrator of the audiobook.

I shared with her that my father had a fourth-grade education and did not read very strongly, but often I would read to him. My reading to him was not about me educating him. My reading was often at his request. He would see his college-boy sitting at the kitchen table leaning into and silently reading some staid textbook or a literary anthology for class. He would ask me, "What are you reading so intensely?" I would tell him the book, the passage, and for what class. Then he would ask me to read out loud. And I would.

Reading aloud for my father took me back to my childhood—when reading out loud in class or church, or even for him, then, was a demonstration of capacity, a pedagogical performance of display. In reading the Bible in front of church, it was evidence of religiosity in a passage across generations, a rehearsal of faith. At times, reading was a performed display of knowledge—the performative inflections and recognition of punctuation—periods, commas, question marks, and exclamation points. It was at times a tongue testing of pronunciations and enunciations presented with the assumed appropriate expressivity and force of delivery for teachers, parents, and communities of faith—to see a passion of learning or of knowing, performed through reading. Reading for my father also played out in other ways, like reading a formal business letter that had arrived with his name on it, reading for content, reading for a notice or notification of action or intent. But in these cases, reading for my father at the kitchen table as I studied for school was different, and maybe not.

Upon his request I would brace myself, returning to old positions of childhood performances. I would sit up and clear my throat. I would attend to the structural components of the passage—following punctuation as performative cues—making the delivery and message entertaining, digging deep into my understood meaning of the text as to relay to the listener through expression—in a cold, and not-so-cold, first reading aloud. And my father would nod his head—at first appearing prideful that his son was reading so well. Then he would nod in a contemplative sense, his pride turning into a deep thinking into the reading and his deep listening. At the end of these little performative moments, my father would commend me by tapping me on the shoulder as he would then walk away to his bedroom. And while I would smile, thinking that I had done something *for him*, I had always known that he had done something *for me*. At the end of those moments, those embodied performative readings, those moments ripe with the oral interpretation of literature that would later become a part of my professional craft. I recognized that I always had a deeper encounter with the text, a deeper encounter with the content of knowing and feeling the meaning of those words as they swirled in my head and out of my mouth. And I wondered. Did he really want me to read *to him* or *for him*—or did he want me *to read aloud and read lively* because I could—knowing that by doing so—I would enliven the knowledge gained from reading aloud—and it would not appear as such a chore—as he had witnessed me sitting at the kitchen table. Did he want me to make reading and learning a public activity (like democracy) and not a private chore (like a punishment and doing time)? Did he want me to work a little harder in reading—under the guise of doing it for him when it was really for me?

I thought about his intentions as I spoke to that colleague who told me of her father reading to her. I thought about this as I became embarrassed in front of her because I started to cry, crying from this sudden and deep realization of my father's gesture. With his fourth-grade education, my father consistently taught me how to read: how to read books, how to read people, how to read culture, and how to read life (or read myself into living). As a college professor I am now reading and writing and teaching my father into my scholarship and classroom pedagogies again and again and again—so that other

Figure 2 In reading (to/for) you.

Figure 3 I am reading you in me.

smart Black college boys and first-to-go students of all races, genders, creeds, religions, and class origins—might also find their fathers and family members written between the lines of their studies and recognize what they were taught at home—long before they too—started to read in college.

★★★★★★

I hope this story makes sense to you.

I hope this story makes sense to you today—as you activate your membership and citizenry on this campus, and in the not-so-always tender bosom of higher education.

I hope this story makes sense to you—as you embrace being the first in your families to enter the university; the first among many *who may not have had* the opportunity, *who may not have had* family members who read as well as you do; the first to have the experience that can transform the pathway of your life and theirs.

I hope this story reminds you—to take the lessons you have learned from home and apply them to what you will encounter here. Apply your indigenous cultural knowledge in relation to this academic intellectualism that often disregards the origins of your knowing along with the materiality of your bodies and the critical cultural intelligence of your beings.

Use your lived experience with the *ones who loved you into being*, as a filter for the academic knowing that you will encounter here (at the university); never elevating one over the other, but always allowing each to co-inform your learning, your being, and your becoming.

I hope that while you are here (at the university) that you will **read deeply, read lively, and read out loud!**

I hope that you will brace yourselves in your studies so that when reading you will—sit up, clear your throat, and clear your mind. And then attend to the structural components of knowledge acquisition—following punctuations as performative cues, unpacking theory, and philosophy like luggage, digging deep into your understanding of the text (e.g., the article, the book, the professor, classroom engagements, and the cultural politics of education) looking for deep meaning—the intended and the unintended; read and then reread every text when necessary. Always ask questions. Always assert and relay your understanding (and your differing experiences) to the listeners in class and to your professors. Do this as a means of introducing and inviting diverse perspectives of seeing and knowing the world into the classroom. And when something is taught or is engaged in class that rubs against your sensibilities, against the physicality of your being, against your lived experience like sandpaper or a knife cutting out your cultural truths and bodily realities—find the right way to call that out, *to read* the moment, and respond with the counternarrative of your lived experience.

And if the notion of pedagogy asks the questions, *What to teach, why to teach it, and how to teach?*[8] then critically read into the answers to those questions to see if *you* were taken into consideration in deciding the—*what, why, and how* of *your* learning, and of *your* presence in the classroom as a knowing, thinking, feeling cultural subject. Ask about the value of *your* cultural knowledge as it intersects with the content matter of the course. Then, regardless of the answer—just insert yourself; insert your body politic in a *kinesthetic and multidimensional* ratio of doing-to-knowing so that you literally embody your learning, so that you are fully present, forcing teachers *to educate your whole person.*[9] And you, as an active learner, involved in a dynamic process in which you integrate what you are learning to your already *internal structures* of knowing—which were derived through your culturally informed particularity.[10] Do that performatively and critically in the processes of learning and teaching—for surely you are always and already both student and teacher for self and others in a dynamic process, always recognizing and celebrating your deep encounter with the text, and your even deeper encounter with the content of knowing and feeling the meaning of knowledge as it swirls in your head, through your own cultural cosmologies and out of your mouth—as you share with others—both here and at home.

I also hope that you will then be able to relate what you are learning here, in the white ivory tower of higher education, to what you were taught at home. Relate the two *sets of knowledges*, like a dialogue that democratizes and further possibilizes the lives and the value of your family, of your community, and of your culture. Do all of that in this place. In the space of higher education that has never *really* anticipated the breadth and depth of your cultural intelligence and the cultural capital that you embody, enact, engage, and enter this place *with*.

[And just so you know, I intentionally ended that last sentence with the preposition *with*. I am using it like my father used it—not just because the word *with indicates association, togetherness, and connection between things and people*. For my father, ending a sentence with the word *with*, in this context, was a reference *to what people carry*. It related to issues of purpose and positionality; it related to integrity and what people had to offer. "What do you carry *with*—as you enter this place? The colloquial language may be considered uncouth and non-academic, but I understood what my father was talking about in his *grammar of motives*[11] and in the social consciousness of a Black man from the South with a fourth-grade education trying to teach his soon-to-be Black-male-professor-son about reading, the world.]

Higher education needs to know what you enter *with*. It needs to know what you bring.

So, Bring It!

Bring your cultural selves to bear upon your educational experience and help us to transform higher education by and through the sheer tenacity and audacity of your presence. This demands your full-embodied participation in your education—in which you become an agent of cultural change both in the university and in your communities.

And if you think that you are coming here (to the university) to be changed—then check yourself! And if you have bought into the elitist and often racist notion that you are entering the university as an empty vessel waiting to be filled—disavow yourself of that rhetoric of disdain. And begin to challenge *the ideologies of institutionalized learning to facilitate your own political agency.*[12] And embrace the *cultural synchrony* of your lifelong learning before you arrived here. Embrace what your family taught you. Embrace what your community taught you as skills of knowledge and the personal dignity necessary to live in the world. And recognize all that has seemingly become instinctual—you have learned. Because they needed you to learn it, and to know it, for you to survive—and for you to make it here, now.[13] And in the academic struggle of code-switching that you will experience between campus to community; in those moments of trying to share with family what you are learning at the university (for surely you will struggle)—remember how family nurtured you into being and becoming. Transform the labor of code-switching back into the love that you have for them; use that moment as your own pedagogical moment to teach as you learn, to lift as you climb. Maintain a deeply felt and organic connection to family because they matter and they are always present in the materiality of your being and the spirit of your possibility. The link between labor and love is most meaningful as it relates to family.[14]

So hold on to the things that matter to you (e.g., your cultural knowledge, your formal, and informal homeschooling, what your family taught you, and even the lessons learned from the streets). Then grab greedily from this place the things that you need (e.g., degrees, theories, skills, and tools for success on your chosen path). And in the process, help us to change higher education for the next First-to-Go student who follows you.

Let There Be More (of Us!)

You see, I know that my father wanted me to work a little harder in reading—hence his request of me to read aloud under the guise of doing it for him, when it was really for me. Now I evidence the many lessons I have learned not just from school but also from home, from my family—and from him—for others including you to see and read, with the notion of reading defined in three additional interlocking ways:

1. Reading, as a multifaceted process involving word recognition, comprehension, fluency, and motivation . . . making cognition, recognition, comprehension, and meaningful understanding from print.[15]
2. Reading, a public performance as an embodied act of presentation with and for effect and purpose.
3. Reading, as an act of attending to the knowledge, realities, and truths of any given circumstance—which sometimes means calling people to task; *to read them*—for their lack of sociocultural consciousness, or the realities of your particularity and, thus, educating them as needed.

So, I ask you to *read* yourself into the processes of education, teaching, and learning towards your own possibility and into the horizon of your potentialities. And in the manner that I welcome you today, I hope that you will join me in doing the same—conjoining your past-present with your future-perfect lives; for yourself and for your people—whoever they may be. So Congratulations—and Welcome! Now, show them what you come with. Bring it!

Tenants of an Activist Critical Performative Pedagogy: A Conclusion

My introduction to CPP came in my doctoral training with Elyse Lamm Pineau at Southern Illinois University Carbondale, an energizing and tumultuous time in which I was negotiating my own integrative approach to critical pedagogical studies through a performance paradigm. It was a time in which I was delving more into my own historical experiences as a Black gay male student in predominately white universities with predominately white straight professors. My doctoral program culminated in a one-man show titled *Putting Your Body on the Line*, a performativity of Black masculinity, and a dissertation titled *Performing Culture in the Classroom: An Instructional (Auto)Ethnography of Black Male Teacher/Student Negotiations of Culture*—each of which explored the tensiveness of being and becoming in shifting socio-cultural-political contexts—especially through the passages of formalized teaching/schooling/education.

During those reflections and through nearly thirty years of teaching pre- and postdoctoral programs—the notion of an activist critical performative pedagogy speaks to the person that I am, and my desire for other students of color and first-generation students to be empowered in their higher education experience. Separate from the timidity of being both "of color" and "first-generation" in the white ivory tower—how can these students (we students) be charged to claim the voice and volition of their (our) lived cultural experiences, to make manifest in/and dynamize their (our) educational experience? This comes through a series of both recognitions and encouragements that lay the preliminary foundation for emerging tenets of an activist critical performative pedagogy.

Such emergent tenets begin to include the following: (1). A recognition that students are activist participants in their own educational experience, that encourages them to speak up and speak out to cultural and racial erasure in the classroom, or the perceived subjugation and demonization of cultural and racial indifference in the curriculum—becoming activist interventionists of the facile cultural production in the presumed-to-be educated person.[16] (2). A recognition that critical performative pedagogy, with all its liberatory intentionality is still not something that is done to students, even through the assumption of enlivening the educational experience and dynamizing learning that calls for teachers trying new embodied pedagogies of engagement. Teachers must acknowledge the actuality of cultural bodies in their classroom and the expectations that they have for students to do and enact exercises that potentially threaten students' cultural body politic for the grade of participation and enactment. (3). A reminder and recognition for students that their critical intellectual learning and training began at home or on the streets, long before they arrive at the university; asking them to recognize the dialogue between culture, community, and campus as a form of honoring family and indigenous knowledge in their quest to advance in their career pathways. (4). A recognition that teachers, artists, scholars—in as the other, and people-of-color and particularity, including members of LGBTQ+ communities in higher education; those who (and we who), have traversed the borders and boundaries of the white ivory tower—must embody an activist affect in welcoming and warning their (our) young brethren about the challenges of educational enculturation and the necessary performative resistance to erasure of their cultural truths and origins.

An *activist critical performative pedagogy* (ACCP) is a (5) recognition that aspects of critical autoethnography, with a particular focus on excavating societal injustice and the struggle for equity, can be enacted by teachers, academic administrators, and students to share their own stories of educational trauma while empowering others as a liberating discourse of discovery and democracy. (6). A recognition that confirms the "interrelationship between cultural studies and critical pedagogy within a language of critique and possibility, a theoretically rigorous discourse that affirms the critical but refuses the cynical, and that affirms hope as central to any sense of human agency and critical practice but eschews a romantic utopianism. The concept of the performative . . . provide an articulating principle that signals the importance of translating theory into practice while reclaiming cultural texts an important site in which theory is used to 'think' politics in the face of a pedagogy of representation that has implications for how to strategize and engage broader public issues."[17] And performative as a critical/creative enactment of the real that stirs the imagination while energizing the possible. (7). A recognition that the aegis of critical performative pedagogy is grounded in the emancipation of educational tyranny and the suppression of the expressive modalities of both teaching and learning.

The (8) dynamism of an emergent *ACCP* is an invitation for students to be fully activated; to become fully alive, fully present, fully embodied, and fully whole in their persons in the classroom without compromising their past, current, or imagined cultural selves. (9). It further recognizes that if universities are striving to evidence their greater commitment to diversity, equity, inclusion, and antiracism, they should also recognize that the classroom is a political space. Thus, students need to engage an activist sensibility to realize the liberatory possibilities of education in their processes of being and becoming without compromise. And finally, (10) ACCP works to help students **read (to/for) educational liberation**: a triple process of pedagogical activism that encourages—*reading educational liberation, reading to educate liberation*, and *reading for educational liberation*—as active agents to elevate the past as they move toward their futures.

Notes

1 Performance History: An abbreviated version of this essay titled, "Reading *(to/for)* Dad-dee: A Performative and Activist Critical Performative Pedagogy" without the broader theoretical frame and concluding tenets, was delivered in a digital symposium titled, *Critical Performative Pedagogical Encounters,* cosponsored by the National Communication Association and the Hugh Downs School of Human Communication at Arizona State University on August 6, 2021—along with Elyse Lamm Pineau and Rachel Hastings. The interior text entitled, "Reading (to/for) Daddee" was presented as the keynote address to the 13th in-coming cohort of the Loyola Marymount University First-to-Go Program on August 9, 2021. The latter preceded the former in construction—then was expanded to theorize on intent and occasion of the former.

2 Wimmer (Eds.). *Teaching performance studies.* Carbondale: Southern Illinois Press, 41–54; Harman, R. & French, K. (2004). "Critical performative pedagogy: A feasible praxis in teacher education?" *Social Justice in These Times.* www.researchgate.net/publica-tion/284287567_Critical_performative_pedagogy_A_feasible_praxis_in_teacher_edu-cation Accessed July 4, 2021.

3 See Alexander and the broader contributing volume: Alexander, B. K. (2021). "Criti-cal autoethnography as intersectional praxis: A performative pedagogical interplay on bleeding borders of identity." In *Critical autoethnography (writing lives: Ethnographic narra-tives),* 2nd edition. New York: Routledge, 32–44.

4 See Pineau, E. L. (994). "Teaching is performance: Reconceptualizing a problematic meta-phor." *American Educational Research Journal,* 31.1, 3–25. doi:10.3102/00028312031001003.

5 First-to-Go Program "At LMU, any student whose parent(s) or caregiver(s) did not receive a bachelor's degree from a university located within the United States is referred to as a first-generation college student. If your parent(s) or caregivers(s) attained an associate's degree from a community college and/or you have siblings who have gone to college, you are still considered a first-generation student under our definition. The First to Go Program at Loyola Marymount University offers first-generation college students—valuable resources and opportunities for their academic, professional, and personal growth. It is our mission to reinforce and build upon the unique sources of cultural capital first-generation college students bring to the university in order to create a community that promotes and progresses our students' successes during their tenure at LMU." https://academics.lmu.edu/arc/firsttogoprogram/.

6 This title should be read as three orientations to reflection: Reading Daddee, Reading to Daddee, and Reading for Daddee)

7 Wilkerson, I. (2020). *Caste: The origins of our discontent.* New York: Random House.

8 Simon, R. I. (1992). *Teaching against the grain: Texts for a pedagogy of possibility.* New York: Bergin & Garvey.

9 "*The education of the whole person*" is included in the Loyola Marymount University Mission Statement along with "the encouragement of learning" and "the service of faith and the promotion of justice"—of which I strongly believe and cite frequently in my scholarship and emancipatory pedagogies https://mission.lmu.edu/mission/missionstatement/.

10 See Rodriquez, V. (2021). "The teaching brain and the end of the empty vessel." 181. https://scholar.harvard.edu/files/vanessarodriguez/files/vrodriguez_publishedmbe-article_11-16-12.pdf. Accessed July 11, 2021, 2:00 p.m. I take liberty with this impor-tant essay to make my point.

11 Burke, K. (1969). *A grammar of motives.* Berkeley, CA: University of California Press.

12 Garoian, C. (1999). *Performing pedagogy.* New York, NY: State University of New York Press; Garoian, C. (1999). "Performance art as critical pedagogy in studio art education." *Art Journal,* 58.1, 57–62.

13 Rodriquez, V. (2021). "The teaching brain and the end of the empty vessel." 179–80. https://scholar.harvard.edu/files/vanessarodriguez/files/vrodriguez_publishedmbe-article_11-16-12.pdf.

14 I entered the reminder about transforming labor into love, after a brilliant first-generation student from Arizona State University asked a question regarding this difficult negotiation of code-switching with family members. This entry was a part of my response to her.

15 Leipzig, D. H. (2001). "What is reading?" www.readingrockets.org/article/what-reading. Accessed August 2, 2021.

16 Levinson, B. A., Foley, D. E., & Holland, D. C. (Eds.). (1996). *The cultural production of the education person: Critical ethnographies of schooling and local practice.* New York: State University of New York Press.

17 Giroux, H. A. & Shannon, P. (Eds.). (1997). *Education and cultural studies: Toward a performative practice.* New York: Routledge, 2.

Section III

Letters to Those Who Mattered

The epistolary style is a literary form that allows for a story to unfold in letters as a direct address of intention and connection to an absent other. The letters that we present in this section are not evidence of nonfictive conjurings or fanciful tales. These are letters of first-person direct address, letters that our souls have longed to write to those who mattered in our lives, only halted in time relative to our coming of age or coming of knowing the import of those past relationships and now missed opportunities.

Letters *to those who mattered*: those of importance, consequence, note, weight, significance in our lives—in the immediate past and lingering presence, those for whom our words of respect and gratitude, or maybe even words of remorse, regret, or disdain may have fallen short in the passage of time or never uttered at all. Only now have we been able to write the direct discourse of our care or concern across time, across generations, and across lived circumstance to bridge the gaps of our loss or distance. *To those who mattered*, in the materiality of their being, in their corporeal presence in our lives, and the difference-making that their physical, psychic, and philosophical presencing made as ballast and beam in the architecture of our being. *To those who mattered*, for whom the substance of their physical presence was as important as their mind and spirit—a holy trinity of their whole persons that could not be separated, each of whom have left a legacy in our lives in the inheritance of biology or the wisdom of knowing; each of whom has left a lifelong affair of the heart, to which we now take up as a consideration of care and caution; to each of whom, have helped us establish arguments of belief and defense that establish evidence as grounds on which we stand.

In presenting these letters before each other, we, the members of this collaborative quartet are engaged in an intergenerational dialogue. We are both writing *to* the ones who mattered at the same time we are writing *about* the ones who mattered to each other. We do so in ways that are both private and public, as well as both particular and plural to Black family experiences that may also be resonant with the reader, maybe even beyond blackness. As we articulate individual experiences we also contribute to a collective, communal, and cultural knowing. We tell the stories about the people *who* mattered in our lives

DOI: 10.4324/9781003274315-12

and *how* they matter(ed). We tell the stories about the people who knew us well and called us by names that mattered in our families, names that no one else use but family, names that signal relationships and histories—middle names, nicknames, pet and play names, and the names that signaled rituals and family connections; a daughter named after a mother, then a grandmother; a son named after a father, then a grandfather. Names that keep spirits alive. *Names that we call home.*[1] Names that we call ourselves for comfort, as we re-member ourselves with those who loved us enough to name us. We tell the stories as communal sharing, and like Dumbledore's *pensieve* in the Harry Potter series, we now place these letters in a reservoir of memories (called this book) to which we can later revisit and retrieve at our leisure to spot the patterns and linkages of our past, our living, and our futures as archives of possible ways of knowing.

These letters stand alone and maybe lonely in the absence of the connecting receiver. But collectively they circulate and create entries in a broader basin or cultural diary to which the authors invite the readers to add. Add your memories as letters of direct address and cathartic process. Add your letters as worship, praise, and gratitude, or add your letters of regret, resentment, and reconciliation to the object/subject of your focus, or as machinations and mechanisms of self-healing. Add your letters as to heal the scars of the past, to liberate the possibility of unburdening yourself from or to remind yourself of the many gifts of memory that you have yet to unwrap—as time capsules from your past as you begin to plan for better tomorrows.

BKA

Note

1 Thompson, B. & Tyagi, S. (1996). *Names we call home: Autobiography on racial identity.* New York: Routledge.

9 To Daddee (*Love Keith*)[1]

Bryant Keith Alexander

Dear Daddee,

It has taken me a long time to write this letter to you. I have written a lot about you in my scholarly work, sometimes trying to remember or memorialize you, and sometimes about the trials and tribulation of being with you.[2] But all those efforts seem to fail to capture the fullness of you to me and in me. So maybe this time I just want to say thank you.

Thank you for being a strong Black father.

Thank you for being a consistently present Black father in my home upbringing.

Thank you for being you, in my own processes of being and becoming, me.

I used to think that we were so different. But now that I am coming closer to the age of your passing. And now that the implicity and complicity of blood are making you more present in my body—the aches, the pains, and the challenges, not to mention that your face appears with more frequency in the mirror when I look; I realize that we were not so different, not just in body but also in mind. The PhD that you encouraged me to complete in relation to your fourth-grade education has finally taught me enough to come back to you, again and again. Maybe you would have predicted that return. You always had that form of intelligence that letters behind names could not achieve.

I was listening.

I was listening, especially in those quiet moments together watching reruns of the same old westerns and military shows in which you deconstructed the ethics of war, race, class, white privilege, and the role of Indigenous people and Black people on the short-end of manifest destiny and Americanism, in the reel and real-life adventures of our experiences in this country—both found and transported.

I was listening.

I was listening when you pointed out military movies with shifting "others" as enemies of war or skirmishes with Native Americans (in those pained cowboy-and-Indian movies) when parties retreated; retreated as a strategy of war, not a complete withdrawal or throwing in the towel or declaration of defeat but a type of military operation that signified a pulling back of forces

DOI: 10.4324/9781003274315-13

and energies while maintaining an obvious contact with the opposing faction. While you liked the strictly military versions in overt wars, you celebrated and cheered when Indians (Indigenous or Native Americans) used the same strategy in covert wars of manifest destiny, annihilating people for their land (like stealing and raping Black bodies for their labor—Daddee, that was also a part of your lesson.) The Native Americans were (also) presumed to be savages with no critical sensemaking skills and thus had no rights. When they retreated, it was a variation of biding time, a variation of suggesting defeat by running away but a reconnoitering of possibilities that came back to occupy a different ground (as in space or argument or position of defense) that was easier or a better positioned for an ambush, for an insurrection—as a strategic and acceptable skill in combat in defending their territory and claiming their sovereignty. When it was obvious that the "Indians" were making a perceivable risky move with some sacrifice to get the greater gain in a perpetual fight for dignity and destiny,[3] you outlined those strategies, asking me, "Do you see it? Do you see what they are doing?" You taught me about the importance of retreat as a strategy of survival.

I was listening.

I was listening to the lessons on performative masculinity which for you was about being resilient and resistive for the common good. You knew I was gay long before I did, but for you, masculinity was not about the directionality of desire but the convictions of the heart. Sitting at your knee watching television, just you and me, when everybody else was gone, I listened about being a man—and staying, and standing strong, against all odds. But when everyone else was home, Mamee and the other six children, I remember that you always seem to be in the process of leaving. Retreating from the activities of the everyday hustle and bustle of a big family. You would stay long enough to touch each; you would stay long enough to claim a certain dominion; you would stay long enough to declare and discipline; then you would retreat, retreating to your bedroom where you listened to music alone; sometimes I would follow you, thinking it was just to be with you. And sometimes you would retreat into a puff of cigarette smoke or into a bottle. I did not follow there, neither then nor now. I wasn't sure, but it appeared that you were running away from the obligations of a large family or maybe the noise, or maybe it was just your need to be alone, a different retreat.

At varying times, when she would see the same behavior in me, Mamee would say, "You are just like your father." And I hated that phrase. I hated it because it seemed like a curse. But maybe she was trying to help me understand you better, especially in those times when I would not talk to you for days because you had said something harsh. Maybe you were trying to get me to fight back. Unlike my four brothers and two sisters, I never learned to fight back with you in the same ways. But maybe you would be happy to know that I have learned to fight—in my own ways, with words, but still with the ferocity of getting even or standing my ground or putting people in their place—which were the postures of self-defense that you wanted to instill. You always said, "That one's got a mouth on him." Maybe my talking back then was a rehearsal for my professional life where words matter in shaping new realities and possibilities for self and others; a different kind of fight—and maybe not so different. Thanks for the early lessons.

Then and now. Then, the fifth child of seven, the fourth boy of five, the sensitive one who ran away to the back room to hide in a book; avoiding being an audience to performances of bravado or shame; never wanting to fully witness because I did not want to later have to testify to what I heard, to what I saw, to what I felt; the anger, the resentment, the hurt knowing that I was never given the same stage. I was not the oldest child or the oldest boy, not the youngest child or the youngest boy, not the presumed talented one or the middle child who demanded attention. I was not the squeaky wheel that demanded oil and attention. I was always a little off-center and different—the one who learned to be self-sufficient but still yearned for the attention of respect. Maybe that is why I followed you when you retreated—thinking that it was just wanting to be with you—it was probably my own need, an impulse that I was rehearsing in my own survival of retreat. *And now*, in my adult/professional life, the only Black administrator at my level and above—at a university engaged in *trans-race-formation* as a reckoning of the current historical moment but still *predominately white*, which is a term that is as much about sensibilities and positionalities as it is about demographics—I also stand a little off-center.

Both there and then, and here and now—I stay/ed to witness and watch, to contribute what I can in a double load of work and representation, and then I retreat. I retreat from large gatherings of mandated sociality saturated with the politics of positionality in which people are still strategically working the room. I stay long enough to touch each; long enough to claim a certain authority of my position. I stay long enough to represent as needed in the politics of difference and diversity, then like you, Daddee, I retreat; retreating to my office, or my car, or my home—maybe to listen to music alone or to write. Sometimes at such gatherings, I would have one too many drinks to lessen my anxieties, then think of you and restrain myself—wondering if your drinking was linked with your anxieties, to calm the social noise, white or otherwise.

Because of this behavior I was once described by a high-ranking university official as being a phantom. He was describing the fact that I seemingly appeared and quickly disappeared at social events. And of course, he was right in his adjectival description of a certain phenomenon. Though he also showed a lack of racial awareness in him being a white man calling me a Black man, a phantom; like the historical reference to Black people being spooks or bugaboos. I understood his description of a certain presencing and absenting, but without the recognition that *I was fully present*. And that *I made my presence known*. Then I made the conscious decision not to linger. Thus, I am not a phantom as *something apparent to sense but with no substantial existence or an object of continual dread or abhorrence*. That is the unfortunate construction of the Black man in the white imagination to which this country is still reckoning with in the year 2021. And whether "just" a poor choice of words or not, he, like so many others, need to dig deep, with the pressure of a root canal, to extract the roots of their own actions that give teeth to impressions of racism or how racism is also linguistically rooted in our references to the presumed other. I am not that kind of a phantom, nor were you, Daddee. *I see you.* And while you retreated from time to time, you stayed with your family, and you were always in arm's reach when needed. I, too, retreat as a form of personal survival: to sustain enough energy to do the work, to mindfully mine future possibilities and support the greater effort for the ones who need me to be fully present, for the ones who are also in the margins, standing on the borders of their being and becoming.

I always saw you in the process of retreating, but you never fully left. You stayed.

I wonder.

I wonder how many Black boys did not understand their Black father's anger or struggles or pains and scars.

I wonder how many Black boys coded on the anger without a deep sense of their Black father's desire for them *not* to relive the same experiences and maybe feeling helpless of that inevitability.

I wonder how many Black boys didn't value their Black fathers because they didn't look or act like the Beaver's father (on *Leave it to Beaver*) or Richie Cunningham's father (on *Happy Days*) or the father of the Tanner kids (on *Full House*), or even Heathcliff Huxtable on that pseudo-rendition of an upper-class Black family (on *The Cosby Show*). I suggest that even the actors who played those fictional television fathers failed to live up to the fictive paternal image that they perpetuated, along with the network propaganda of the ideal American family, which was typically white or engaged in a performative whiteness. We know for a fact that Bill Cosby failed miserably in living up to the idealistic Black man he played on *The Cosby Show* or even as the moralizing ranting and demonizing public figure who critiqued other Black men about how they treated their women and children and not standing up as Black male role models. This is the same actor playing the same role on television and in the public sphere—demonizing/demoralizing other Black men, only to be revealed [*allegedly*] as a philandering man who drugged dozens of women in service of a necrophiliac-type sexual desire to have sex with their comatose bodies, all of which shattered the hypocrisy of his crafted public persona and his constructed social mobility. He served two years in prison and was released on a procedural technicality against the three counts of aggravated indecent assault to which he was charged.[4] I always hated Heathcliff Huxtable anyway. There was something unreal about the character. There was something in the refractivity of the moralistic induced rhetoric that Cosby rehearsed on Thursday nights and his celebration of selective parts of Black culture (through Heathcliff Huxtable) that did not bend to shine the light on aspects of everyday Black culture and of everyday Black people.

Cosby seemed to believe that his class-based moralistic ranting through his fictional character of Cliff authorized his grandstanding in the everyday life of Black people, never deflecting from the actuality of his private practices as a [*presumed and convicted*] serial rapist. But maybe that did not impact the actuality of him being a particular kind of Black father to his own Black children. Maybe we, or some people, can separate that aspect of his private family life from the other aspects of his *other* private activities made public—to avoid the *destruction of a legacy*.[5]

We used to watch *The Cosby Show* as a family, aspirational in nature because of class and the representational politics to see Black folks living well. But, Daddee, I remember that you didn't like Cliff Huxtable either—you said the character *didn't sit right with you*. But you reminded me that you first introduced Cosby to me years before through his comedy albums, where he was touted as a "clean comic." We would listen to the albums on your portable record player in the back room, on one of those days when we were both retreating. Then, when you were home on Saturday mornings, we would watch Cosby through another alter ego, *Fat Albert and the Cosby Kids*. The animated cartoon that featured poor Black kids who often circulated in and around a Philadelphia junkyard.[6] The show always had an educational lesson through the frame of Dr. Bill Cosby, EdD. You preferred that version of Cosby more, maybe because that rendition of his public efforts and education still cared about representing and uplifting everyday Black folks, or at least those who were makin' it-by-the-hardest. I clearly remember you entering the house from time to time pronouncing in a guttural sound: "Hey, Hey, Hey, Daddee's home"—a variation of the signature *Fat Albert* opening. The irony is that when Bill Cosby was released from prison—he invoked the same triplet, "Hey, Hey, Hey," through the feeble and crackled voice of a former childhood icon turned ex-con-rapist. I cried—not because of his demise, but of what that took away from my childhood memories of watching, *Fat Albert and the Cosby Kids* with you. But my memories of your entering announcement into the house, "Daddee's home"—stands strong with me to this day.

And maybe there you were, Daddee, less Cliff Huxtable and more Fred G. Sanford (of *Sanford and Son*). Fred, that somewhat sarcastic Black male junk dealer who operated a junkyard with his son Lamont in another Black television series. Fred, who was always a little cantankerous and grumpy but with a heart of gold and fully present for his family.[7] Fred G. Sanford's flaws were obvious as he continually worked, episode by episode, to address his biases without claiming high moral ground but continually grappling with his humanity in family and the Black community where he lived. In the year 2021, when the challenges of being a Black person in America are still real, when Black people are still being killed under the regimes of racism and white privilege, the lessons you taught me about being steadfast in your commitments and the honor of being a Black man and father are clearer to me today than when I was a boy, because I understand more fully your struggle and your scars and what you did to protect me for as long as you could. I stand stronger for possible futures. I am happy to claim you as more Fred G. Sandford than Heathcliff Huxtable—and I do so with great pride.

I listened and I remember. I remember how many Black boys flocked to the corner lot of our humble house. The fact that you had five biological boys of your own increased the metric odds of the number of friends we would attract. Maybe it was the basketball court or the card games on the front porch or the tournament-style marble games of my childhood that attracted them. But I also think that they were attracted to you. I remember so many of them were from homes with an absent father, with a turn style of new uncles or play daddies or nasty old men entering and existing in their lives. They saw you as a Black father who stayed. I remember you telling them to "Pull up their pants" or "Put on your shirt," not in a Bill Cosby–like moralistic rant but as a set of expectations for your yard, in front of your wife, and in front of your daughters.

I remember that you kidded and jived with them, and you knew their names—because you also knew their parents. They called you "Mr. Joe." And when they saw you coming around the corner, they adjusted themselves. Sometimes you made them help clean the yard or pick up pecans after a rainstorm or pick mulberries and figs from the trees for preserves. You said, "If you are going to spend so much time here—you might as well earn your keep." And they did, with no complaint or talk back. It is no wonder there were always a few extra mouths around dinnertime. You would grumble because that was your way, but they would stay because they knew they were welcomed. And even when one of them knocked at the door late at night, because something was happening at their house—you would grumble about the time but would pull them into the house—sometimes to talk, other times just to say, "You alright? Go in the back room and sleep—we can talk tomorrow." They knew there was love in the house because among other things, this Black daddy stayed. And I knew that as well. And you provided them, like you provided your children, a template of the Black masculine that they/ we could pivot off in finding our own sense of being and relating to Black men in the world. At your passing, these boys, now men, cried, and they squabbled for positions to be your pallbearers as a final act of appreciation for "Mr. Joe."

Daddee, I don't know how to end this letter, so I won't.

It is an ongoing dialogue between you and me and maybe with myself that I will continue to write and unravel as evidence of my being and becoming in your absence. I will continue being or trying to be the man that you and Mamee wanted me to be.

I cry for you and Mamee on the regular. I miss your physical presence in the world and my ability to retreat with you into quiet spaces of our own.

With deep love and respect,

Your boy,

Keith

Figure 4 Joseph Junius Alexander Sr, passed April 11, 2001

Notes

1 In the writing of this piece, near to the construction of the first iteration—I lost the text. Somehow my computer rejected the document in saving, and I could not recover it even with the help from IT. So, after a level of personal frustration and anger, I started another version of the paper that I called, "Reconstructing Dadee"—which also seems like an apt alternative version of my original intent. This piece was originally constructed for this book section; then during the compilation of the volume, I included the piece in a keynote address for the 1st Annual Advanced Methods Institute Conference (Theme: Culturally Responsive Research and Researchers) sponsored by the Ohio State University, College of Education & Human Ecology—June 2, 2021. Columbus, OH [online due to the Covid-19 pandemic]. The keynote titled "Teaching and Engaging Autoethnography as Qualitative Methodology" with a frame and explication of critical autoethnography will be published in the conference proceedings: Pasque, P. A. & Alexander, E. (Eds.). (2022). *Advancing culturally responsive research and researchers: Qualitative, quantitative and mixed methods.* New York: Routledge.

2 See Alexander, B. K. (2000). "Skin flint (or the garbage man's kid): A generative autobio-graphical performance." *Text and Performance Quarterly*, 20.1, 97–114; Alexander, B. K., Moreira, C. & Kumar, H. S. (2012). "Resisting (resistance) stories: A tri-autoethnographic exploration of father narratives across shades of difference." *Qualitative Inquiry*, 18.2, 121–133. doi:10.1177/1077800411429087 (On Line First); Alexander, B. K. (2013). "Stand-ing in the wake of my father's silence (an alternative eulogy)." In S. Malhotra & A. Carrillo Rowe (Eds.), *Silence and power: Feminist reflections at the edges of sound.* New York: Palgrave Macmillan Press, 230–238.

3 I use the Wikipedia reference only for the reader. My father outlined these logics for me long ago in my youth. https://simple.wikipedia.org/wiki/Withdrawal_(military).

4 https://nypost.com/2021/06/30/bill-cosby-freed-from-prison-after-court-overturns-sex-assault-conviction/.

5 A phrase used by Phylicia Rashad in defending Bill Cosby: www.vulture.com/2021/07/phylicia-rashad-changes-bill-cosby-sexual-assault-statement.html.

6 See *Fat Albert and the Cosby Kids*: https://en.wikipedia.org/wiki/Fat_Albert_and_the_Cosby_Kids.

7 See Sandford, Fred G. "Sandford and sons." https://en.wikipedia.org/wiki/Fred_G._Sanford.

10 Dear Grandpa (*Love, Cookie*)

Mary E. Weems

(Born April 20, 1916, to Leroy and Bertha. Died in October 1978, holding his wife Mary's hand)

All my memories of you are part of me. Hard to believe you've been gone forty-three years. I miss you terribly, Grandpa. I wish we'd spent more time together talking about your life as a child, teenager, and young man. I wish I knew more about you than Granny shared over the years and/or I overheard the two of you talking about when we were all supposed to be in bed. Not sure if you know/knew this, but I've always been nosey and what Mama used to call too much into grown folks' business. This is how I know your mama, Great-Grandma Bertha, who was born in southern Ohio, could have passed for white; in fact, her birth certificate reads 'white,' even though Granny said she had several brown-skinned siblings. She died before I had a chance to meet her, but she was Mama's best friend, just like Granny was mine. I know that when Great-Grandma agreed to marry your father, her family disowned her, that she never had anything to do with them again. I was able to conclude without being told that she and Great-Grandpa faced some of the most devastating relationship racism thanks to miscegenation—kind reserved for Black men (light-skinned or not) who were married to "visibly" white women toward the end of 19th and the beginning of the 20th century.

Beyond that I know you met Granny on Halloween night at a party where you were playing guitar in a band, and after dating each other less than two months, you got married on Christmas Day and remained in love and together, never spending even one night apart for forty-two years until you died from complications due to colon cancer. Granny told me once that the two of you had an agreement—even if you had to stay up all night, you never went to bed angry, and since I never even heard you raise your voices to each other, I'm guessing the two of you kept that promise to each other.

Since you were a doer and not much of a talker (except when in the company of my brother, your son, or other men in the family), I don't remember many conversations with you but, rather, either listening to you talk about something in the local news you read and watched every day, something that needed fixing in the house, or something I or my siblings brought to your attention about our lives. You were always brief, honest, and encouraging.

DOI: 10.4324/9781003274315-14

Plus, you had a sense of humor, which helped me laugh when I was worried about school or crying about something. For the most part, though, I talked to Granny about any and everything, never realizing until I was long grown and you were gone, that you were like the strong glue that held us all together.

Grandpa, I remember that like me, you wore glasses for nearsightedness; and dropped out of school in the eighth grade to help your family during the Great Depression. You told me once that during that time Black men had the hardest time finding jobs but that Jewish business owners would hire you, even though at times, you were paid in food.

Alcohol was a big problem on your side of the family. I'm not sure why, but you lost your older brother to drink, and you lost your dad at a young age—just not sure how he died. You drank too, shorties, sometimes pints of Wild Irish Rose every day, and, occasionally, a beer or two. I remember because Granny used to fuss, not because drinking "ever" stopped you from doing anything— you always protected and provided for Granny, your children, and us, including the four-bedroom house you bought so mama and the four of us could have a stable place to live—she fussed because she loved you and worried all that drinking would hurt you.

As a result, you would hide it from her as much as possible, doing a lot of your drinking in your car either going to and from your job or to and from the some "place" you were always going for parts, to shop for groceries, to pick one of us up for a ride, to help someone else in the family. On the many occasions you were riding me from point A to point B, you'd always take that last swig before we went into the house, put your bottle back under the seat of your car (Granny didn't drive), and tell me, "Don't tell your grandmother."

You loved to play guitar, and some of my earliest memories are of you seated with your pick in your right hand, cradling the guitar on your lap and playing. I remember the time you spent on the porch steps, teaching a friend of my brother's, who went on to become the member of a popular soul music band. Even though you never went to church or talked specifically about God or religion, one of the songs I remember you playing and singing was "An Old Rugged Cross," the lyrics "On a hill far away, stood an old rugged cross, the emblem of suffering and pain . . ." always heard in your voice.

When you weren't working away from home, or at home on something that needed fixing inside or in the driveway on your latest hooptie, your favorite thing to do was be with Granny, who always called you "Duffy," in response to your "Honey." When you came home from work before you spent any time with us beyond giving us pieces of Beeman's gum that you kept in your pocket, your first thing was "Honey, I'm home," as you headed to the kitchen, where she was cooking whatever we'd be having for dinner. Granny would stop and take a seat at the table with you so the two of you could talk about your day. I only know this because I'd often listen from the dining room, knowing better than to interrupt your time together.

I'm not sure why but you were always a man of few words. I'd often see you quietly sketching the heads of people with a pencil, reading the newspaper, or just sitting cupping your head with your left hand—a Black man's version of

"The Thinker," sculpture. You used to tell us that there're three questions no one can adequately answer about human beings: (1) Where did we come from? (2) Why are we here? and (3) Where are we going?

I always had the sense that you cherished time you were able to spend alone—and while I'm just making the connection as I write this letter, I'm the same way, an odd combination of extrovert and introvert—I love being by myself and am always one of the first to leave an informal or formal gathering of people.

Figure 5 Grandpa and Granny Owens

Grandpa, you were the best, brightest, most giving and loving grandfather anyone could have. Every night, before we went to bed, I got to kiss you good night, and any time we left the house you always said, "Be careful," the "why" of which I didn't understand until I was grown and experienced how cold-blooded and cruel life can be.

You blessed my life forever by providing a beautiful home with Granny that us kids could feel safe in by being there when we got home from school, since Mama worked the 3 to 11 p.m. shift at Stouffer's, by passing along life lessons and advice that I've used repeatedly to develop into the kind of woman I hope you can be proud of: Look out for your family, follow your dreams, work hard and save some money, stay out of trouble, keep your word, and give everything you do your best effort.

When you died, my brother said he lost a father and a grandfather. In many ways, I did too, and I'm writing to let you know that even though we lost you before I got the "good" job with Chevy, became a homeowner, went to college and earned three degrees, and got married and became a mother—none of this would have happened without the support you unselfishly gave and gave and gave.

Grandpa, I always told you I loved you, but I never got a chance to tell you how much you meant to me. Even when you were sick in the hospital, I refused to accept how ill you were, to wrap my brain around the possibility that one day you would die and leave us.

I'm so glad I had the chance to see you in your hospital room, right after you passed away. I'd never seen your face when it didn't have some kind of worry in it—a wrinkled brow, a serious, distant look, a frown living in the corners of your mouth. I knew as soon as I looked at you that you were at peace—rested—ready to be with God, Great-Granny, Great-Grandpa, and your only brother. I kissed your forehead—I kissed your cheek, I said, "See you soon."

I'm sorry, Grandpa, thank you. I'm sorry, Grandpa, thank you. I'm sorry, Grandpa, thank you.

See you soon. Give Granny and Michelle a hug for me.

Love, Cookie

P.S. A few years ago, I tried to empathize or more closely identify with your life filling in the blanks of what I don't know with imagination, and wrote:

Grandpa:

I was born to a light-skinned Black man
and a looks-white mother in 1916
fifty-one years after Juneteenth, 1865—
Mother's family disowned her like she'd committed
blasphemy when she married my daddy, even though
damn near her whole family was passing for white
always one child away from being exposed.
What they'd been doin' for years was shipping the dark children

off to relatives in California, the ones who had too much color
to be invisible. I lost my daddy when I was a boy. Mother
had my brother, then me, and before I turned 7 years-old, my father
had drank himself to death.

*(Takes a short of Rose out of back pocket, in
brown paper bag and takes a swig)*

I knew something was wrong because mother let me and my brother
sleep in on a Sunday. When I woke up and saw the sun shining
through the window, I ran into the kitchen and there was mother, her best
friend Ruby
and Pastor Price seated at our table full of coffee cups, shot glasses, ashtrays
and half-eaten
plates.
When I met Mary on Halloween night over forty years ago—I recognized
her beauty underneath her homemade mask. She told me she was supposed to
be somebody. But since my feet stuck to the ground and my eyes were glued
to her red mouth—I didn't hear a word she said. We married on Christmas day
and from that moment she was my Honey for life. She blessed me with two
children, a daughter, and then a son she named after me. Spent my whole love
for life with Mary, taking care of my kids, then my grandkids. Left this world
in a brand-new suit she bought for me, glasses, and my favorite hat.

Family Portrait

My young cousin sent me this photo in a phone text months ago. She lost her
mother, my second cousin, a few years ago and had found it among the numer-
ous photographs her late grandmother had passed down.
Every time I look at it, I feel closer to heaven than here, closer to my grandparents, all my grandmother's "ten" siblings and their children, closer to my late
daughter who joined them on January 3, 2017.
Several months ago, a friend of mine lost his ex-wife. They'd been divorced
a while, but when she got sick, he moved her back into his house with his son
and daughter and took care of her as long as he could. After she died, I saw him
out in the streets, and he shared how he'd been feeling since her passing. He
said, "I'm trying to get as close to death as I possibly can." Revisiting this pho-
tograph for this piece, I have a sudden, spiritual, clear understanding of what he
meant. I'm reminded of the true circle life is—that like my great-grandfather,
James Owens, who is in the far right corner, dressed in a three-piece pinstriped
suit, white carnation in his lapel, his head gray-haired and tilted up with pride;
my grandfather, the light-skinned, short-haired man stands in the same row
as Great-Grandpa but more to the center—Grandpa, who taught me how to
whistle; my mother, the little girl in the first row in the short dress, who had
me right after she turned seventeen, standing beside my late, favorite great-
uncle, in shirt, tie, and knickers with his hands around the neck of the family

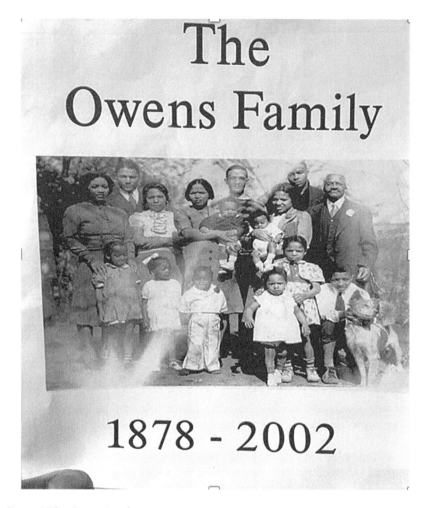

Figure 6 The Owens Family

dog, my beloved and everyday-missed grandmother, my granny—at the far-left side, dark hair carefully coifed, hoop earrings, capped-sleeved top, arms crossed—who taught me almost everything, standing next to my uncle, the eldest and junior to their dad, and all the family in this image I can't name—I'm reminded that I, too, am going to join this photo one day, I'll take my place beside my granny and stand still with my daughter, surrounded by eternal, familial love, while God snaps our picture.

11 What Becomes (Possible) When a Black Woman Sees You

A Gratitude Meditation for Mama Crystal

Dominique C. Hill

After standing up in court and telling the white woman judge for the umpteenth time, I don't want to go home. I am ready to go to a placement.	"You don't belong here."
Eyes likely rolling out of exhaustion and anger. Preparing to be taken back to the single-sex cell where we wait until all the other young folk, "juveniles" they called us, had their moment before the judge. A familiar-but-not-supposed-to-be-there face looks me in my eyes.	"You don't belong here."
Mama Crystal was not one to play with, so I likely straightened up just enough to not be disrespectful and still indicate disinterest in what more she had to say. My mom stood within feet of her, likely asked her to come there (so I thought).	
The possibility that now my enrichment program knew I was in "juvie," that my history and geography teacher definitely knew I was locked up, that my mom called her to talk some "sense" into me (read: convince me to listen to my mother and deny my feelings, my knowledge) made me sick to my stomach. I wanted to get as far away from that courtroom as possible, wanted to be unseen by my teacher. Some part of me wanted to be alone with her, though, and find out the deets—Like, who sent her? Why did she agree to come? Who was she finna tell? And whose side was she on?	"You don't belong here."

(Continued)

DOI: 10.4324/9781003274315-15

(Continued)

Sitting in the cell waiting for that moment of protocol where we stand and are fastened to the person in front of and behind us (unless you were the leader or the rear of the line), a warm feeling rushed through me. I couldn't describe it then and wasn't about to share it with the other girls in the cell. It lasted through my wait, through the ride back to East Ferry, and evaporated somewhere between the unmemorable dinner and waking up on a thin mattress at 6 a.m. for calisthenics.

I continued to think about the Black woman adorned in African cloth with draping locs, my then history teacher in Buffalo Prep—an enrichment program for inner-city youth. She was unlike any other woman I'd ever spent substantial time with and demanded respect in ways unfamiliar to me. There was something about the strength in her calmness—oooooo it was creepy. She did not raise her voice, did not curse, and charged us 25 cents, 25 push-ups, or 25 sit-ups—you choose—for being caught saying "shut up." Mama Crystal didn't eat meat like the women in my family, didn't drink like the women in my family, didn't have a perm like the women in my family, didn't prioritize her feelings over mine like the women in my family. I loved the women in my family and came to love her just the same.

"You don't belong here."
You can come home with me.

At my next court date, there she was again. Before returning to my cell, I learned Mama Crystal was also a social worker, that when I stopped coming to class, she sought out to find me. I also learned that she came on her own accord and made an agreement with my mother that if I told the judge I changed my mind and wanted to go home, I could move in with her until I was ready to actually return.—*I never wanted to go home, but that's a different story for a different day*. I listened and in disbelief reluctantly turned to read my mother's face; she was in agreement.

"You don't belong here."
You can come home with me.
Your attitude doesn't have to be your homeplace.

I never knew my mother to listen to anyone at that time in our lives, but whatever Mama Crystal, my then teacher and eventual mother, told her, it registered.

Shook. I said I'd think about it. Inside, I was floored and frustrated. If only my mother fought for me that way. Disappointed and hopeful. The weight I carried was evident in my walk, eyes, and cocked lips.

"You don't belong here."

Figure 7 Crystal "Mama Crystal" R. Austin-Seymore

What kind of spell had this woman put on
   my mother? How could my teacher be
   my guardian? What type of food do Black
   women absent of spicy mouths and draped
   in long dreadlocks eat? No doubt fear
   lurked in every corner of my body, and
   yet the idea that she came to see about me
   comforted me at night.
Four days before my fourteenth birthday
   I stood before the judge with a new tune
   and lied. Four days before my fourteenth
   birthday, I said yes to living with Mama
   Crystal because when a Black woman
   comes to look for you to announce,
you believe her.

(*Continued*)

(Continued)

When a Black woman goes out of her way to find you, it's almost impossible not to locate pieces of yourself you didn't know exist, pieces that comprise pride, a soft-not-weakness, and forgiveness. Saying yes to my teacher ushered in a new way of living, of doing school, and of doing Blackgirl.

Mama Crystal, a hardcore vegetarian, loved and made a loving home with Poppy, a science wizard, math teacher, and beef burger connoisseur. In their home, I realized effective responses emerged from me with expressed disappointment (*not raised voices*) and sustained deliberate eye contact. I learned that mothering and parenting were other dimensions of teaching while Black.

Because mother/ing is an action; it is about nurturing and creating spaciousness in the lives of youth and ourselves. I received an *other* mother[1]—another and different opportunity to be taught survival strategies and to learn what mother/daughter love (could) look like. After two years as her student, six months living with her, and becoming one of her children, I started to see myself more clearly. I didn't belong in juvie or a funk.

No longer mad at the world (*just mainly my mother, still*). No longer sabotaging my life (*I returned home to attend the high school of my choice. That was the deal my mother offered*). My lips weren't poked out, and the chip on my right shoulder had smoothed out a bit. I still ate beef (*although I don't currently*) and developed an appreciation for reflecting on my mistakes and bad decisions—*these were standard practices in Northumberland.*

Even after leaving Northumberland, her words stayed.

They became a reminder, a checkpoint even. Oftentimes I would find her words while reflecting on a relationship I'd outgrown or after acknowledging a low vibration feeling I'd laid in for too long.

You don't belong lost. Anger don't own you.

"You don't belong here."

Last time her words bubbled up inside me,
   I was sitting next to her in awe of her
   strength and angry at cancer and whoever
   the hell created it (*you know it likely came*
   from someone's lab), wishing I knew before
   that very moment, before it got this bad,
   that my mother was dying. There's lots
   of travel, misplaced paperwork, possibly
   some hurt feelings, and for sure immense
   grief that copped a squat between this
   moment I mention and my whispering to
   her, this and more:
Mama Crystal, you don't belong here
   (anymore). You can let go and trust your
   children will all be alright. I rubbed her
   hand, looked into her eyes, and, before
   returning to the family business a few
   steps away of how to care for her, the will,
   and her wishes, I kissed her on her head.
I never imagined I would be responsible for
   gifting her words back to her.

Note

1 Gumbs, A. P. (2016). "M/other ourselves: A Black queer feminist genealogy for radical mothering." In C. Martens, A. P. Gumbs, & M. Williams (Eds.), *Revolutionary mothering: Love on the front lines* (pp. 9–31). Oakland, CA: PM Press.

12 A Praisesong to Softness

Reflecting on Soft Black Masculinities and Survival

Durell M. Callier

In the now famed edited collection of essays of Black gay men, edited by Essex Hemphill and conceived by Joseph Beam (1991), *Brother to Brother*, readers experience entryway into the interiority of Black gay men's lives. A collection of poems, essays, and fiction, we grapple with the hopes and dreams of Black gay men, their search for community, coping with HIV/AIDS, creating family, looking for love, and surviving the rejection of society because of their race and sexuality. What I continually come back to in the text are the whispers of longing and hallelujah exhales of how they made it over, with chosen family, friends, finding each other, learning to love themselves fully and unlearning so much of what society said was an impossibility of their being. One poem, "Brothers loving brothers," so aptly illustrates this.

> Respect yourself, my brother,
> for we are so many wondrous things.
>
> . . .
>
> You previous gem,
> black pearl that warms the heart,
> symbol of ageless wisdom,
> I derive strength
> from the touch of your hand
>
> . . .
>
> Brothers born form the same earth womb.
> Brothers reaching for the same star.
>
> Love me as your equal.
> Love me, brother to brother.
> *(Vega, 1991, p. 106)*

The essay that follows moves through autoethnographic vignettes, reflexive poems, and epistolary narratives, echoing the unlearning of hate we are made to digest because of race, sexuality, gender performance, and so on and learning of acceptance

DOI: 10.4324/9781003274315-16

and love in *Brother to Brother*. Staging a different set of intergenerational dialogues, "a quartet of saxophones blowing red-blue squalls," "A Praiseong to Softness" explores (soft) Black masculinities, what is taught and unlearned in order to survive more whole, more free (Hemphill, 1990, p. xxx). It also juxtaposes the various words, saying, phrases I have heard and had to hold in navigating my own sense of self regarding how my body was read, what I could do with it while also highlighting the love and protection of Black families in support of their queer kin. This is accomplished through the three movements used in the essay, "Softness," "Protection," and "Invocation." These headings act as themes of the writing contained within connecting back to the larger commentary on the creation and sustenance of soft Black masculinities and ending with a hope of softer Black masculinities and femininities so that we might be tender with ourselves and each other as Black people.

Softness

Dear Gran,

Today I ate a plum and it made me think of you. Unfortunately, today's weather signals to me that it is almost the end of summer. Child of the summer that I am, those are perhaps some of my fondest memories of you. From the summertime fun in the apartment complex pool to the multiple simultaneous and at times overlapping vacation Bible schools you would enroll me and my sister in to staying out later because the streetlights came on later. And how could I forget all of our summertime eats, Gran. Watermelon. Strawberries. Peaches. Nectaaaarines. Plums. Grapes. Oranges. Grapefruits. Cantaloupe. Honeydew, your favorite. You'd always let me cut up the watermelon, my favorite. I know I ate just as much as I would put away. Skimming mine off the top with each slice, a piece for me, five others in the bowl. I don't know if you knew this. My willingness to cut up things and put things away was also about how I knew it meant I could have first dibs to see if we had picked ripe fruits or not. Chowing down nearly to the white of the rind, you'd let me. Just shy of a tummy ache, most times, you'd usually remind me with a "Boi, if you don't finish cleaning up all that mess," or "Keep eatin all that watamelon and yo stomach gonna hurt."

Oh and how could I forget all of the fresh things from Uncle Arthur's garden like peppers and string beans you'd teach me how to snap one day and tomatoes and cucumbers that we'd cut up and soak in vinegar and pepper. I almost forgot about how much I enjoyed cucumbers in vinegar, or a tomato with a schmear of mayo, pepper, and salt. Delicacies. And crabs! How could this Bmore boy ever forget. Us splaying copies of free newspapers we had collected from around town across your dining room table after we had cleared it off with all the mounds of your important papers—from the extra Bible you kept there to your Baltimore School for the Bible notes from the classes you were taking to the extra programs from church, Daily Words, and other inspirational tracts.

But the plum I had today was soft. Very, very, very soft, and juicy. The type of softness that reminded me of your arms. I think my plum was soft because it was overly ripe, and I carried it in my lunchbox today on campus. So it probably got a little bruised. And there is even something there we could say about the softness of you that I've carried with me, despite how the world might have treated you while living. That excess. Your excess weight, water, salt, cholesterol, heart size, joint swelling and stiffness that even through that you found, we found a way to be soft, to be sweet, to be viable if yet bruised.

But the plum I had today. The plum that brought back all these memories of you, of us. It was very, very, very sweet and soft. And it is both the sweetness and the softness that I have been wanting to write about here.

But first, I want to say thank you. Thank you, Gran, for protecting my sweetness, for protecting my softness. I somehow have survived to still be sweet and soft, and I no longer run from it as if it is something I should not be, should be ashamed of—and for that I am grateful.

With Love,

Durell

PS: I still know and believe that the best is yet to come. For that hope too. Thank you.

Figure 8 a time for everything (2018) mixed media collage by Durell M. Callier, pictured Gran (Silvine L. Bradford 1935–2008) and younger artist

Protection

You must got sweet blood!
         If you was a girl, legs probably wouldn't be so shapely
You have long pretty eyelashes. Ever notice how most men have pretty eyelashes?
You must
        How you and your girlfriend doing? Y'all still together?
        Got sweet
He got a lil sugah in his tank.   *It's like Prego, trust me, its in there.*   *You*
keepin your nose clean?
       Only girls can . . . .   *You sing like a girl . . .*   *Go sing*
with the girls. . . .
      Sweet blood
If I had your range, do you know what I would do with it?
Stop etting that boy carry your purse like that.   *Let's fix your walk.*
      You just sittin up there, legs crossed like Jackie Kennedy.
       Only HE is good.
        You sweet
How you doin in school? You still keepin those grades up. Alright. Here take
this . . .

Dear Cousin Ricky,

When I read my cousin's Facebook post about keeping the family in prayer. I was worried. When she said on the next day, that her father had passed, and that at this time the family needed a moment I was shook. I wanted answers. Had you been sick, and I didn't know it? Was there a tragic accident that we were all just learning about? A stroke, a heart attack, an aneurism? COVID. It was COVID. And I was angry—not at you but at what we know now has been an avoidable set of tragedies. You had been vaccinated, took the necessary precautions. And they say we are coming out of this pandemic, but I can't tell. You aren't here, and there doesn't seem to be a bottom anymore.

I still can't believe you are gone now. Neither could I fathom the depth to which our small interactions would matter. In a sea of words, tossing me to and fro, communicating to me what boys should and should not do, who I was and should be, what was a feminine yet desirable trait to have, and those that were transgressive for bodies marked as male, your actions shone through. There are very few details of our exchanges that survive my memory. Only that each occasion, no matter what it might be, you were always kind to me, an unusual gentleness, when measured in relationship to your Apostolic upbringing. The other side of the family as we call y'all, given our Baptist upbringing and way-wardness. Somehow, though, I never left your presence feeling less than, feeling wrong, feeling inadequate. You, with your quiet grace, poised laughter, and humor, were good-hearted, benevolent. That's what you gave your wife and two daughters. That's what you gave us. What you gave me. A photographer by training, you, I think, knew how to capture the essence of others, how to hold the beauty that was there, not to make us something else but to see us, as we were. That eye, I think, saw me at times when I didn't quite see myself. And without prying or forcing an answer of whatever was working itself out, you would look me in the eye, and say, "Here take this . . . you need anything, man . . . proud of you . . ." as you slid $20 in my hands. Thank you.

In loving memory,
Your Cousin Durell

Dear Nang,

Although our time spent together was not long, there is a memory enlivened by a photo that I have always gravitated toward. The two of us, you smiling, beaming, laughing, as I, a wee-toddler probably no more than three or four years old, wore a hat of yours. And as far as the story goes, as it was told to me, there was no calamity, nobody snatched it off or decided to gather me and let me know that this, I, was *wrong*. You let me play, you let *me be*.

your smile
reassurance
that whatever i was dressed in
or out of
whoever i chose to be
was alright
you tiding me over
sticks and stones
that tried to break my bones
and words that tried to kill me
a steady presence
made manifest in your daughter
and her daughter
letting me be
laying a foundation
that that
it's alright
that that
you alright
that that
is right

We don't talk enough about how Black families make room for their sweet, eccentric boys, their hard irreverent girls, and all-around peculiar kin. We've always been there. Under approving eyes of matriarchs, at their hemline, in their garments, in and outside of their closets and our own, dancing right there in the living room, in our homes filled with laughter, saying in hushed and thundering tones, we love you, just as you are.

Love you always,
Durell

Mommy,

Look how far we've come, each of us charting paths across the stars finding our ways back to ourselves, back to each other. This constellation fixed by silent glances, deep breaths inhaled together in our embrace, deliberate talks, and

Figure 9 Nang (Florence Bradford, 1913–1989), Durell, and Kelvin R. Callier (1963–2021)

Figure 10 Mommy and Durell

setting straight, long phone calls where we called for nothin and didn't want to bother, presence as the present, slight gestures all our love language studied, passed down and perfected, your prayer of protection. Of all the words I've ever heard that have meant me no good, there you've been, a shield and banner, wit and retort, teaching the possibility to bob and weave, and never let em catch you. These are just an abridged version, the ones I am conscious of now:

1. Are you happy
    A question to guide and ground. No judgment. Like that time, I told you I was dating someone (news flash to you), and how I had decided to move on. And you simply wanted to know was I happy.
2. Use what ya got and be proud of it
    Remember that time, I was looking real sad on the way to school and you pulled over the car, just as "Silent Night" by the Temptations was playing and reminded me that there was this famous man who sang real high. Did you plan that? 'Cause it stuck.
3. Love is sometimes a quiet presence
    We are not a touchy family, and we don't always say, "I love you." Not aloud, verbally, every chance we can. And that's alright. Because what I also know is that sometimes a quiet presence is all you need in your corner to weather a storm and know who and whose you are.
4. You're never too old for me to worry bout you.
    How many of us can say we have someone who still worries about us, how we're doing, if we're eating, got our mind right, are out of harm's way? One day in my mid-20s, as I was home for the holidays from grad school, I in my new "grownness" decided I was going out for the night. You, after watching a horrible accident on the 11 o'clock news, text to ask if I was safe, if I was alright, letting me know that there was a car that looked like mine that had been in a "real bad" accident. Continuing to text while I'm *out* in the club, you said, "I don't need to know all your business just tell me you are safe when you go out. You're never too old for me to worry about." A pact we made then to let you know that I was safe. One I use now almost no matter when and where I travel to, one of the reasons I decided to invite you into the fulness of my life. I didn't want some tragedy to happen and everybody who cared about me not be able to show up, or show up fully because you didn't know, because I wouldn't let you worry bout me.
5. Cry sometimes it helps
    Goodness knows you and I take the cake for crying. Just the other week, something moved me so in my writing, I was sitting in the café crying. I don't hide tears or run away from them when they come. I think it makes people uncomfortable. I think people don't know what to do. They don't know like we know. Cry. You never hid your tears from us growing up, and that has had a profound impact on who I am today.

6.   Thank-you makes room for more
     No matter how little or how much of something we did or did not have, you were clear, be thankful. Folks now talk about it as keeping a gratefulness journal, practicing what you taught in a simple way to keep us.
7.   "Opinions are like assholes, everybody's got em and most of em stink"

Now I am not sure if you learned this yourself or if Uncle Mikey is the reason you knew it and passed it on down. But wherever this knowledge came from, it has made ugliness roll like water off a duck's back, squashing attempts at other people's projections, diminishment, backtalk, downright nastiness to take root in my spirit.

Thank you, for the lessons. Thank you for the protection. Thank you for loving me as best you knew how, and for growing to love me in the ways I need/needed.

Love ya,
Your eldest, Durell

Invocation

I know that little Black boys don't often get to grow up and be who they were, who they would be without the harsh realities of the world. I know that because I've had to fight to not become a lot of things—terrible monsters and Bigger Thomas, a hypocrite and liar, a hardened shadow of myself, and shrinking violet. I know that we don't always survive tenderhearted, our innermost vulnerable selves intact, because I see it in the eyes of my lovers, in the recoil of my care, in our inability to find the language of love and concern, in our unnecessary quarrels, in their breaking apart in my arms, a dam that could not hold anymore, that had to give way to feeling, to vulnerability, somewhere along the way they/we learned to discard something we so desperately needed—our softness. And I know this because I see it in my younger brothers. And not just them, my sister too. Eyes grown a tad less joyful, bodies made harder, to calcify the air around them, the suffocating weight of not being able to be handled gently, handled warmly, handled with love. Who gets to survive this world unharmed by the messages of not being "enough" of not playing a "proper" role? We all been touched, and yet some of us have had others gift us the freedom to be something different, to hold onto the clouds of our inner child, that wonder, amazement, love, tenderness.

This is my prayer.

may you know
that sweetness saves
your sweetness
can hold
can carry

can save
you
    unload that weight

float
transform
lead light
iron cotton
feel unburdened

    release

be newborn
gentle with yourself
gentle with others

    return

saccharine silk
velvety caramel
Sister Louise poundcake moist

Figure 11 Durell + siblings (Eddies Dett, Dominic Dett, Sheenan Callier)

delicate
uninured

don't you know you deserve it baby

you deserve
you
still soft
still sweet
still

13 A Tribute to Franklin[1]

A Comic Appreciation

Bryant Keith Alexander

Dear Franklin,

You have always been my hero.

But, oh, how lonely it must have been as the first, and only, Black *Peanut* on the Charlie Brown cartoon series, being the perpetual other. But you always presented with such style, grace, insight, and character. I wanted to be you when I was growing up. You gave me great joy. A boy with few words but great presence.[2]

Figure 12 The Peanuts gang sits down to eat in *A Charlie Brown Thanksgiving*, which aired in 1973

DOI: 10.4324/9781003274315-17

They say that you were a fictional character, but to me you were real. You were real because in some ways, I became you. I became the only Black guy sitting at the table, and you gave me early lessons on dignity and decorum.

I am told that it was a Los Angeles schoolteacher named Harriet Glickman who wrote to Charles Schulz, your popular creator, on April 15, 1968—eleven days after the assassination of Martin Luther King Jr.—telling him that he needed a Black character.[3]

Maybe as a moment of racial healing and maybe to fulfill King's dream that someday we could *be measured by the content of our character and not the color of our skin.* The content of your character was a testament to possibility—though, of course, the color of your skin drew attention. I was told that Schultz was later contacted by a southern newspaper editor who covered the comic strip and said something about *not minding a Black character, but he didn't want to see the Black character in school with white kids.* A more-than-residual display of the racial animus of the day that reinforced the logic of *separate but **never** equal.* But there you appeared in the same class with the white kids, sitting near Peppermint Patty—that ambiguously queer character and her sidekick Marcie, who also gave me joy. When I was old enough to go to school, I thought of myself as you—and every time I sat in the front or behind a redheaded kid—I giggled privately—channeling your presence in the classroom. My father used to point you out in the comic strip to me and say, "See he looks like you."

I know and remember that you always seemed a little confused or baffled by the strangeness of Charlie Brown and his all-white crew; a dirty boy always in a cloud of dust, a silent boy who played the piano all the time, pushy girls (who presented freely), an overly erudite white boy with no common sense and always in praise of pumpkins, a black-and-white beagle personified as human.

Trust me, I understand.

But, oh how discrete you were in your negotiation of difference. Recognizing your own difference, embodying an acceptance that was still not modeled on the national front.

I know that they featured you as a skilled dancer, maybe partially racist but evidently true. You had a stylistic rhythmicity that even transcended the rudimentary animation of the time—evoking an undeniable Black expressivity that tickled me and inspired me through your range—from the waltz to breakdancing—*rapping and representin'* for us all. Beyond tokenism, you showed up and showed out with envious musicality that was both embodied and instrumentalized. I wanted and received my first guitar as a little kid because you played the guitar.

While your arrival to the series was late, delayed by the racial politics of the times and the separated invisible and unimagined lives of Black people—when you did arrive, you did just in time for a little Black boy born in 1963 to be ready to recognize your arrival and understand the importance of your inclusion.

You arrived with a question.

Figure 13 Franklin Armstrong

Figure 14 Franklin's first appearance

You arrived with a level of assistance and observation.

You arrived with a calm clarity and offered a counterpoint to a self-deprecating lovable loser.

And in the move from comics to animation your true skin tone was refined to show the beauty of your person, and not the reductive blackness of skin—which once made you just look dirty to the always lily-white cleanliness of Charlie Brown, a name, that for me, suggested a diminutive non-distinctness. But in character—you were the counterbalance. Your full name was Franklin Armstrong. What a powerful name for a little Black boy character, a name to grow into, a name to make an impact. Yet while I know that your introduction into the comic strip came with an intention of integration, it also came with an intention of colorblindness—the performative stigmatism of the times, the myopia of the masses cloaked as inclusion, a seeing and not-seeing of difference. This to the point that your playmates did not note your blackness; *a matter of the peculiar disposition of their eyes, the of eyes those with whom you came in contact and on the face of the nation. A matter of the construction of their inner eyes* that saw you but did not politicize the full reality of your Black presence in the fictive reality of the comic strip,[4] thereby rendering your blackness invisible. But of course, I saw you and was not blinded to the rhetorics of the time.

For years I have kept little mementos of you with me, a lapel pin that I wear from time to time that just tickles me. And when people say, "*What* is that, and *why* are you wearing it?" I say, "You mean, *who* is that? His name is Franklin Armstrong, the first Black *Peanut*. And why are you *not* wearing him?" Franklin, you are also a part of Black history.

One of my prize possessions is my cut out of you. It sits approximately 19 × 12 × 1 inch on a hardboard surface. Like the infamous "Elf on the Shelf," my Franklin cutout moves to different places in my house, most times seated on a high-back mission-style chair in the living room near my guitar, sometimes on the couch upstairs, and sometimes at the dining table—always re-creating scenes of daily living. My cat Piper has become accustomed to your presence. It is a little trick that I play on myself, and sometimes my partner joins in—if only for the ticklish moments of rediscovery. It reminds me of my childhood joy with you.

Figure 15 Franklin in play

Franklin, you have always been a hero to me, maybe even a monument to a shifting historical moment of possibility. And even though some people might want to critique your isolated presence or your awkward positionality in certain comic-made-dramatic frames of racial politics, I say, "Thank you."

Thank you for being a trailblazer in your presence, in your defiance, and in your articulately controlled sensibilities that made the little Black boy that I was smile, and the older Black man that I am—remember you as a role model. The presence and materiality of your character mattered.

Your friend,

Little Keithy Alexander, almost grown up.

Notes

1 See Wikipedia: https://en.wikipedia.org/wiki/Franklin_(Peanuts)
2 Solis, J. (2020, February 21). "Snoopy trends on Twitter after 'racist' franklin Armstrong tweet angers Charlie brown fans." *Newsweek.* AT 3:00 PM EST. www.newsweek.com/snoopy-trends-twitter-after-racist-franklin-armstrong-tweet-angers-charlie-brown-fans-1488517.
3 See "How Franklin, the black 'Peanuts' character, was born." *NPR,* November 6, 2015. AT 4:58 AM ET. www.npr.org/sections/codeswitch/2015/11/06/454930010/how-franklin-the-black-peanuts-character-was-born.
4 See the prologue of Ellison, R. (1972). *Invisible man.* New York: Vintage Books, 3.

Section IV

Monuments of Memory and Remorse

"Memory and monument are to each other as process and product, although not necessarily as cause and effect, for circularity often obtains. The two terms are etymologically related and descend from notions of remembering."[1] This key phrase from *Monuments and Memory, Made and Unmade* by Robert S. Nelson and Margaret Olin is important to this section. While their project primarily focuses on the symbolic physicality of buildings and world structures of social investment and the political impulse to both construct and deconstruct such monuments through and over time, their important reference signals the relationality of monuments to memory.

Here we are interested in the monuments of memory and remorse that we build as psychologies of knowing ourselves in relation to an absented other, or local/national monuments that emerge as historical landmarks or the communal like roadside memorials that sprout as immediate public mourning, remembrance, and riot, some of which are signified by flowers, balloons, photographs, stuff animals, and other artifacts that connect the living to the dead at the time of the dying; some of which are renewed and refreshed in continued grieving, or the active process of sustaining of anger and outrage, often becoming more formal monuments to memory—epitaphs on headstones, funeral programs, statues, murals, T-shirts, tattoos, and posters as anthems, as a political *activist affect* those vows to remember and then act on the happening as object lesson and grievance.[2] Like saying, "I Can't Breathe" or "Black Lives Matter" or "Say Her Name" or "Know Their Names." Maybe they become structures of assumed permanence—on highways and byways and town squares of social infraction, prominence, or providence. These monuments to memory linger with relative longevity to the political investment in the telling and retelling of the happening—as abject lessons for the living, as *sites of memory*.[3]

Monuments tell stories, passing on the word of a happening of a had been as tragedy or an investment in the possibilities of being that we keep alive. Their presence always challenges the confirmation of the story being told and why, with the impulse of telling how one *reckons with history's legacy*[4] and *the inventing and reinventing of truth*.[5] **With that noted, how are we all monuments to history? How are we in our living, monuments to those who lived**

DOI: 10.4324/9781003274315-18

before us; those who birthed us into being; those who preceded us and who persevered for our possibility; the courageous and the everyday warriors of living? We stand as generational and intergenerational markers on the physical and psychic terrains of their lives, standing strong to both *write* and *right* the impact of their being. We commemorate their legacy extending it into the future offering a glimpse into their "interior life" that informed their exterior realities that impacted so many of us. Toni Morrison states:

> Moving that veil aside requires, therefore, certain things. . . . I must trust my own recollections. I must also depend on the recollections of others. Thus, memory weighs heavily in what I write, in how I begin and in what I find to be significant. Zora Neale Hurston said, "Like the dead seeming cold rocks, I have memories within that came out of the material that went to make me." These "memories within" are the subsoil of my work. But memories and recollections won't give me total access to the unwritten interior life of these people. Only the act of the imagination can help me.[6]

So, within the pieces that follow in this section, we blend and bleed the borders of memory and imagination in the historicizing of monuments in our private, public, and political lives. We memorialize as an active process of remembering who we have lost and what we experienced, and we engage *imagination as a faculty of reknowing* realities lived and as a *revelatory capacity of invention and innovation.*[7] Such engagement of imagination helps us travel back and then forward to a Black futurity—taking the memory of those who have empowered the energy of the possible in us and thus activate "dreaming of a different world where justice and freedom prevail" and joy lives.[8]

BKA

Notes

1 Nelson, R. S. & Olin, M. (2004). *Monuments and memory, made and unmade.* Chicago, IL: University of Chicago Press, 4.
2 See 1. Harris, A. & Holman, J. S. (2019). "Activist affect." *Qualitative Inquiry*, 25.6, 563–565. doi:10.1177/1077800418800753; Harris, A. & Holman Jones, S. (2021). *Affective movements, methods and pedagogies* (A. Harris & S. Holman Jones, Eds.). New York: Routledge, xii–xiv.
3 See Morrison, T. (1995). "Sites of memory Toni Morrison: The site of memory, taken." In W. Zinsser (Ed.), *Inventing the truth.* New York: Houghton Mifflin Company.
4 See Smith, C. (2021). *How the word is passed: A reckoning with the history of slavery across America.* New York: Little, Brown and Company.
5 Morrison, T. (1995). "Sites of memory Toni Morrison: The site of memory, taken." In W. Zinsser (Ed.), *Inventing the truth.* New York: Houghton Mifflin Company.
6 See Morrison, T. (1995). "Sites of memory Toni Morrison: The site of memory, taken." In W. Zinsser (Ed.), *Inventing the truth.* New York: Houghton Mifflin Company, 191–192.
7 See the short article: "J.K. Rowlings Notes Importance of Imagination at Harvard Graduation", June 6, 2008. www.foxnews.com/story/j-k-rowling-notes-importance-of-imagination-at-harvard-graduation. A similar definitional frame of "imagination" with similar features also appears as common word serve www.lexico.com/en/definition/imagination.
8 Dyson, M. E. (2004). *The Michael Eric Dyson reader.* New York: Basic Civitas, 481.

14 Monuments to Living (or Finding and Reviving the Dead in a Graveyard)

Bryant Keith Alexander

There is a precariousness about graveyards, burial sites with monuments to the dead. But not just the random dead, the dead of those who we cared enough for to engage the ceremonial rituals of death commending souls to God and ground, laying bodies to rest in fields of mounds with headstones; headstones marked with names and dates of existence, maybe with a photo that fades over time, maybe with a sentiment of relationality, mother of _____, father of_____, or divine wishes to rest in peace etched in marble and memory; monuments that we tend to with flowers, a coat of paint, and weeding away the vestiges of time. The precariousness of graveyards pivots between monuments to the dead and embodied monuments to legacies of having lived in those who tend to memory. Every time I visit home, the home of my childhood in Lafayette, Louisiana, my first stop from the airport (or my first pass on days when my soul cannot bear the pain of reentry and remembrance enough to stop) is the graveyard. There is a certain path from the Lafayette Regional Airport on Surrey Road that takes me directly to the graveyard, as if a strategic path of remembrance on a ritualistic pilgrimage, a return to home. Before visiting the living, I visit the dead.

The graveyard of my family is adjacent to Immaculate Heart of Mary Catholic Church. It is the church that was the site of all things that were community in my Catholic upbringing. The site of mass every Sunday and on holy days of obligation. It was the site of baptisms, first communions, and confirmations. It was the site of service on the alter and in the choir. It was the site of a lifetime of catechism as a child and adult, the site of weddings and funeral rights. The graveyard is next door. It is the graveyard that holds the final resisting place of my family: parents, grandparents, a sweet auntie, a contested uncle, and two of my siblings, some who still live in the visceral every day with pictures on the surfaces of my home—with them I do daily visitations. And others are much further in my memory, and some I never met, like my mother's parents or my father's father. Yet I visit with them in monuments of memory that circulate not only in my head and my heart—but also through my body with family histories of blood pressure issues, eye issues, diabetes, and arthritis. Many of them live on my body in the image of me, like that of my remaining siblings that invoke remembrances of them (past/present *familia*) to some of the old people

DOI: 10.4324/9781003274315-19

who say, "You look so much like _____." You know what I mean; when the materiality of your presence reminds other people of your people who have passed; sometimes people you never met, and along with the ones you did know and love, and the ones who loved you long before your being; like the grandparents you never met who yearned for the idea of you in the birth of their own children—your parents. They are present with/in/on your body, my body. In such recognitions—our bodies, your body, and my body become monuments to their have/had lived/lives.

The graveyard of my childhood was adjacent to the playground behind the church, which was adjacent on the other side by the community hall and the Catholic school. No fence. No wall. The playground, which was also the site of the annual carnival almost bled into the site of the graveyard. Maybe there were piddly low shrubs that were supposed to define a border but not a block. And while some of my childhood playmates were afraid of the graveyard, it was a place of exploration for me. The told and imagined stories of so many who had gone before me. The stories their tombstones told, how long or short they lived; grandparents, parents, children, and babies; an intergenerational cluster together in a family plot; each a monument to the other, some who passed in the contiguity of time or the consequences of circumstance. And the condition of the plots spoke to monuments of care or neglect or that difficult reality of when all who cared have also passed; what remaining monuments are tended by the obligatory maintenance of appearances to which all communities must address—either as care or as caution to our own mortality.

As a child, I remember creating fanciful tales from the headstones, using the lexia of thought and biography to *spinstory* the lives of the dead, a play on names, on age, and on assumed relations. In southwestern Louisiana—graves often tower above the ground, above the waterline; family members are sometimes stacked atop each other. I would imagine the figurative family trees rising to the sky in a reverse natural order anchored by ancestors and family, which are, of course, our roots. I also imagined with those graves that were still low to the ground, who might be the next family member to join, to stack, to piggyback in the family reunions in the graveyard. These were not the maudlin preoccupations of a dark child, but ways of living and playing with the dead that reveled in their being or had been—that protected me in some ways from the delusions of immortality. In church, we were taught that in death, we are reunited with our families who preceded us (in heaven or ground). So this gathering of souls in the graveyard seemed normal.

The graveyard of my return home operates in a space of memory and mourning, a space of silent intergenerational dialogues, a *Spoon River Anthology* of family and communal stories.[1] In my first stop from the airport, dead relatives wait for me before I visit living family members. My mother always taught me that no matter how far I traveled, returning home is required. From my car, I walk the distance of my memory to the location where she lays. But she is not alone. She lays stacked atop my father, and he atop my brother, Nathaniel, the first of their seven children to pass away before them. Each taken by grim reapers called AIDS, called alcoholism, called a drunk driver—in that order. Every time I visit, she is the one who greets me. She is atop, not just in order of sequence but somehow also willing my father and brother to stay in place—each, restless souls who in life were apt to stray. I stay for a while. I stand before them crying. I speak to each about my loves and my regrets. I move to the next, a single grave of my older sister that is set apart, a disbursal of family monuments. She was the eldest child, the most recent in passing, and maybe her separation from the three is indicative of her living. But in the end, we all come back into the fold. I repeat the gesture: stay, stand, speak, and move on. Then I look for the others—the parents of my parents, the favorite auntie I loved, and even the uncle that I didn't. Because this is a family reunion, everyone gets visited and everyone receives a prayer. In the end, these dialogues with the dead are renewing. They prepare me for dialogues with the living. The generational and intergenerational dialogues across time and space—siblings and their children and their children. I am the only one without children—so I engage them with dialogues of remembrance and possibilities, grounding us in the realities of dying but instilling the commitment to living and thriving. I procreate generational legacies, but only in story. When I get home, to the homes of the living, I rejoice in their presence. I see how we are all becoming our parents, becoming the old people surrounded by children and grandchildren. Each of us says, "You are looking more like _____ each day."

And when I am home, I always take the chance to visit the real old folks, the ones who were my parents age or older, the ones who, when I knock at the door—it takes them a long time to get there—saying, "Wait I am coming. Wait I am coming. Wait I am coming." Then they ask, "Who is it?" And when I try to tell them, they don't remember, until I say, "I am one of Joseph's (Red) Alexander's boys". Or I say, "I am one of Velma Bell-Alexander's children . . . we use to live on the corner of 12th and Simcoe, across from Winfield-Syrie Funeral Home—remember?" And then I hear the door unlocking and through an old screen door, a pair of eyes stare back. Then the screen door opens to take a better look at me, to (re)cognize me in their memory. Then they say, "Oh yeah, I remember you. Keithy, right? The one that went off to school, right?" I acknowledge and smile, thinking that they look the same. Were they always this old? And am I always the one that went off to school in their memory? Well, each to their distinction, and Black community investments in memory and education run soul deep.

I am always beckoned into the house and offered coffee or sweet tea, into a house that smells the same since my childhood—when my mother would send me to deliver a pie or pecan candy sold outside of church or fresh put-up fig preserves. Then as the ultimate display of their memory, they begin to tell me about myself, about the memories when I did this or that—not all good and sometimes mistaking me for one of my four brothers. I never correct them. We smile and laugh, maybe at the same thing and maybe at very different things. Then they tell me something about growing up with my father or mother or something about my father's father or my mother's mother, some I met and never met but monuments to memory in *the telling of the told*. There is some-thing in their memorializing that gives them and me joy. And those monu-ments stand strong like figurative family trees rising to the sky, and these old people become monuments to longevity and community and culture. They have become the grandparents I did not know. In what they taught me then and now, they were *otherwise*,[2] not always determined academically trained but intellectually powerful with a wisdom that was always mind-boggling. They offer(ed) other ways of possibilizing everyday Black life. They were wise in other ways, that if you were/are really listening (then or now), they outline(d) the kind of lessons that others would later theorize in academic ways, the stuff taught in universities that never cite the old folks as the source. I cite them here—not as a scholarly requisite but as a cultural necessity. They along with my parents were *otherwise*; they were the first real teachers of *all I ever really needed to know*.[3] So I visit and worship there with them in their homes, until later when I visit them in their final resisting place, and even then, I continue to listen and learn.

There is a precariousness about graveyards, a precariousness of graves that are clearly located within a grounded stability but still likely to fall from memory or collapse under the weight of sorrow or remorse—if we don't mine the importance of the legacy of those who lie there. Graveyards are the gardens of sad dreams and sweet memories that I visit first when I go home, visiting with the dead before I visit with the living, re-membering them in me as monu-ments of their being and my becoming.

Notes

1 See *Spoon River Anthology* a play by Edgar Lee Masters structured as "a collection of short poems that collectively narrates the epitaphs of the residents of Spoon River, a fic-tional small town named after the Spoon River, which ran near Masters' home town of Lewistown, Illinois. The aim of the poems is to demystify rural and small-town American life." https://en.wikipedia.org/wiki/Spoon_River_Anthology.

2 During the writing of this piece I was introduced to this exhibition, "OTHERWISE / REVIVAL 04.09.21–07.31.21—that focus on visual images and representation of the Black Pentecostal movement www.bridgeprojects.com/exhibitions/otherwise-revival.

3 Here, I am alluding to Fulghum, R. (2004). *All I really need to know I learned in kindergarten: Uncommon thoughts on common things*. New York: Ballantine Books—but in the important sense of Black intergenerational dialogues.

15 Rice

A Visit to a 12-Year-Old Black Boy's Memorial

Mary E. Weems

On November 22, 2014, **Tamir E. Rice**, a 12-year-old African-American boy, was killed in Cleveland, Ohio by Timothy Loehmann, a 26-year-old white police officer. Rice was carrying a replica toy gun; Loehmann shot him almost immediately after arriving on the scene. Two officers, Loehmann and 46-year-old Frank Garmback, were responding to a police dispatch call regarding a male who had a gun. A caller reported that a male was pointing "a pistol" at random people at the Cudell Recreation Center, a park in the City of Cleveland's Public Works Department. At the beginning of the call and again in the middle, he says of the pistol "it's probably fake." Toward the end of the two-minute call, the caller states that "he is probably a juvenile", but this information was not relayed to officers Loehmann and Garmback on the initial dispatch.[1]

I have visited the Cudell Recreation Center on the westside of Cleveland, Ohio, a few times over the years at the invitation of its former director, who hired me to design and implement poetry writing workshops for local poets, and I am familiar with the small park area behind the building where children and teens spend time together playing and interacting with each other. It's an integral part of the community and one of the few areas in the city where programs designed for young people and adults are regularly provided.

The first thing I thought about that did "not" occur to me at the time, because I was too busy being outraged about what happened to an innocent Black boy at the hands of yet another white police officer, *is* if it's true, as reported in the earlier quote from Wikipedia, that the man who called told the dispatcher that it was a *juvenile* and the gun was probably *fake*—why did the man call the police in the first place?

Also, something I did think about back then, especially after it was reported that the officers lied in their report about approaching Rice several times and asking him to show his hands while the boy appeared to be "drawing" his weapon when a video showed that they started shooting before the vehicle even came to a stop—is how possible is it that the dispatcher whose main "job" is to relay all pertinent information to the police officers who pick up the call did not share the two most important pieces of information, that it was a juvenile and the gun was probably fake?

DOI: 10.4324/9781003274315-20

It's far more likely that this information was shared, and hindsight being "cover-your-ass" 20/20, the officers compounded their lie about approaching Tamir by stating they were never told. Given the long history of police killing innocent Black boys/men and women in this country and then lying about it, even in the face of video recordings of the incident, I find it difficult to believe anything except that officer Loehmann and his partner were fully aware of the situation and didn't care. As for Tamir waving the gun at people, this makes it sound as if he was on a busy street and waving at people passing by instead of the truth, which is Tamir Rice was playing with a toy gun behind a "recreation center" that has an entrance on a "side" street, in a space designed for play.

In spite of the video, a grand jury declined to indict officer Loehmann, because Rice was apparently trying to "draw" the toy weapon as the police approached in their patrol car.

Interesting and tragic, too, that Loehmann had previously been determined emotionally unfit to be a police officer at his previous job in Independence, Ohio, and was hired by the Cleveland police department, which didn't bother to read his personnel file from Independence as part of its hiring process.

Subsequently, Rice's mother filed a civil suit against the city and was awarded six million dollars, which did nothing to bring her son back, while officer Loehmann only lost his job and remains free. Even though this could change if Samaria Rice's recent request, backed by several politicians to reopen this case is granted—as of this writing and "since" being found not guilty—

Loehmann is free;

Tamir Rice is dead.

What are the possibilities that this could have "ever" happened to a white boy?

Two years after Tamir Rice was killed and the officer who shot him was exonerated, I was approached by a young white woman and community activist who hired me to design and implement a healing workshop for some of the boys in the neighborhood who either knew Rice personally or had heard about what happened to him. She'd already worked with others thanks to the local councilman and the Cudell Center to build a beautiful garden behind the building, filled with the kind of wildflowers that attract butterflies. The old, weathered wooden gazebo located right in front of the garden had been turned into a memorial, which included lots of teddy bears in various stages of wear and handwritten notes either on the concrete of the back lot or on the banister and benches of the gazebo. When I arrived that afternoon, a young white woman was there with her little girl. I overheard the mother telling the daughter about what happened there. As I set up on the gazebo, I heard the two of them praying for Tamir. There were Black kids in small groups playing together, sharing the kind of young folks' banter I'd heard hundreds of times before. It was obvious they all knew each other and were enjoying some Saturday morning downtime.

The space in that moment held the vibe of peace, as if it was part of the air we were breathing, as if Tamir Rice hovered somewhere close by watching and wishing he were here.

As the time for the workshop approached, the boys started approaching the gazebo one by one. All of them were between 11 and 13 years old, and as I introduced myself, gave each of the high fives, and asked them to sign in, I was struck by how young they all looked—no way I could mistake any of them for anything but a child. Unfortunately, I turned the writings over to the woman who hired me, as we agreed and am unable to share from them, but I recall the sense of what they talked about during our group discussion before I asked them to write. I posed the following questions one by one and while I was concerned about whether it would be difficult to talk about how they were feeling, as it turns out they were all anxious to talk, and I did more listening than moderating.

Focus Group Questions for Boys
10–13–16

1. What is a policeman or policewoman's job?
2. Who do the police work for?
3. Do you know any police officers?
4. Most police officers are good guys or women. What would you like to share with police officers who help people when they're in trouble?
5. Have you ever been helped by the police?
6. Have you ever seen the police help someone else?
7. How did you feel about the police before Tamir Rice was killed?
8. How do you feel about the police now?
9. If you had to describe the police in one word, what would you say?
10. If you could speak one on one with a police officer about the shooting of unarmed Black boys and men, what would you say?

I designed the questions to allow for a wide range of responses, and that's what happened. Some of them thought Tamir should not have been waving a toy gun and understood why the police shot him, something they didn't think would have happened without Tamir's actions. The boys who knew Tamir either from school or from playing with/seeing him at Cudell thought the police were dead wrong and should be punished. Not a single boy ever recalled being helped by the police, and several said they'd always been afraid of the police. One boy in particular I remember because he said his mother no longer allowed him to play outside, and he described what it was like in their hot apartment day after day, after school and on the weekends.

Overall, it was a healing time for the boys and me. One of the prompts that worked the best of the three I gave them was writing a letter to Tamir and telling him how they feel.

Long after they'd left the park, I sat in the gazebo, and then in my car, reflecting on the loss of this one boy, and the effect it's had on the community at large.

I was disappointed to learn that Tamir's mother moved the memorial out of state. It was her right to do what she wanted, but I heard that the kids and adults who frequented the space miss it a lot.

I wrote the following poem, long before the workshop and several months after Tamir Rice was killed. I had an artist friend of mine hand print it on a white T-shirt I planned to wear at the time, but I've yet to wear it.

RICE

Violence has become
A staple in the U.S.
Black Bodies Falling
Graves. . . . . Pots
Bullet Shells. . . . . Curse Words
People Carrying Signs
Miserable Excuses for Guns
So Many Dead
Black Names Blur
While Country
EATS

The list of innocent Black boys/men and women killed by police in this country has grown by leaps and bounds since Tamir Rice's tragic death.

When will we get tired of eating?

Note

1 "Killing of Tamir Rice." https://en.wikipedia.org/wiki/Killing_of_Tamir_Rice. Accessed July 14, 2021.

16 The First Time . . .

Durell M. Callier

On June 21, 2021, I witnessed the culmination of several projects. As part of Miami University's Truth and Reconciliation Project and the Equal Justice Initiative's (EJI) Community Remembrance Project, a narrative historical marker was unveiled in Dr. Martin Luther King, Jr. Park in Oxford, Ohio. The marker recognized Henry Corbin and Simon Garnett, two victims of lynching in Oxford. As the ceremony unfolded, in which descendants of Corbin and Garnett spoke, alongside representatives from the university and the EJI, I was struck by the palimpsest of history and racial terror unfolding across multiple scales in this quaint college town. Nationally, Oxford is the site at which Freedom Summer 1964 training took place; locally, the university also has been embroiled in a variety of conversations and scandals related to race and interpersonally; Oxford is the first place I was ever called a nigger. Despite this violence, I chose to teach at the very site of personal racial terror. Equally so, Oxford is much more than my past and continued experiences of racial animus. I know this because in my first trip to Oxford, I was part of a group of youth organizers from the Baltimore Algebra Project. Bob Moses, civil rights leader and organizer who was instrumental in training Freedom Summer participants, created the Algebra Project as a continuation of the civil rights movement. Because of the work I did regarding fostering equitable educational opportunities for Black youth in Baltimore, applying similar ideas and practices of civil rights activists and organizers in our context, and then meeting them in Oxford for the fortieth reunion of Freedom Summer, I also know that Oxford is a site of tenacity, strength, and radical transformation.

The photo essay which follows bridges these complex realities and their afterlives in our contemporary moment. Recognizing important sites of blackness and Black history manifests in small triumphs, daily individual actions as well as in spectacular collective actions of survival. The decision to be "out of place" and work "within place," at the individual level, is as important as collective acts of survival, joy, freedom making. Equally significant are our rituals to honor and remember tragedy and success. Ultimately, this chapter provides multiple scenes of racial terror, recognizing how history is always present, unfolding, and undone. It is perhaps in the nature of history as undone that the chapter leaves us to take stock of where we've come, how near the past is daily,

DOI: 10.4324/9781003274315-21

Figure 16 Soil from the lynched sites of Henry Corbin and Simon Garnett

where we might go, and how. The chapter is anchored by personal memory, photographs personally taken from significant sites of Black history on my university campus and the surrounding town, and includes a reimagination of archival documents on racial terror to create a narrative of words and images. Choices were made regarding the placement and usage of language, asking readers to consider what is discernible and perceptible in violent rhetoric and actions, where, what, and to whom do we place value.

     Nigg _____ er
           Sails across the sea of smiling white faces
  Uninterrupted by the words which
     Arrested
     Us
We who sojourned here
   to commemorate the
      40th reunion of Freedom Summer
That momentous joining of young people
picking up
Freedom's plow

Figure 17 Freedom Summer 1964 Marker, Oxford, Ohio

> undoing a history of
>   wrongs
> seeking to forge a
>   bolder
>   better
> path together

Nigg _____ er
probablyoneofthelastwordsuttered
afirsthailingandfinalsalutation
lookMaa _____
seePatherehangsa _____
letsgogetusa _____
that_____theredidit

wefixingtotringusupa_____

_____refusestosellland

_____bitch

lazy _____s

uppity _____

As I walk uptown in the college town where I work. The same college town where I experienced for the first time in my life being called a

_____.

I often wonder

Figure 18 Freedom Summer Memorial on Western Campus in Oxford, Ohio

Figure 19 Curbside between Peabody Hall and Freedom Summer Memorial

Figure 20 Lynchings in Oxford, Ohio, Marker

Figure 21 Peabody Hall entrance

did it happen
     here
     this alley
was   it   near
     this   bar
     this

frat house
     this

Figure 22 Freedom House Call Freedom Summer Memorial, Oxford, Ohio

street corner
    block
    where
    did
    the
  assault
take   place
the   violence
the spiritual   lynching

Today another negro was lynched
What
were
the
last
words
they
heard

                James Chaney
                Andrew Goodman
                Michael Schwerner
        What were their last thoughts
                Henry Corbin
                Simon Garnett

Figure 23 Freedom Summer Memorial, Oxford, Ohio

Today we gather on soil stained
descendants of a history
    of words
    of actions
that have foreclosed possibilities and lives
Today we gather
they say for
    truth
    and reconciliation
I still want to know who the cowards were
Do I now teach them? Their child? A friend or family member of theirs?
What does our blood know, our hearts and spirits of this land, of these
    word grenades
                    the fall
                         out
    marked
    here
  in this park

  in this   memorial

Figure 24 Freedom Summer Memorial, Oxford, Ohio

each time I assume the lectern.
Today we chose to face each other
to face
   our
history
to make change
Today
we
moved
one step
   ever so gingerly forward in that long arc of justice
      stirring up good trouble

Figure 25 Freedom Summer Memorial, Oxford, Ohio

we
a
    host of angelic troublemakers
remembering lest we do it all again
        remembering
re-membering.

17 Going There

Bryant Keith Alexander

(*Written after reading Durell M. Callier's "The first time I was ever called a nigger."*)
Let me "go there" with you.

I've always loved that expression. "Go there"—as in, "Oh, you wanna *go there* with me?"

There, being that place of raw direct address.

There, being that place where people "tell it like it **t.i.is.**"

There, being that place where people untie their tongues to say what they had been itchin' to say.

There, being that place or moment in time when people throw caution to the wind to just say what is on their mind, on their tongues, on their stomachs—all places of delicate balance that create a pressure forcing a necessary release, thoughts, and impulses that become guttural utterances in the realities of the moment, or when historical aches, pains, traumas, bruises, and scars are reopened with a sudden jarring reality check of remembrance. When the memory of the first time you were a called "nigger" or "faggot" or "bitch," or "foreigner" comes rushing back, or you pass that place again; you know that place—those places marked by the stain of your blood or tears (that become *monuments of memory and remorse*); that location, those locations where you encounter the phantom of that person again (as *an emblem of suffering and pain*); that person who named you, maimed you, or shamed you, or took advantage of you (*former friend or foe, no longer hiding in the shadows but in the light*). And in that moment, you reclaim your dignity to say, "What did you call me?" "You know what you did to me!" "Do you know what you took from me?" "Today I take it back!"

Oh, I want to "go there." But not just in anger and disregard or wild abandon losing my shit without control. I want to "go there" with all my facilities, with all my talents, with all my intellect, with all my accomplishments, with all my positionalities, with all my control, intentionality, and yes—even with all my restraint and still "**let . . . you . . . have . . . it**."

"Let you have **it**!"—Another one of those phrases in which "It," becomes something active and animated—not just a pronoun used to replace an object that has already been mentioned or can easily be known but the actuality of the offense that is also always known, always felt, always and already in the dailiness

DOI: 10.4324/9781003274315-22

of experience; that which is so insidiously present that it goes without saying because it is always felt (by many of us). But let's call it by its name—*racism, sexism, homophobia, xenophobia*—not implicit bias. Implicit bias is the polite way to discuss it (without really talking about it). It is the polite and maybe sanitized way to ease into the reality of its habituated performative antecedents; the manner that the roles of protagonist and antagonist/perpetrator and victim—get muddied—to suggest, in some psychological and clinical way, that "we all have implicit biases." Thus, redirecting the attention from the particular to the plural, from the raced-based, gender-based, sexed and sexuality-based, origins-based biases to which our intersectional selves suffer in relation to the diminished hierarchical values that undergird history—to suggest, to state that the experience is the same as a bias against—let's say—vegetables or fruit or pork, the predisposition to respond to stimuli in the same way. The same attitude as when I, in my particularity and plurality; when I, in my intersectionality am the stimuli to which you have an attitude: an implicit bias. Hence, in implicit bias, everyone is called out for their social and psychologically induced "biases," reducing or forgiving their complicity for overt actions and behaviors, without blame or shame or consequence. And the particular we—we who have been historical victims to *the implicit **made** explicit* (fill in your name here: _____)—we are left uncompensated and at the same time told that "we too" have implicit biases that inform our explicit actions (so maybe we should be sympathetic to the struggles of others). Maybe these are *the protective pillows of whiteness*[1] or heterosexuality or being in the privileged class of being American (or, fill in the blank, _____)—that activates address without redress or the institutional strategies of addressing history's legacy in delicate ways without owning the perpetuation of pain. I do understand that discussions of "implicit bias" is a starting point of discussion, a recognizing of the psychology of the brain to generalize in ways that may have both positive and negative impacts; I am just pushing for the reckoning (after the recognizing), the intervention and transformation to end the impacts of such biases in their more explicit manifestations—to get at **IT**.

   "Gettin' it" becomes something that you deserve—that you didn't think that I could give you. Maybe because you thought I was just a "nigger" or a "faggot" or a "bitch" or a "foreigner"—*in your terms*. Maybe because you didn't think I had the "nerves" or the "balls" or "the fortitude" (*that last one being my word that shows you that I can use restraint*)—but what the fuck? (or is that "what the heck"?)—

   You don't deserve my restraint—because you depend on my restraint.

   You depend on my politeness.

   You depend on me *not* acting like a "Nigger" to your accusations of calling me "a nigger" (and the other things you call me).

   That is where your power resides—in my restraint not to be that thing that you call me when you are acting out your own fantasies under the guise of white power or heterosexual propriety or class privilege or Americanism (or

_____), because you can. Not all, but *you* know who you are. (See, that is my qualifier not to generalize. That is my performative *resistance to the implicit made explicit*.)

My performance of politeness is historical. I have mastered it under the *threat of law*.

So maybe, from time to time, I will "**go there**" with you—just to show you that I can. And maybe, just maybe, you will then appreciate the restraint that I perform—everyday, with grace.

Note

1 Fine, M. (1997). "Witnessing whiteness." In M. Fine, L. Weis, C. Powell, & L. Wong (Eds.), *Off white: Readings on race, power, and society*. New York: Routledge, 57–65.

18 High Bar Love

Dominique C. Hill

Poised and Intentional

Her entry into rooms and conversations,
deliberate and matter-of-fact.
Her words,
non-prescriptive guidance on self-improvement.
She held no punches.
Without profanity, aggression, or yelling
she'd tell you about yourself,
read you the riot act,
shame you into telling the truth.

Careful and Quiet

Her movement,
firm grace.
Her steps,
ordered and purposeful,
reflecting deep consideration of context and culture.
She knew her history, our history.
With no soapbox or mic,
adorned us in encouragement,
Black genius, and love.

Mindful and Steady

Her pace in classrooms and conflicts,
measured and grounded.
Her strategy,
set the bar high and remember who you are.
She made no room for excuses from any direction.
Without bribery or deceit,
she'd allay your self-doubt,

DOI: 10.4324/9781003274315-23

Figure 26 Mama Crystal + Daughters

bolster your confidence,
remind you of your power.

Mother and Educator

Her voice,
the sound of truth.

She made history each step,
each class, each challenge
she took under her wings.
Made space for each parent,
each tear, each dream
that needed recognition.
She shared what she knew.
She made us family.
She was home.
She left the bar high.

Dominique C. Hill
©2019

19 Standing at the Intersection of 38th Street E and Chicago Avenue S

Bryant Keith Alexander

July 16, 2021

I am standing at the intersection of a *beatdown*: 38th Street E and Chicago Avenue S in Minneapolis, Minnesota, the location where George Floyd was murdered.[1] A beatdown that ended when a police officer knelt on Floyd's neck and back for 9 minutes and 29 seconds; a beatdown punctuated by the repetition of his gasping cries of "I Can't Breathe" in a rhythmicity of labor, suffering, and dying that has become a main beat, as in im/pulse, to the **Black Lives Matter** movement that has catalyzed our national sensibilities about police violence against unarmed Black people in America with shock waves felt around the world.[2]

I am standing as a Black man in America at a memorial site at the intersection of memory and monument, each stands to the other as process and product in a circularity of remembering and a desperate act of not forgetting.[3]

I am standing in this now sacred location witnessing a monument to brutality built through psychologies of knowing ourselves in relation to an absented other, and the ugliness of the continued racial struggle in everyday society.

I am standing at a site of trauma in the confluence of COVID-19 with masked citizens of the community and inter/national visitors who tend to the monument (raised fists of deviance, power, and solidarity; images of the dead; icons of faith, resistance, and hope; markers of caution; clouds of heavenly glory; directional insistence in a turnabout that points to the location of the death)— all marking the scene of the crime along with the litany of names of those who preceded him in policed-to-death Black tragedy.

The monument is to George Perry Floyd Jr., but in the location as I stand, I am transfigured not just as mourner or tourist but also as a Black male survivor for a yet-undetermined future. My PhD does not protect me in any way from the everyday acts of violence to the Black body. And through seeing and being there, I am now further imbued, empowered, and energized with the responsibility to tend to both memory and memorial. *That is the heart of the matter,* and the still-beating pulse of energy to which this monument gives

DOI: 10.4324/9781003274315-24

Figure 27 Memorial site in America

life to activism. The monument that has been built and maintained, and the pilgrimage of my presence from California along with countless others from around the world, is not just the obligatory maintenance of appearances or the ritualistic paying of respect to which all communities must address their dead. It is also an *activist affect* as commitment, care, and caution to Black survival— to which we must all heed.[4] Because in such a beatdown, all our humanity is defeated.

Figure 28 Monument to brutality

(Photos taken by the author on location at the intersection of 38th Street E and Chicago Avenue S, Minneapolis, Minnesota.)

Notes

1 See Murder of George Floyd https://en.wikipedia.org/wiki/Murder_of_George_Floyd.
2 George Floyd memorial www.georgefloydglobalmemorial.org
3 Nelson, R. S. & Olin, M. (2004). *Monuments and memory, made and unmade*. Chicago, IL: University of Chicago Press, 4.
4 This piece is drawing on sentiments from "Monuments to Living (or *Finding and Reviving the Dead in a Graveyard*)" this volume. New York: Routledge. Please see: Harris, A. & Jones, S. H. (2019). "Activist affect." *Qualitative Inquiry*, 25.6, 563–565. doi:10.1177/1077800418800753.

Section V

B(l)ack Talk

The construction of "B(l)ack" is a two-sided co-informing of meaning that signifies for us a doubling effect. The immediacy of seeing "Black" signifies the subject of focus: Black people and the essence of and/or the performativity of blackness, not as monolithic, reductive, or restrictive but maybe as a cosmological configuration of being; an acknowledged being with a groundedness in African roots filtered and tainted by the American experience, forged through the caldrons of slavery, struggle, survival, and the diaspora—(re)cognized; a process of not just recalling or seeing and making known but also a double cognition as in "the mental action or process of acquiring knowledge and understanding through thought, experience, and the senses"—of the Black self—again and again and again. The Black self, which is not an artifact of materiality but of origins and the influences of blood and history that signal the particularity, plurality, and performativities of our being, and in being Black in these United States of America, as well as the multiple borders to which we all cross to get in here or to get out of here.

So, within the construction of "B(l)ack," the reference to "back" is not a coincidence. It is a charge of remembrance—to look backward to (re)member the self in history (the past), in community (to the present), with a forward thinking toward our collective futures. The doubling recognitions of positionality and action demands the triple stages of seeing as a thrice relational orientation that includes the subject of experience and being, the moment of reengagement of histories, and the reorientation to knowing of that experience through a critical memorialization of the self as an active agent. The process includes the tripartite of *reflection, refraction, and reflexivity*. The difference between reflecting or looking back on experience linked with memory and recall then refractively bending and turning those memories to crack open meaning and significance, followed by engaging in a reflexive turn of *looking at the self-looking at the self* in a twice removed level of critical self-objectivity.[1]

The reference to "back" is also then a charge to "talk back": to talk back to history, to talk back to racism, to talk back to authority, and thus to talk back to oppression in those ways in which we engage in continual dialogues with our ancestors and histories. Talk back to our current situatedness in America in a time with continued racism in which we still fight, march, and declare that

DOI: 10.4324/9781003274315-25

Black Lives Matter and, in the process, talk back to the systems and structures of oppression that restrict our social mobility—and, in fact, continue to threaten our continued existence. Talking back is a charge: to speak truths, to challenge the conditions of living. And as our recently departed sista-friend bell hooks writes,

> In the world of the southern black community I grew up in, "back talk" and "talking back" meant speaking as an equal to an authority figure. It meant daring to disagree and sometimes it just meant having an opinion. . . . Moving from silence into speech is for the oppressed, the colonized, the exploited, and those who stand and struggle side by side a gesture of defiance that heals, that makes new life and new growth possible. It is that act of speech, of "talking back," that is not mere gesture of empty words, that is the expression of our movement from object to subject—the liberated voice.[2]

The following pieces "talk back" in ways that are also about "talking Black," through aspects of the vernacular of Black cultural life.[3] Hence, "Black talk" is quintessential to Black people, as both colloquial and stylistic, as well as a focus on issues that matter to Black people. The pieces in this section bleed the borders and boundaries of all other sections to address the issues, the Black issues that are most pertinent to these four Black persons engaged in this dialogue. Sometimes, the issues are addressed directly, and other times, they are addressed indirectly—through play, parody, or parable that is also a part of the Black dialect.

To whom or what do you talk back, or maybe even—as appropriate, "talk b(l)ack?"

BKA

Notes

1 Here I also use this construction of "a tripartite of *reflection, refraction, and reflexivity*" in my discussions on autoethnography as qualitative methodology. The most recent of such discussions will appear in Alexander, B.K. "Teaching and engaging autoethnography as qualitative methodology" in the conference proceedings: Pasque, P. A. & Alexander, E. (Eds.). (2021). *Advancing culturally responsive research and researchers: Qualitative, quantitative and mixed methods.* New York: Routledge. From the 1st Annual Advanced Methods Institute (AMI) Conference (Theme: Culturally Responsive Research and Researchers) sponsored by The Ohio State University, College of Education & Human Ecology—June 2, 2021. Columbus, OH.
2 See hooks, bell (1989). *Talking back: Thinking feminist, thinking black.* Boston, MA: South End Press, 5, 9.
3 See Smitherman, G. (1994). *Black talk: Words and phrases from the hood to the amen corner.* Boston: Houghton Mifflin Company.

20 April 20, 2021

On Luther and Chauvin

The Black Quartet

Durell M. Callier wrote on Tue, Apr 20, 2021, at 12:09 PM:
Subject: Re: Fw: Just saying hey

Hey Y'all,

On this the 70th birthday of THEE Luther Vandross, I thought of you all when I saw this animation/celebration by Google.[1] I think it's sweet and creative. It's rainy here in upstate NY, but I am doing alright, and this just brightened up my day.

As an aside, I am thinking about the queer reading of Donny Hathaway that Bryant did a few years back, regarding lyrical autoethnography.[2] Watching this Luther tribute, while working with you all about Black notes, forms another type of opening in Vandross's music for me. Placing the specter of who was receiving all of Luther's loving and crooning, and who might be loving him aside (if at all). Today, "Never Too Much," reads like a love letter to Black folks. More specifically, given my/our being Black scholars, this intergenerational dialogue/quartet rifts on the melody, that "a million days in your arms is never too much." I could say more, but "Never Too Much," reads/feels like a classic gold standard on being loved on/by/with Black people in and beyond the academy.

Hope you all are doing well. Gotta head in to teach, or rather head over to Zoom. Will get a script out to you by the end of the week.

Take care,
Durell

Mary E. Weems wrote on April 20, 2021, 9:46 AM
Subject: Re: Fw: Just saying hey

"Everybody wants me to be what they want me to be, I'm not happy when I'm trying to fake it" damn . . . so many, many folks afraid for complex reasons to just "be" . . . Yes! Loved Luther and all you share on this vibe makes sense Durell. Thanks, for sharing. And damn, Bryant, I'd love to read that piece. . . .

DOI: 10.4324/9781003274315-26

Donny Hathaway and "gay" never even crossed my mind, but I loved his music and am remembering now how he died . . . Lord.

Cold and shitty day here, but I'm good too Durell. See ya'll soon Family!
Mary

Dominique, written from a place in time to inform the now.

Greetings Blacktastics.

Just caught my breath. Just caught up on some missed emails and thankful that upon arrival, we are all still here together. I'm counting on joy and holding firmly to the queer found poem that is us. "For all we know," we may be a poem that helps Luther find his way home to a past life lost lover of 22½ years. For all we know, our coming and going, and going there (together) to locate pleasure amidst anger, tears, and mounds of unacknowledged solutions is an algorithm. To climax over and again—through songs on repeat, guttural laughs, and clanging mason jars—might be the Black notes needed to move us all closer to feeling free enough to be who we are right now and to be something else in another moment. "Tomorrow was made for some / Tomorrow may never come / For all we know" and still Donny is here with us and we are here loving on and loved by each other.

Dom

Bryant Keith Alexander on Tuesday, April 20, 2021, 11:17 AM, Subject: Re: Fw: Just saying hey

Oh, Sweet Young Brother,

Your message is received with great joy as I sit at my desk hearing the church bells from my campus tolling the time in the near distance of my home to campus. I am sitting with my fist raised **Black Lives Matter** framed poster on an easel behind me. It serves as a very real background in my everyday Zoom meetings as reminder and resistance to the time we are marking. This in the times in which we are living. And the in-between times of waiting the outcome of the jury's verdict in the Chauvin trial in Minneapolis, which is really the George Floyd trial, which is really the trials, tribulations, and traumas of Black folks in these United States of America.

I am taken with your reference to Luther in both memory and memorial. I am taken with the quest and question of "who was receiving all of Luther's loving and crooning, and who might be loving him aside (if at all)." And like Mary's reference—I am taking your "just saying hey" cue to also turn to Lionel Richie saying "Hello" as he also ruminates and asks, *can you love me (?)* when he writes: "I've been alone with you inside my mind, and in my dreams, I've kissed your lips a thousand times, I sometimes see you pass outside my door, Hello, Is it me you're looking for?"

Which is how I always listen to and read Luther—through a queer lens of my desire framing and reframing his quare desire in relation to the utility of his query and how other people fill in the blanks with their desire. The soundtracks of our lives are mostly Black notes from our historical musical collection from church to the club and the energy and wisdom of lyrics yet to be spoken. Our intergenerational dialogue is like the black notes hanging in the air and on the musical bars of our collective past, present, and future. Let us continue to sing, chant, and wail together in mournful remembrance, warning, celebration, and worship. Let's continue to do so together as we brace ourselves for what is to come in relation to our inheritance of resiliency and love from the past.

And here I echo Dom: "Tomorrow was made for some / Tomorrow may never come / For all we know" but we can reach for it and will it into being.

Mad love,

Bryant

Durell M. Callier wrote on Tuesday, April 20, 2021, 2:33 PM
Subject: Re: Fw: Just saying hey

Just catching up, and . . . just yes. I'm not sure what it means that my attention was focused on us today and not Chauvin. I knew last night there was a verdict forthcoming. I think it wasn't until your post Bryant, that I recalled, today is the day. Or rather it is simply a day in which we will find out what jurors decided. I don't want to wax long about that. Guilty is a start, truly not the destination.

Bryant Keith Alexander wrote on Tuesday, Apr 20, 2021, at 5:24 PM
Subject: Re: Fw: Just saying hey

The halo effect on my "Black Lives Matter" poster is indicative of a blessing that must continue to abound above us all. Above all Black peoples in this critical historical moment. Today and beyond.

Your "focus on us" (a Black Quartet) and the national focus on "Chauvin" are entangled in the same set of issues: freedom, accountability, recognition, life/liberty/pursuit of happiness.

Figure 29 Day of the Chauvin Verdict

You wrote: "Guilty is a start, truly not the destination." Yes, and I present it here again as a triune of repetition to match the poignancy of the message and outcome of the verdict:

Guilty is a start, truly not the destination.
Guilty is a start, truly not the destination.
Guilty is a start, truly not the destination.

Love and respect you all more today than yesterday (if that is even possible).
Bryant

★★★★★★

There is a seamlessness in this dialogue or maybe even a seam*full*ness of call-and-response to which we are grateful, grateful for the technology that allows us to engage in the immediacy of an organic dialogue in time and place across a practiced space of community celebration: one in Los Angeles, California; one in Cleveland, Ohio; and one writing from upstate New York, each stopping for a moment in the continuation of our day to mark time:

to mark time in a national moment of recognition and acting on the impulse to signal each as a form of outreach,

to mark time in the moment of memorializing and witnessing—the passing of life and the implementation of the law,

each mapping atop the other,

each notable—the memorialization of a famous Black crooner and the other who took the life of an everyday Black man, making both their living and their dying iconic. The verdict in this case is a memorialization of the right side of justice. Derek Chauvin (himself) is not iconic, only emblematic of white crimes against Black humanity to which the verdict only begins to regulate.

Each is a moment we take to mark, looking through a different lens but feeling into mourning and remembrance to celebrate Black life.

Mary's response does something: a move from Luther Vandross to Lionel Richie to Donny Hathaway—the felt remembrance of the power of music to signal and signify the shaping of cultural memory as we each read and reel through how those lyrics and the delivering vessels penetrated our lives, activating our desire—he to her to him to they to each their desire and sensed interpretation of need.

She cites, Lionel: "Everybody wants me to be what they want me to be, I'm not happy when I'm trying to fake it." The lyrics key into the struggle to live, to love, and to be. All for very different reasons. "Damn," she writes. "So many, many folks afraid for complex reasons to just 'be.'"

We hear and listen to the music through the lens of our desire and disdain.

So many, many folks afraid for complex reasons to just "be." **To be real?**

So many, many folks afraid for complex reasons to just "be." **To be gay?**

So many, many folks afraid for complex reasons to just "be." **To be Black in America?**

We remember how they lived.

We remember how they died.

We remember how it makes us all want to say, "Lord, Lord, Lord."

So, on this day, or maybe that day, April 20, 2021—when the memory of Luther and the Chauvin verdict after killing George Floyd came into confluence along with the rage (and exhale) of a nation.

On that day, in the confluence of memory and memorial when melodies of faith served as a reminder and the rhythmicity of "guilty, guilty, guilty" read like lyrics, read like the reframing of a new song of justice (or the beginning of justice).

On that day, we were all willing to sing that new song of justice, wondering how Luther would have sung it better.

Best, Bryant

Postscript: *June 25, 2021: Derek Chauvin sentenced 22½ years in prison for the murder of George Floyd.*

Postmortem: *The life of a Black man killed by a white police officer reduced to only 22½ years.*

Notes

1 www.youtube.com/watch?v=69KrkMpvZdg&t=89s; www.artbysambass.com

2 Alexander, B. K. (2016). "Introduction: 'A song for you'/'killing me softly': Lyrical dialectics of design, desire, and disdain (a performative introduction). In the special issue: The song book of our lives: lyrical autoethnographic performances." *Qualitative Inquiry*, 22.10, 771–774.

21 *Trilogy of Terror* on the Black Hand Side

Bryant Keith Alexander

Many people might be surprised that I am a fan of old horror/terror movies and similarly made-for-television dramas, although I cringe throughout watching them—the attraction–repulsion effect is core to the genre. Along with the old westerns that I watched with my father, I also watched old vampire and terror movies with my grandmother, his mother, and the only grandparent that I knew. One of her favorites was called *Trilogy of Terror*, a 1975 made-for-television horror film directed by Dan Curtis and starring Karen Black. The trilogy featured three short films presented in sequence, each based on presumably unrelated short stories by the same author but the three are tied together by the same white female actor of the day, Karen Black—who plays the protagonist in each. While the stories stood alone—the drama and trauma of the protagonist tied them together in a broader narrative of terror—that, for me, bled the borders of each into the realness of the experience in watching the whole. The first film follows a college professor who seeks sexual excitement with her young male students and eventually kills them in her insatiable lust for play and control. The second is about twin sisters who have a tensive relationship on opposite sides of a spectrum of repression and expression—only to realize that it is a case of split personality and one kills the other, ostensibly killing the self. And the third focuses on a woman terrorized by a Zuni fetish doll in her apartment, which serves as a different story about being consumed by rage, revenge, or desire.[1]

Every time my grandmother saw that the movie was coming on, from the old *TV Guide* of the day, she would call me over to spend the night. We would sit in a darkened room with popcorn and watch it. There were no Black people in this production, though, of course, the lead actress in all three had the last name of "Black." My grandmother, the consistent storyteller and cultural critic, would offer her own reading of the short films using them as object lessons to Black people—using the last name of the actor as her signifier. To her, the first film was a lesson about white women who sexually lure Black men and then claim rape to defend the honor of the presumed image of white female fragility against Black bestiality. And while their claims of self-defense and victimhood always paid off with the destruction of the Black man, my grandmother would say that they (white women) did not realize that it was not always their desirous

DOI: 10.4324/9781003274315-27

white beauty that lured the Black man. Sometimes it was his form of revenge to whiteness—and particularly to white men—who systematically took/take advantage of Black bodies—in slavery and beyond both sexing and *ungendering* the Black female body as recreational play and tortured as "unprotected female flesh"—relative to the white female body, which must always be protected.[2] The attraction–repulsion effect again. But even so, in a white capitalist society—a Black man's revenge most often ends in his own annihilation. My grandmother would later repeat stories about Emmitt Till and other local Black men in the Lafayette, Louisiana, or Breaux Bridge, Louisiana, area, who fell fate to a flirtation with white women—then had to deal with their menfolk or the police—who were always and already the same—who were sent to revenge her virtue.

My grandmother's interpretation of the second film in the series was really about the double consciousness of Black people and how we needed to reconcile our own struggles in this country before we become our own worst enemy and hence the source of our own self-destruction. She saw the presumed twins in this film, who were never shown in the same scene but always referencing their disdain for the other, as Black folks, Black folks who had somehow separated their actual self from their imagined self, either by choice or as an effect of trauma—failing to reconcile the wholeness of their being. The consequence for her was that we, Black people, would then engage in behaviors that threatened our own personal survival. And while others could be blamed for the trauma of our schism, we were responsible for reconciling our wholeness into a single consciousness of survival.

For the third in the trilogy, my grandmother interpreted the Zuni fetish as the repressed rage of Black people and the desire of white people to fetishize natives and particularly blackness by keeping and collecting *insidious iconographies* of their own social construction of Black people. You know what I am talking about—the Mammy images, the Black sambo images eating watermelon, the lawn jockeys, the Aunt Jemima relics, *ceramic uncles and celluloid mammies,*[3] or even the occasional severed digit from a lynched Black person, hung for his/her/their presumed offense to whiteness (e.g., a finger, a toe, a penis taken)—a souvenir by any other name that "saves the past and represents it in the present . . . to be revisited over time."[4] Not unlike the life of our sista Sara Baartman, whose body in whole and part was displayed in her living and after her death.[5] My grandmother grew up in a time when these relics mimicked the actuality of racial oppression, suppression, and repression in the daily lives of Black people, everyday reminders by white folks of their own presumed superiority to the hyperbolic black features that they promoted (in exaggeration) in relation to their own presumed refined and contained features and how white folks kept the mementoes as signifiers on their lawns, front porches, coffee tables, shelves, and under glass. She told me of serving as a domestic, a maid in the houses of white people—and the special attention that they wanted her to give in dusting these items as in a double parody of pain and intended humiliation.

In the film, my grandmother loved the moment when the gold chain from around the neck of the Zuni fetish doll falls off. The chain that supposedly contained the actual spirit of the Zuni hunter named "He Who Kills." My grandmother would become more animated in that moment and would gesture toward the television as if she was removing the gold chain herself so that the hunter became alive and would then chase and terrorize the white woman who wanted an ethnic fetish, and she does get it. I often wonder what would happen if the Mammy images, the Black sambo images eating watermelon, the lawn jockeys, the Aunt Jemima relics, *ceramic uncles and celluloid mammies* came alive—shooting watermelon seeds like bullets, spilling syrup like blood, and Black lawn jockeys speaking with a dandy eloquence to tell their complex contested origins and travels.[6] And what would happen if the gruesome souvenirs from lynchings—severed fingers, toes, and the legion of angry Black penises were reanimated and sought their revenge? Well, you should watch the old film, because after a terrorizing chase and a series of defensive actions on the part of "Amelia," the name of the character and the episode—the spirit of the hunter becomes reanimated in her—thus making manifest her own anger lust in more overt ways.

My grandmother loved this film not only because of the shock of horror and terror to excite the spirit but also because she found ways to read these films as allegories to the Black experience in America, the reel (real) and the surreal. These were the intergenerational dialogues that we had using old horror/terror films as pivot points for cultural studies. I marveled at the ways in which she would lean into the narratives and pull back insights and comparisons that served as lessons for living. During it all, my grandmother was an old woman who tickled and inspired me. She tickled me with her unregulated tongue that talked a whole lotta shit, and she inspired me with a whole lotta wisdom along with a killer sense of humor that fused and manifested in a complex *wit*.

My grandmother suffered no fools, and she felt that through the survival of old age, she had earned the right to tell-it-like-it **t.i.is**; fearlessly speaking truth to power.

Notes

1 See "Trilogy of terror." https://en.wikipedia.org/wiki/Trilogy_of_Terror.
2 Spillers, H. (1987). "Mama's baby, papa's maybe: An American grammar book." *Diacritics*, 17.2, 68. doi:10.2307/464747.
3 See Turner, P. A (1994). *Ceramic uncles and celluloid mammies: Black images & their influence on culture*. Charlottesville, NC: University of Virginia Press.
4 Young, H. (2010) "Housing the memory of racial violence: The black body as souvenir, museum, and living remain." In *Embodying black experience: Stillness, critical memory, and the black body*. Ann Arbor: University of Michigan, 181.
5 See Crais, C. & Scully, P. (2010). *Sara Baartman and the Hottentot Venus: A ghost story and a biography*. Princeton, NJ: Princeton University Press; Holmes, R. (2007). *African queen: The real life of the Hottentot Venus*. New York: Random House.

6 Goings, K. W. (1994). *Mammy and Uncle Moses: Black collectibles and American stereotyping.* Bloomington: Indiana University Press; Hampton, C. M. (1970, September 23); "Black man proud of statue of black boy holding reigns." *Austin American- Statesman.* www.news-papers.com/image/355948667/?terms=jocko+graves; Halligan, W. T. (1972). *A horse for the general: The story of Jocko Graves.* Unpublished. In the archives of the Alaska Pacific University/ University of Alaska-Anchorage consortium library; Koger, E. (1976). *Jocko: A legend of the American revolution.* Hoboken, NJ: Prentice-Hall; Ridder, K. (1988, February 22). "Black lawn jockeys pointed to freedom." *The Province,* Vancouver, British Columbia. www.newspapers.com/image/505940543/?terms=%22Green%2Bribbons%2Bwere%2Btied%2Bto%2Bthe%2Barms%2B%22; Turner, P. A (1994). *Ceramic uncles and celluloid mammies: Black images & their influence on culture.* Charlottesville, NC: University of Virginia Press.

22 Feel/Think the Kink

A Dialogue with Jubi Arriola-Headley's *Original Kink*[1]

Mary E. Weems and Bryant Keith Alexander

Mary

> Original: n. 1. Existing from the beginning
> Kink: n. 1 a. Twist or bend in wire etc. b. tight wave in hair 2. Mental twist or quirk, esp. when perverse ([origin] Low German or Dutch])
> Oxford English Dictionary, 1996 Edition

The amazing cover of this book, a well-built (and I mean cut!), nude, mature Black man posed on a silk-draped bed or table, with long thick, black twisted hair falling over a face that ends in a nappy gray chin, begins to tell its story. Like the poems in this collection, he is fine, well built (or constructed), naked as truth, and he's lived long enough to know who he is.

I found this brother's work when I happened to watch a YouTube of a brief interview with him about this book and heard him say that when he writes he never writes alone, he's always writing, drawing on his experience, the experiences of family and other Black people he knows and the ancestors, which is exactly what Bryant and I argue in our book with Routledge Press *Collaborative Sprit-Writing: Performance in Everyday Black Struggle*. During the interview, Arriola-Headley shared a short poem, and I loved it. As soon as I could get to my phone, I ordered the book, then emailed Bryant to tell him about it, suggesting that we consider including our individual responses to it in this book.

There are no poems about hair in *Original Kink*. There are a lot of poems about being "original" that, here, I interpret to mean that queerness has existed from the beginning of humankind, and many of them have an element of "kink" inspired by an experienced poet who showcases his "mental twist or quirk, especially when perverse," in poem after poem.

Creating "Found Poetry" from the writings of someone else is a way of more deeply engaging the work by bringing one's life experiences to the material, creating an intersectionality between, in this case, Arriola-Headley's life and mine, using selections of his words as a means of expressing what I experience in the moment.

My goal is to more closely identify or empathize with Arriola-Headley's experience as a queer Black man while culling connections on the vibe to my

DOI: 10.4324/9781003274315-28

own life and staying open to receiving some of his more personally challeng-ing poems, for example, the one where he describes his first sexual encounter with a grown man at fourteen years old, in another his penchant for S&M, and last a section that's part of his "Daddy" poem where his description of "Queen Tony" sped me immediately back to my memory of the late Miss Tony, some-one I grew up seeing and caring about—someone who lived their entire life as a woman. I've heard many stories about men and/or from the mouths of men about being 'fooled' by Miss Tony—I'd never heard the term 'transgender' back then and don't recall her being referred to as anything but "Miss Tony." She was beautiful in figure and spirit and unfortunately my last memory of her is attending her funeral, walking up to view her and realizing that her family had buried her as a man. . . . .

This is a brilliant, in-your-face truth-telling, risk-taking, wonderfully writ-ten first collection, one I'm certain I'll read and reread in the future, one that's given me a lesson in what it means to write the stories you want to tell as a Black queer man in the United States without fear or concern for what the public's response might be.

"I once was lost . . . but now I'm found, was blind, but now I see."

Amazing Grace

Found Poems:

1.
I play with myself out of context like peacocks
in the Artic, or tenderness in baritone
A single word—*boy*
Gothic arches penciled in where eyebrows once grew;
Boy had lingered lusting, fingered the fabric
as the man I can't imagine.
This boy, broken
while some woman guided her gaze toward anywhere.
I wish I didn't know his story
how butterflies slit their own throats for fear
How a boy must fashion touch.
How quick we are to teach a boy to cradle hurt
in his hands
& preen.

2.
Smell my swagger
like ripe fruit
split fat
Wield praise

like sparrow
you martyred me
blind to bullets
Tell, I loved you
Tell, you betrayed me
Tell, I forgave
Tell, my name—Joy

3.
I will never consider suicide.
I love rainbows
but what I really miss
is cum.
I've dreamt your murder
a tiny death, America
I fashion fetish outta outside
looking in
I'm America
Thirteen going on gutted
fast talk & first kiss &
last to. . .
I'm a cowboy, America
all curse words
& swagger.
I'm a symphony of shredding skin,
concrete canvas
I'm a teaspoon of history
whisked into a pound of lies.
I am kink, yes
I am shackled, yes
I'm Jesus to your Judas, yes
I'm the patron saint.
America.
This is a dare.
I dare you to love me, America—
love me like it's legal.

4.
I claim fuchsia
I'll drape my dick in it
I'm no novice
But neither am I your *nigga*
Your palm prints, secret
On my thighs
Call me. I may kiss you.

5.
Winds worry his bones.
Him, a failing structure; his
Floorboards his [one] act.

6.
Patterns in flesh, sick
symphony in bile. Swollen
punchline yawn toward.

7.
Stench of sycophant
read wretch. *Croon into chaos.*
Resist. Prolong pain.

8.
The language in which I'm most fluent is. . . . . silence.

9.
I got something to tell you [daddy says]. *I have cancer. I'm a warrior
Baby. & one more thing, I love you.* & that's how I know he's dying.

10.
How may I love, Shall I kneel?
Spread thighs, expose?
Shall I slip hands into hips
Claim my body, break it?
I long for the lash, sting of skin,
Stiletto. Peg, spank, spare me that longing
that comes on parting.

11.
So much of who we are is birthed.
Watch those hands soothe grease along roots,
an anointing, a blessing, a psalm. Steal
through the dust of the day, gossamer over
this world, how much it hurts to be a girl.

12.
When he entered
he became
source of light & I
would thirst swallow drown
I loved him like humans let gods do
when their light fades to a bastard ember

what we call a galaxy
their carcasses populate the inky between
a crown of thorns
what we can hold. We
fetish his piercings, swaddle in notion,
but death is coming, we
smell it on our god like shame.

13.

I have seen song rain
brings like my open palms
like I'm unbreakable.

14.

Think of it, breeze
rouging your cheeks for others
leaves blushing
shield your eyes from the neon pink
DIE FAGZ tag . . . the man
not spat inches from your feet.
None of this stops you from pity
though you would not stop to give him
a dime.

15.

You loved Him like them church ladies in their pressed red skirt
Suits & their jute & feather crowns love to gossip.
You couldn't think of him without a capital H.
His eyes was like this particular brown you get when Daddy
pour his bourbon & the light catch it just so.
How did He know how to mother you?
How was his arms strong enough to lift you off the ground?
How'd you know to wrap your arms round His waist, imagine
this moment a sacrament?
If only you knew His name.

16.

Wash a dish every now & when.
Race me to this inescapable.
Let's hope, sing, limerick.
Tease me out of my miserable busy.
Let me hold you.
Say yes.

17.

All we can pray for is dance:
our bodies hungering, hips, jukebox
pose and grind
street names for genuflection,
call & response—we sing,
I see the god in you.
Sweat like worship is labor,
beat, praise song.

18.

Wear something loose to dance in,
shower in shimmer & spectacle. Take
this body to the nearest ocean, set me ablaze
at sunset, my body bathed in bonfire.
Swap stories about me.
Make love near my ashes,
Blow me like an eyelash,
a wish.
Don't forget me.
Let me go.

19.

My laugh takes no blame.
If my laugh was a nation
it would be Palestine
My laugh forgets to shrink
My laugh takes names
My life like a balm, baby,
like a balm.

20.

What you call me is not who I am.
My name is sunk deep in the Atlantic.
Knock over each & every Confederate monument
& place it next to a statue of Harriet Tubman
scar spangled banner
Daddy.

21.

Before this world
there was Darkness.
Just. Like. You. Girl

You were not made in God's image—you
are God.
You are Black.
This is our origin story.

Bryant

I repeat, or is it reiterate or meditate or hallucinate or fantasize?

The amazing cover of this book, a well-built (and I mean cut!), nude, mature Black man posed on a silk-draped bed or table, with long thick, black twisted hair falling over a face that ends in a nappy gray chin, begins to tell its story. Like the poems in this collection, he is fine, well built (or constructed), naked as truth, and he's lived long enough to know who he is.

And I am wondering about this man on the cover who beckons me to uncover,
to pull back the sheets,
to spread open,
and peel back,
the cover . . . of this collection of poems.
Enticing me to wonder my imagination and to wander in his uncoveredness.
It is not just because he is naked and "*well built (or I mean cut!)*, as she says. It is because he is a grown-ass Black man poised, posed, and punctuated in his steadfast masculinity speaking a naked truth that foreshadows the content of the volume that he himself un/covers. He is not being commodified in this piece in a Mapplethorpe-kinda way. He seems to present himself—but not too present in himself, presenting himself as truth-ta(l)king, as a truth-making template, a sage or griot, a modern image of Rodin's statue of *The Thinker*, or maybe a more *awakening* ancient version of *The Black Man Thinking*, often ignored or fetishized but seldom contemplated. Here he is played but not displayed with intentionality, a clarity and voracity that lead the reader into the volume to which he beckons with the same charisms.

I imagine him sneaking a peak through his twisted kink, *scanning silhouettes* to see if you are/if I am interested,
interested in entering,
interested in uncovering, maybe more images of him,
maybe more interest in the articulate tongue that is put to work. . .
on paper in the volume.
He entices you to *cum*, to enter. He entices me. . .
I am interested.
I am interested in the collaborative impulse that plays out and splays out throughout this volume of poems. The relationality that is at play in every poem that speaks to/at/with/about a lost, active or passive other in the discovery of the self.

I am interested in reflecting on how we be, and how we be-come—in our personhood, in our blackness, in our sexuality, in our desire, in our disdain, in our *body politic*, in our humanness.

She writes as a Black straight woman: *My goal is to more closely identify or empathize with Arriola-Headley's experience as a queer Black man while culling connections on the vibe to my own life and staying open to receiving some of his more personally challenging poems . . .*

I write as queer/quare Black man: *My goal is to more closely identify or empathize with Arriola-Headley's experience as a queer Black man while culling connections on the vibe to my own life and staying open to receiving some of his . . .* experiences: same and not the same; the often unspoken, the often presumed to be taboo, but the real and surreal of desirous maturation or is that the maturation of desire; a cuming-of-age-story; *our origin story?*

In every poem I see myself. Not always in the same position or positionality, but not not.

In every poem I see, and feel, and re-member. Not always the same sensations, but not not.

In every poem I see and say as he does. "I'm no novice, but neither am I your *nigga*. Except when I am." (19)

In every poem I find myself in a relational dialogue that speaks to a collective sense-making that is both particular and plural, dry and moist, as am I, as are we—sometimes in a variation—*like a cactus hoarding water in our belly, longing to be touched.*

In our book *Collaborative Spirit Writing* Mary states:

> One of the results of the diaspora of slavery is that those of us who were dragged here have been scattered through sale and/or escape throughout this country, making it difficult—if not impossible—to know who belongs to who.

But somehow in this text/body of *original kink*, we come to recognize each other again—across gender, sex, and sexuality.

In our book *Collaborative Spirit Writing* I respond to Mary, saying:

> Yes, working collectively with Mary is in part bridging the diasporic disbursal of our shared origins with lived experience mediated by time and distance. We find a recognition of the self in our co-writing, our co-presencing, our co-performing—each embodied and voiced—and in our recognition of the self in/as the other. It is that dialectical performativity of Black people that is so familiar no matter where you travel. It's as if you have met before, even though you haven't, *but of course you have*—because recognition, like memory, is more than just skin deep. It is soul deep.

And I imagine Jubi responds, "Ride on, King Jesus/No man can-a hinder **me.**"

In reading Jubi Arriola-Headley's *Original Kink*. I recognize him as my people.

I see him. I see you. I see me.

We meet and greet on the stage of the page; writer/reader, viewer/viewed/ voyeur. And then we immediately continue a conversation with each other as if we have not been separated by time, place, space, and the broad circumstance of *diaspora*. We are now not only engaged in collaborative writing, but we are also engaged in an *inter/intragenerational dialogue* that sustains and extends the story of our lived experiences from shore to shore, between bodies/borders/ boundaries on issues of *race, gender, sexualities, and culture(s)*. Same and not the same but all true. Necessary dialogues to break the silence of oppression, opening spaces for possible futures.

Maybe we can be *acolytes* to/for/with each other.

Note

1 Alexander, B. K. & Weems, M. E. (2021) are the authors of *Collaborative spirit-writing performance in everyday black lives*. New York: Routledge, Qualitative Inquiry and Social Justice Book Series. In writing this piece we are extending our collaboration, celebration, and communal dialogical engagement with Arriola-Headley, J. (2020). *Original kink*. Little Rock, AR: Sibling Rivalry Press, LLC: little Rock Arkansas. And the cover art of the book, "Awakening," by Andrew Graham.

23 Spell Casting as Talking Back

Dominique C. Hill

> now why dont you put me back & let me hang out in my own self
> somebody almost walked off wid alla my stuff
> & didnt care to send a note home sayin
> i waz late for my solo conversation
>
> (Shange, 2010, p. 63)

These days, I've been reclaiming intimacy. Talking (more) to my mother about the weight she carried and still carries in her body from childhood, about being the "brown-bomber," the darkest of her sisters. These days, I've been making room for the necessary ruminations about collective care, about being a scholar, about family ties, and about the work of healing. I listen to my spirit (more) these days and offer my attention to the advice, loving care, and possibility built into the living words, creativity, and survival of Black women. Specifically, the women whose hands have literally and figuratively clasped my chin to hold it up, angled to the sky or the mirror not made of glass, to remind me of myself, my power to see *and feel* and create what I need. And amidst the incessant antiblackness and other machinations of spirit-murdering[1] amplified during this pandemic, my vigor to talk back has heightened, its direction and aesthetics expanded.

To "talk back," as bell hooks articulated, is a form of resistance and self-defining practice. So, I conceptualize the many smacks in the mouth I received from my mother as a necessary chain of reaction to make clear to me the costs of being myself. Rooted in cultural expectations, gender-specific racialized forms of knowledge distribution, and what happens on the corner shared by these two, talking back is a mode of self-naming, giving birth to self, of standing ground to maintain the right relationship to oneself and not allow parts to be stolen, walked off with, or blotted out.[2] These days, my talking back and Black has felt different when inside and pouring out of me. It has entailed a conjuring of and listening to my mother tongue, no matter how fearful, vulnerable, hesitant, sexy, unrelatable, or outrageous it may sound. Talking back is methodological, pedagogical, spiritual; it is an incantation and portal building

DOI: 10.4324/9781003274315-29

I learned from the same women who dared me (you bet not!) to employ it in their presence.

I regularly turn to these women to check in, connect, and create new memories. They are my heart. These days, I find myself afforded access to the histories, happenings, and hurts that provide a thread to suture strewn-around pieces of my mother's childhood and broken heart. I open, I speak, I inquire, but mostly, I hold space. I listen acutely for ways to apply salve and insight that I might take with me as I do this thing called the academy on my own terms, as I grow a loving partnership with a woman too fluid for any one referential pronoun, as I drop into myself and feel and be and breathe beyond default while also being a scholar, an educator, a creative, a dancer, and a wanderer. These days, I'm standing face-to-face with spells I didn't mean to cast, unintentional incantations so powerful that they made their way into my bones. And these days, with the help of time, pandemic ponderings, and quality conversations with loved ones, I'm writing new ones.

Today, I talk back so that the women in my family might unravel so that my mother, in particular, might give birth to herself. Like the lady in green, my mother talks about what got lost and what was stolen while Auntie's and Granny's eyes shine in want of something on the other side of squelched needs, desires, and yearnings. Through conversation, I learn that they imagine their time to have passed, that if anyone brings that piece of them to life, it will be my generation, specifically me. Through choreopoem, I cast a spell, Family Recipe #19, as a rune for rebirth. Remembering secrets revealed to me—on

Figure 30 The garden from which Dominique C. Hill grows

paper, by six women in my family, almost twelve years ago, in my mother's living room, where we talked, danced, wrote Black girlhood, family wounds, and future visions—I crafted Family Recipe #19. Blending our silences, yearnings, shame, and strength into a roux for returning unraveling and returning to one's essence, this spell is also homage to Ntozake Shange. The choreopoem[3] fuses music, poetry, and motion as counter-discourse to talk back to people, wounds, communities, systems, and fears. This culturally specific form is used to create, critique, and conjure and renders holistic, sacred, and honest visions for and representations of life. Disappearing the particular name attributed to an experience, the choreopoem relies on what Nikky Finney referenced as "first person plural"[4] (Finney, 2009), in which the individual particularity is held in the arms of the collective. Family Recipe #19 is a poem and spell crafted in honor of the collective yearning I heard and continue to hear from the bold, brilliant women in my family and a metaphorical testimony of why I continue to live.

The room is dark and
lurking between the shadows cast from a cracked door
is a combination of whimpers, short quick breaths, and gasps.
A pale and then red light rises to reveal a
girl seemingly asleep in a closet.
The room darkens again.
The whimpers and breaths turn to sobbing laughter.
A pale-yellow light rises to reveal a
girl disrobing herself from her skin.

(Nina Simone's "I Put a Spell on You"[5] plays—
"And I don't care / If you don't want me/ I'm yours right now")

The girl asleep in the closet awakes and starts to try on clothing.
The girl steps out of some of her skin.

(Sudden dead disturbing silence)

*Sunshine and Wind (*whispering*)*

Turn On Tha Pot
It must be boiled down to nothingness

Sunshine

gotta simma for some time
cook down,
like gravy, like greens
like meat released from the bone

Wind

Make certain it's on low

> *Sunshine starts twisting—first at the wrists, then the neck, waist,*
> *her body is jerking as if in an attack,*
> *until her skin lays in a pile on the ground.*
> *At the bottom of the pots sit silences and shame*
> *carried in tow from generation to generation from youth.*
> *They sit heavy, the texture of molasses,*
> *the smell of bitter love rottin atop a dead cabbage.*

Wind

Two big mounds of audacity
A shot of bourbon, make that three
Two fa me and anotha to create the punch
the slap
the bass,
no coming back from here
Lots of minced menses—the kind after an overdue release, the kind that
stores unrequited encounters, shimmy them in
Drop in a heap of love
and anotha
anotha
Stir

> *the air in the room circulates, fanning the fire, the heat*

Wind

Stir until the shame and silence clump with the menses
Let it bubble up
Sprinkle in mo' love
Let it all clot
Like stopping a slow death,
like healing,
like a body that knows how to mend itself
Add garlic, onion, and honesty,
the spice purifies the blood,
flavas the meal
Stir

> *the air in the room circulates,*
> *the lights suddenly fail, darkness.*

(Lucille Clifton is heard reciting her poem "What the Mirror Said."[6]—
"listen, you a wonder/ you a city of a woman/ you got a geography of
your own")[7]

Wind

Cover
Do not conceal

> *Wind's stirring turns to an aggressive*
> *rhythmic whipping stir,*
> *Whip whip, stir.*
> *The contents at the bottom of the pot*
> *rise as smoke,*
> *moans, sighs, and cries.*
> *Wind covers the pot, leaving the top slightly off*
> *for what boiled down to release itself.*
> *The top whistles.*
> *Bubbles, steam, and a gray liquid rises*
> *up and out of the pot, filling the air,*
> *hanging in the balance.*

Wind

remember before
remember you
remember your gait,
your smirksmile, your curiosity,
your heart.
Go back to floating
remember the sky you slept in,
played in.
You wanted to come here, *remember?*
to make things.
to bring things to life.
to see your thoughts become things,
and feel it, *remember?*
Remember what you wanted
Remember you wanted to feel it!
"you not a noplace
Anonymous girl"[8] not ugly,
empty, in the wrong body, nor just
flat–out wrong.
You a whole wide world
by your damn self

Simmer, simmer
Simmer on that
Simmer into that
(*whispering*)

(Nina Simone's "Here Comes the Sun"[9] starts to play—
"It's been a long, cold, lonely winter / Little darlin' / Feels like years
since you've been here")

> *The gray liquid*
> *hanging in the balance begins to move.*
> *It starts to fill in its empty spaces,*
> *spread out. Other colors emerge in the space*
> *Between the gray—all of it a liquid-like substance.*
> *The texture of clotted blood but not sticky.*

Simma
Simma
Simma
Sssssssssssssma
Sssssssssssssma
Sssssssssssssma
Sssssssssssssma

(Re)member yourself
(Re)member yourself back together
Simma
Simma
Simma
Sssssssssssssma
Sssssssssssssma
Sssssssssssssma

> *The skin on the ground vanished.*
> *The pot is empty and atop it sits a wing of the sun.*

Wind

(Re)member your essence
Simma
Sssssssssssssma
Who you be
(Re)member your gifts
Simma
Sssssssssssssma

Sunshine and Wind (whispering)

Turn. Off. Tha. Pot.
There's nothing left to boil down.

Sunshine (whispering)

I Am. I did not die.[10] Still here.

Notes

1 Williams, P. (1987). "Spirit-murdering the messenger: The discourse of fingerpointing as the law's response to racism." *University of Miami Law Review*, 42, 127–158.
2 hooks, b. (1986). "Talking back." *Discourse*, 8, 123–128 (p. 126.)
3 Shange, N. (2010). *For colored girls who have considered suicide/when the rainbow is enuf.* Simon and Schuster.
4 Finney, N. (2009). "Foreword." In R. N. Brown (Ed.), *Black girlhood celebration: Toward a hip-hop feminist pedagogy.* New York: Peter Lang, xiii–xxii.
5 Simone, N. (1965). *I put a spell on you [Song]. On I put a spell on you [Album].* UK: Philips Records.
6 In "What the Mirror Said," Lucille Clifton offered a litany for Black girls and women, wherein she reminded us of our bigness, beautiful geography, and value. Within Spell #19, it serves as a cleansing agent, a wiping off the soot of the lies and weight held that sometimes stops us from saying what's necessary, walking away from harm, and even taking pleasure in ourselves.
7 Clifton, L., Young, K., Glaser, M. S., & Morrison, T. (2012). "What the mirror said." In *The collected poems of Lucille Clifton 1965–2010.* Rochester, NY: BOA Editions, 199.
8 Clifton, L., Young, K., Glaser, M. S., & Morrison, T. (2012). "What the mirror said." In *The collected poems of Lucille Clifton 1965–2010.* Rochester, NY: BOA Editions.
9 Simone, N. (1998). *Here comes the sun [Song]. On sugar in my bowl: The very best of Nina Simone 1967–1972 [Album].* Culver City, CA: Sony Music Entertainment.
10 June Jordan (2003) in *Some of Us Did Not Die* reminds us that despite the real pain and trauma endured, those of us still here have a responsibility to imagine anew. Within the context of this spell, it is a recognition that after being boiled down to nothingness, we remain, this time ourselves without the weight of the world.

24 Admirable or Ridiculous

Talkin Black, Back, & Between Kin Folk

Durell M. Callier and Mary E. Weems

Maya Lewis: Damn shame. I tell you. Being a black woman. Be strong they say. Support your man. Raise a man. Think like a man. Well damn, I gotta do all that. Hmph. Whose out here working for me? Carrying my burden, building me up when I get down. Nobody. Black women out here tryin to save everybody. And what do we get? Swagger jacked by white girls wearing cornrows and bamboo earrings, ain't that a bitch? But we still try. Try to help all y'all, even when we get nothing.

Is that admirable or ridiculous. [*laughs*] I don't know. I know me sitting here is ridiculous, when I could be helping. [*mockingly*] But you don't want my help. You want to do it all by yourself. Mr. Big Strong Black Man. [tone changes, serious] God forbid you let a sister like me help you out. Nah. You don't want that. Don't let me put you on my back when you fall. Wipe the crust outta yo eyes. Put a pep back in yo step. Because when we do, you resent us for making you better. Smarter. Stronger. Then drop us so you can be with someone basic, someone without all that baggage you left us with. But we still try. Takes in breath. That's why I'm here. Trying and saving. And trying to save, like we do. Here I am.

Admirable or ridiculous. Baby you tell me. . . .[1]

In Shonda Rhimes's syndicated political thriller television show, *Scandal*, audiences witness the fictitious inner workings of Washington, D.C., politics and the White House through a Black woman fixer—Olivia Pope. The art of *Scandal*, which aired for a total of seven seasons on ABC TV from 2012 through 2018, oftentimes imitated life. Real life during those years was punctuated by rising backlash to our nation's first Black president—Barack Obama—and Black family—wife, Michelle Obama, and two daughters, Sasha and Malia—in the seat of the nation's power, alongside continued losses in Black economic growth and wealth, an elite class that was growing richer as the poor got poorer.

It was also during this time frame that we saw growing divides in tribalism based on those ancient evils that have yet to die—hate based on difference, the need to have someone's foot on someone else's neck just to feel stronger, better, good about yourself—were all on the rise.[2] So were shootings of young people and queer people and Black people in our most sacred spaces—the church,

DOI: 10.4324/9781003274315-30

night club, home, school—where we practiced freedom and liberatory education despite societal constraints. And here was *Scandal*, archiving, signifying, and remixing all this, holding up a mirror for us to stop and think, piercing the fourth wall now in our everyday talk via our *Scandal* watch parties, during which we donned our Olivia Pope–sized wineglasses, with our heavy pours of red wine, listening to a Black soundtrack of genius old-school R&B, Motown-era music—soul—rocking our souls speaking back to the soul of our nation.

The preceding excerpt references one of those touch points in the show, when we as an audience are witnesses asked to contemplate the connections between our lives and the show. In one of the many explosive scenes of the Season 6 Finale, we sit with the protagonist—Oliva Pope—and her mother—Maya Lewis—as Lewis remarks on the state of Black womanhood. The scene gave us as an audience a lot to feel and think through, particularly the monologue that Maya expertly delivers.

The show became known for its scathing monologues deployed as wit and as reading down the house, with Olivia's parents—Rowan "Eli" Pope and Maya Lewis—known for some of the most iconic monologues of the show. In the described scene, Maya's been arrested and sits in a secret facility prison. She is a wanted "terrorist," and the villainess, whose character is a fulcrum of other dynamics, reveals an absent mother–longing daughter dynamic between herself and Olivia, as well as a jaded lover and betrayal between her and Eli. As each of these dynamics is on full display, so, too, are the fraught relationships and political realities between Black women and men.

A classic Black feminist reading,[3] Maya asks us, Is it admirable or ridiculous? Her words provide a refrain to the section that immediately follows. In this section, both authors reflect on the question posed regarding the relationships of Black men and women, particularly as those relationships are constrained by systems of power. Offering personal reckonings with these relationships as they bump up against systems of power, Durell provides a series of autoethnographic vignettes in the forms of poems, in which he wrestles with an admirable—lifesaving/affirming role—of Black women in his life juxtaposed to the ridiculous—death dealing and diminishment of quality of life—Black women in his life have experienced by men and at times inclusive of himself. In this vein, Mary interjects her own biographical reality of moving through and from the ridiculousness of these relationships under the duress of US empire, colonization, and racism.

Wrestling with the possibilities of Black love, care, joy, in the US, despite these forces, the authors interweave narrative, reflection, poetry, and analysis between. Whereas two distinct voices emerge, the writing seeks to provide a form that offers the semblance of dialogue and ease of reading, asking readers to stick with the gravity of shared yet diverging lived realities. To demarcate the individual author's voice, the corresponding author's text are formatted differently. Italicized words, right justified, represent Mary's words and the nonitalicized left-aligned words represent those of Durell. Illuminating more than what has been done, whether good, bad, or ugly, the authors also address what we as Black people deserve—each other in earnest mutual love, respect, building up, nurturing, and affirmation.

admirable[4] [adjective]
ad·mi·ra·ble | \ ˈad-m(ə-)rə-bəl

>*deserving the highest esteem: EXCELLENT*
>*obsolete: exciting wonder: SURPRISING*

I

i am approximately one billion, on hundred forty-three million, five hundred seventy-seven thousand, eight hundred fourteen seconds old and assuredly no less than all my time here there stands a Blackwomangirl

Her
be true to yourself, be who you are
Her
boy don't you sit up there and lie to me
Her
the best is yet to come
Her
be unfuckwithable
Her
don't let nobody steal your joy
Her
take your time
you KNOW how
Her
don't get out there and eva act like it wasn't a Black woman who put you on
Her
own your shine
Her
i love you
Her
i love you still
Her
i'm proud of you
Her
look and live
my brother live
Her
look how far you've come

Her
i'm proud of you
we're proud of you
we love you
we we   we
we we
we we
we
be here
don't forget about us

He

Told mama I was too dark to be his
His skin the kind of chocolate that's healthy
Mine an in-between him and moma

Loved me best he could, useta say it
All the time followed by the kind of absence
That makes you wonder

He

Like a Black Peter Pan
Never, never grew up
The surprise baby at the end
Finer than wine
Mama's baby

He

Walked me down the aisle first time
Only person crying in my wedding pictures

He

Was the only one I'll ever have
He's dead and gone
*and **so** missed.*

II.

i'm the eldest
but
i don't throw hands

my lil sis does
for all of us
and don't you forget it

Oldest

> *If in fact, I find out during death*
> *I can come back for another try*
> *It will be as the youngest child*
> *of any mama who will take me*
> *inside and cherish me like I'm*
> *a child*
> *and not a grownup.*

III.

i broke her heart
millions of pieces
our high school turned college love
like a star
its shining brilliance
an actual death
marking time
illuminating
the possibilities of rebirth
in our truths

i could not love her as she needed
as she desired
as she deserved
i chose me instead

she with this revelation
now naked before her
because clothes are for closets
took my hand and said
i still love you
and still
drove me to the airport
and still
hugged me
and
still

Heartbreak

> *I've loved more than one man, married thrice*
> *but my heart, the gut of me, where I come from*
> *has only broken once*
> *my first love*
> *who didn't believe a lie I told about a date,*
> *and moved to Chicago without saying goodbye—*
> *married a girl from Cleveland*
> *I didn't even think he liked.*

ridiculous[5] [adjective]

ri·dic·u·lous | \ rə-ˈdi-kyə-ləs

arousing or deserving ridicule: extremely silly or unreasonable: ABSURD,
PREPOSTEROUS

I.

she—my great grandmother
so i am told
so i believe
so i know
use to endure abuse by our
"loving" great grandfather

a split in the family tree
this matriarchal line
carrying the knowledge of terror
terror
in his hands
terror
by not paying the oil bill to freeze her out
terror
as in the choice to stay or leave and go where
terror
loss of newborn children
terror
cold prying shrew hands

the patriarchal split only knows the glory
the "provider"
the "benevolent"

the —
horseshit

they are buried
side by side

What Durell shares is bits and pieces of the story of so many Black women I know/have known/will know including my own. The global epidemic of sexual/emotional/physical abuse against women is rarely referenced in the news media, and when it is—the only difference is the city, town, state, country—the gist of the story repeats like someone just copied and pasted the details and changed the names and locations, and other than the 'rare' prosecution of the perpetrator (think Bill Cosby, Jerry Epstein, Donald Trump, R. Kelly and etc., etc., etc.) nothing changes. Terry Crews was still immediately believed when he accused a powerful white man of violating him, and no one challenged why he waited so long; dozens of women still have to "prove" what they share when they finally summon the courage to speak out and in the end are typically devastated by the lack of accountability for their abusers. The saying "rule of thumb" comes from the fact that it used to be okay for a man to beat his wife/woman with anything as long as it wasn't larger than his thumb. And rape has only been against the law in this country during my lifetime. Sexism and misogyny are alive and well and given the fact that men continue to rule this world—I pray for change but have little hope it will come.

II.

she the youngest
of four
only girl
biggest heart
who gave and gave and gave
when she didn't have to give
when her children might not have

and when she turned to them for help
for a space in the heart
returned
just a bit of the plot she so richly gave
often
she the only girl
youngest of four
single mother
big hearted
learned that
apples don't fall far from their trees

I am the oldest of four. Mama had me right after she turned seventeen; by then my father, who wanted her to have an abortion, had already been in the army long enough to win a Golden Glove championship in his weight class. I am the orange on Mama's apple tree. I jumped soon as I could, found a different kind of tree—grew into me, her seeds planted in my heart.

III.

confession

i didn't know how to love her
love licks are just hits
a consequence of time and messaging
that i know better than now

but he did not

my sister almost blinded in one eye on Mother's Day
her big-hearted self
only girl of four
learning that
we still have an apple/tree problem

I never met a man who knew how to love me until I finally met one who knows how to love himself. My third husband.

I Atlas Shrugged the user-abuser-lost-kinda Black man off my back a long time ago, turned my life over to God the Creator of all things and figured out who I was and what my purpose in this life is. One of the first things that happened is I re-met my husband, a man I'd known since my late daughter was five, a man who loved and looked out for his late mama and daddy; loves and looks out for his sister and niece; and, most important, loves, protects and provides for me. My biggest fan, the wind beneath my wings. Our marriage a partnership of commitment—he looks out for me, and I look out for him. The closest I've been to happiness with a man— twenty-one years and counting

IV.

would there be apples or trees
lest She

held him down
me down
us down

I can't make a grown person nothing. Used to think if only I could love a man enough, good-sex him enough, take his shit enough waiting for him to change—he would. That's bullshit. My stepmama used to say, "Man don't change nothing but his socks." Person don't change until and unless they want to—applies to me, applies to every man and woman I've ever known. Change is a choice, and it takes acknowledgment and hard work.

Watching You/Watching Us an Afterword

When Mary said,

I've never heard of Scandal *watch parties (I'd use my age as a reason but one of my closest friends who's two years older than me watches religiously) but am reminded of a long time ago when Black folks being on television was so rare, each week* Jet Magazine *would publish the names of the actors who'd be on television the following week and the names of the television shows. People who at the time didn't have television, would visit family and/or friends, share food and drinks, and party together. A celebration of even the brief presence of somebody who looked like us,*

she conjures for us the reality that we yearn to see ourselves reflected back to ourselves. But, at times in our desire to see our Blackness in all its splendor and diversity celebrated, we, because of racism, sexism, misogyny, homophobia, transphobia, and other systems of power, fail to see and value one another. Essex Hemphill's (1992) declaration in his poem, "To Some Supposed Brothers," admonishments remain that "we so-called brothers / wonder why it's so hard / to love *our* women / when we're about loving them / the way america / loves us" (p. 146).[6] Extending Hemphill's admonishment, and the gravity of the conversation staged here, we leave you with Lewis's question reframed—Is it admirable or ridiculous, the way we try to love each other the way America loves us? Baby, you tell us.

Notes

1 Taken from Shonda Rhimes (2017) Season 6 finale, *Scandal*. ABC Network (2017, May 22). "Mama Pope speaks her mind—scandal season 6 finale [Video]." *YouTube*. www.youtube.com/watch?v=jgm9X3BDeT0&t=3s. Accessed October 11, 2021.
2 See Parker, P. (1978). "Have you tried to hide?" In P. Parker (Ed.), *Movement in black*. Trumansburg, NY: Crossing Press, 47–48; Toni Morrison, YouTube [Alex Hyman]. (2019, August 6). "White people have a very very serious problem—Toni Morrison on Charlie Rose." *YouTube*. www.youtube.com/watch?v=n2txzMkT5Pc. Accessed October 11, 2021.
3 See Bowen, S. (2017, November 16.). "Why can't Olivia Pope be more like this character on Scandal?" www.refinery29.com/en-us/2017/11/181577/olivia-pope-maya-lewis-black-women-feminism-scandal. Accessed October 11, 2021.
4 Merriam-Webster. (n.d.). "Admirable." In *Merriam-webster.com dictionary*. www.merriam-webster.com/dictionary/admirable. Accessed October 11, 2021.
5 Merriam-Webster. (n.d.). "Ridiculous." In *Merriam-webster.com dictionary*. www.merriam-webster.com/dictionary/ridiculous. Accessed October 11, 2021.
6 See Hemphill, E. (1992). "To some supposed brothers." In E. Hemphill (Ed.), *Ceremonies* (pp. 145–146). Jersey City, NJ: Cleis Press.

25 Feeling Real

Reprise (Talking B[l]ack to a Younger Brother)

Bryant Keith Alexander

I: I Apologize

The younger Black gay man said: "Nobody ever told me Langston Hughes was queer."[1] And my immediate response as a Black gay man of a certain age was, "I am sorry. I apologize." The impulse to apologize came from a sincere place of remembrance, knowing the feeling and yearning to know that others were what I knew I was and not having the words to ask or define the parameters of my desire or fixing my mouth to ask. The apology came from that place of harboring the sentiments of Hughes in my boy bosom, knowing there was a resonance of something that spoke to deep places in my person, wondering what that kinship was about beyond the poetic, beyond the poetic blackness, and within the poetic performative blackness of his words that danced in my spirit.

I went *Looking for Langston*[2] through a monochrome cinematic vision of *dreams deferred*[3] in which raisins dried in the sun and were rehydrated with bodily fluids of desire.

I went looking for Langston through his poetry, prose, and plays.

I went looking for Langston through *the weary blues*,[4] but *not without laughter*.[5]

I went looking for Langston as a I *wondered and wandered*[6]; learning *the ways of white folks*.[7]

I went looking for Langston in the process of being reborn in a *Black Nativity*[8] and yearning for *America to be America again*,[9] but not Trump's MAGA.

I went looking for Langston and I found him, but I didn't tell you about the search and the discovery, which was not so much about him but about me.

I didn't tell you because despite my public persona, I am really a private person. Now I come to know better that such privacy can create gaps in our shared histories and perpetuate complicities of silence that become intergenerational.

*I wish that someone had told **me** that Langston Hughes was queer.* Or is that Langston was *quare*, recognizing the intersectionality of his blackness, gendered identities, and all other political aspects of his real and imagined selves to which we cleave.[10]

DOI: 10.4324/9781003274315-31

II. Re/Membering

When you talk about childhood recitations during Black History Month celebrations, I, too, remember being that erudite, articulate, and desirously performative young Black boy reciting Malcolm, Morrison, Martin, Maya, Ellison, Langston, and James Baldwin along with Gil Scott-Heron, Huey P. Newton, Angela Davis, and Audre Lorde—each a revolutionary in their own way, each parting waters with words and calling people to attend to desire and disdain, along with claiming their power and striving towards possibility in *shadow and act.*[11] Those recitations were rehearsals for living, and the writings were lessons for action.

In talking to you now, the you who is particular and the you(s) that are plural, I am also remembering myself through the journey of your wonder and discovery, and re/membering myself to the responsibility of community.

Mentioning our brother Dixon, you reminded me that "[y]ou [I], then, are [am] charged by the possibility of your [my] good health, by the broadness of your [my] vision, to remember us [them]." I know the spirit and the standpoint of that charge. My biological brother, Nathaniel Patrick Alexander, died from HIV/AIDS in 1994. At that time and following, as I was *Standing at the Crossroads*, I wrote:

> I am standing. I am standing at a crossroads between my brothers: the married brother, the dead brother, the jailed brother, the dropout brother. I am standing at the crossroads between my biological brothers and my cultural brothers. I am standing, looking through a window to another time onto a dust basketball court, seeing young Black Olympians in the prime of their manhood perform the pageantry of youthful dreaming and the ritual of growing up. I am standing at a crossroads of my life as a Black gay man living in the age of AIDS. I am standing at a crossroads looking through the window, seeing myself engaged in the pageantry of death and the ritual of saying good-bye. I am standing at the crossroads between Simcoe Street and 12th Street, between my childhood home and the funeral home, between boyish dreams and adult realities. I am standing at a crossroads-looking, reflecting, remembering, moving and being moved, but standing still at an intersection in space and a breach in time.[12]

I remember and I re/member not only those who have passed but also we who are present and living to breach the intersection of space and time of their *sojourn*[13]; to live boldly, to live out loud; to remember each other in living, dying, and the *ceremonies* of our community.[14] No shade, or maybe all *shade.*[15]

III: You Make Me Feel

> You invoked Sylvester, and something in me moved.
> I moved to the dance floor
> that space of comingling desire where bodies move not just to the music

but to culture and desire.

Bodies as spectacle and cat call.
Bodies *feelin' the spirit in the dark*.[16]
Bodies feeling bodies, grinding
under the guise of dance.
Bodies simulating sex on the dance floor.[17]

I remember seeing that video. Yes, that video that for me was an
awakening.[18]
Woman/man/woman/man? It did not matter to me; his salacious beauty
overwhelmed.

"You make me feel mighty real."
An anthem.
An anthem to the question of realness in the farce of gender.

Real, the partner of authenticity.
Mighty real—uninhibited contact.
An invitation.
A permission.

He pushed me over the edge
Beyond possibility to a chameleon realness.

I had almost forgotten what Sylvester did for me.
He made me feel mighty real (and seen).

IV. Against Monuments of Remorse

I apologized as a memory of remorse for all the times in which the casualness
of my Black gay self may have gone unrecognized or un-declaimed; times
in which I did not mentor out loud, not proclaiming the presence of other
Blackqueer/quare folks living to be out loud, the ancestors, the **br**others, the
sisters; the **bristers**.

I don't want to build further *monuments of memory and remorse*, not just to
the overt atrocities of violence or the isolation and tragedy of invisibility and
loneliness or cloistered identities dancing or *playing in the dark*.[19]

I want to recognize the ways in which we all become walking monuments
of memory and remorse—when either we don't speak our truths and suffer for
it or our silence hurts others in their knowing or not knowing that *Langston
was queer*, as an analogical reference to Black lives/knowledge that move from
generational dramas of living to intergenerational traumas—learning lessons in
isolation of broader cultural knowing.

Together, let us be living monuments for each other.

I will tell you, the truth.

Notes

1 This is a reference and response to Durell M. Callier in the introduction of this book. Or see: Callier, D. M. (2020). "Feelin' real/unbroken: Imagining blackqueer education through autopoetic inquiry." *International Review of Qualitative Research*, 14.2, 330–336.

2 Julien, I. (1989). *Looking for Langston*. Produced by Sankofa Film & Video, British Film Institutes, United Kingdom.

3 Hughes, L. (1998). "Dream deferred (Harlem)." In A. Carroll et al (Eds.), *Great American poems*. New York: Mineola, 75, 101.

4 Hughes, L. (1926). *The weary blues*. New York: A.A. Knopf.

5 Hughes, L. (1930). *Not without laughter*. New York and London: A. A. Knopf.

6 Hughes, L. (1993). *I wonder as I wander: An autobiographical journey*. New York: Rinehart.

7 Hughes, L. (1934). *The ways of white folks*. Chicago: Vintage.

8 Hughes, L. (1992). *Black nativity*. New York: Dramatic Publishing.

9 Hughes, L. (2013, May 7). "Let America be America again." *Poets.org. The Academy of American Poets*. www.poets.org/viewmedia.php/prmMID/15609. Accessed October 8, 2021.

10 Johnson, E. P. (2001). "Quare studies, or (almost) everything I know about queer studies I learned from my grandmother." *Text and Performance Quarterly*, 21.1, 1–25.

11 Ellison, R. (1953). *Shadow and act*. New York: Random House.

12 Alexander, B. K. (1999). "Standing at the Crossroads." *Callaloo: A Journal of African American and African Arts and Letters,* 22.2, 343–345.

13 Hunter, B. M. (1993). *Sojourner: Black gay voices in the age of AIDS*. New York: Other Countries Press.

14 Hemphill, E. (1992). *Ceremonies*. San Francisco, CA: Cleis Press.

15 Morrow, B. & Rowell, C. H. (Eds.). (1996). *Shade: An anthology of fiction by gay men of African descent*. New York: Avon.

16 Johnson, E. P. (1998). "Feeling the spirit in the dark: Expanding notions of the sacred in the African-American gay community." *Callaloo*, 21.2, 399–416.

17 See: Alexander, B. K. & Weems, M. E. (2017). "Special issue: Terrorism and hate in Orlando, America (poetic and performative responses)." *Qualitative Inquiry,* 23.7, 483–571.

18 Sylvester—"You make me feel (mighty real)." www.youtube.com/watch?v=oG2ixYJ79iE.

19 Morrison, T. (1993). *Playing in the dark: Whiteness and the literary imagination*. New York: Vintage Books.

Section VI

Voting Rights and Writing Volition

Mary starts this section with the question, *Why Did Black People Vote for Trump?* A question that at first seems perplexing, so we explore that question in a four-way dialogue of speculations that don't necessarily demonize but don't necessarily redeem the act or motivating intentions. We don't seek to alienate, as much as speculate on, the ways that Black people are not a monolith; we are not the same—so when we resist the collectivizing of us all—we cannot also resist the individualization of attitude, beliefs, and values that make us so different—yet tied together by histories and origins, or needs and desires, that are also variable in our politics of difference and diasporic disbursal.

We also find ourselves asking about "voting rights"—which, in many ways, are being challenged again in this country: again, suppressing the voting rights of Black people, discouraging or preventing other special groups from voting, reducing the numbers *by hook or by crook* of those who might vote against a candidate, a party, or a proposition. Gerrymandering practices are still popular as intentional redesigns to redistrict voting zones to establish knowingly unfair political advantages for one political party over another by manipulating the binds, borders, bounds, and boundaries of electoral districts—most often used to control the Black vote/the colored vote, to suppress the Black vote/colored vote, to keep suppressed People of Color and our voice through our vote in the determination of local, state, and national elections. As well the locational politics of polling stations that have People of Color standing in interminable long lines in nearly unbearable conditions to vote, along with the sometimes indistinguishable ballots to which people must decipher and decode referendums to understand when a vote of "YES" means no, and a vote of "NO" means yes—usually an intentional strategy to confuse the raced or uneducated—voter suppression and the act of insurrection run hand and hand these days. Because if you can suppress the vote then you engage in the repression of voter effects. Thus, we are also thinking about the historical struggle to get the vote, the historical struggle for equal representation under the law, the historical struggle to get People of Color to the ballots and the conditions of their (our) participation in the legal processes of democracy, and the ability for the write-in vote, all of which draw race lines and class lines through the democratic process of the

DOI: 10.4324/9781003274315-32

vote. The vote linked with *life, liberty, and the pursuit of happiness* which is usually a vote against hate and for a freedom of possibilities. In the years beginning with 2020, voter suppression feels too familiar, like a *posttraumatic stress disorder* that haunts Black people in this country. For many, it is the war after the war: wars of military aggression or the daily struggles of living Black in the United States of America.

And it makes this Black Quartet begin thinking about *writing as an act of voting*, writing as volition, writing as a means of *righting* ourselves in history, writing as a means in which we practice our power and to assert our will on determining the direction of our individual and collective futures, writing as taking a stance. This last section of the book initiates a response to the informing question: *Why did [so many] Black people vote for Trump?* But then it moves to offer a set of perspectives and possibilities, a set of manifestos on Black influence through critical creative writing, through activism—and differing perspectives on practicing the vote, voice, and volition. But it also speaks to the choices that we make toward our personal happiness and/or our personal salvation. In many ways, this last section signals back to the first section in which we celebrated the originating *Black Quartet*—and the stance their work took to contribute to a broader artistic activist affect.

How did you vote? What would you stand in line for, or cross lines for, or put your body on the line to vote—for" *(Dangling proposition intended, or maybe I should change this to a "hanging participle")?*

BKA

26 Why Did Black People Vote for Trump?

The Black Quartet

Mary: A couple of weeks ago, a white woman bartender at a local bar over-heard me sharing me and Bryant's new book *Still Hanging: Using Performance Texts to Deconstruct Racism* with a friend and asked me if I was a Trump fan before she showed me her anti-Trump poem. During the 2020, campaign, I noticed that one of my Black neighbors, whom I've never met in the seven-teen years we've lived in our community, had a yard filled with Trump signs "Blacks for Trump," and so on. These two disparate experiences (the first one long after Biden was elected) prompted me to ask: Why did Black people vote for Trump?

The first time Trump ran for president, I was so traumatized by the fact that President Obama and Frist Lady Michelle were leaving the White House and so convinced that the orange-pumpkin-head-white-man I kept hearing about didn't have-a orange-snowballs chance in the desert of beating Hillary Clinton that I didn't pay much attention. This certainty was reinforced by the constant feedback from political folks in the field, and the numbers crunchers who were tracking various national polls. After all, Donald J. Trump, or T-rump as I like to call him, was totally unqualified to hold any kind of political office, let alone the most powerful position on the planet. While Trump has long boasted of being a successful real estate mogul, Trump has never been success-ful at anything in his life other than the reality show *The Apprentice*, which ran for thirteen years from 2004 to 2017. The tragic irony of the show's premise is that each season a group of professional hopefuls competed to prove they had the business acumen to win, yet every business venture Trump has ever participated in has been an abject failure, often leaving small business owners unpaid and struggling as a result of working for Trump. Yet the show made Trump a celebrity in his own mind and in the minds of millions of Americans who tuned in each week. Trump became a symbol of popular culture, includ-ing being referenced in rap songs by Black artists and embraced by a small number of famous Black entertainers, including Kanye West, Steve Harvey and other Black comedians. Even Dave Chappelle, who hosted *Saturday Night Live*, shortly after Trump was elected said, "We should give the man a chance."

DOI: 10.4324/9781003274315-33

Watching Chappelle, one of my comic heroes, say that, I thought, "Chance, what the fuck is he talking about?"

When the Central Park 5—Korey Wise, Kevin Richardson, Raymond Santana, Antron McCray, Yusef Salaam—were convicted accused of gang raping a white female in Central Park, Trump immediately began exacerbating the situation by calling for the reinstatement of the death penalty and letting it be known that he wanted the teenaged men punished before the trial even started. Their subsequent conviction and years in jail ended when the "Innocence Project" picked up their case, and in 2002, Matias Reyes plead guilty to the rape, which was supported by DNA evidence. Their convictions were vacated, and the now fully grown men were released from prison without any acknowledgment from Trump of his unjust accusation and outcry. It's common knowledge that Trump's rental property applications were marked with a 'c' for colored to ensure that Black applicants were denied an opportunity to rent/lease from him, and when applicants challenged this racially discriminatory practice, he spent thousands of dollars in attorney fees to fight them in court.

Prior to and during his campaign, Trump claimed to believe Obama was born in Kenya rather than the United States right up until Obama produced his birth certificate to quash a birtherism myth that remains true in the hearts and minds of millions of Trump supporters today. I could go on and on and on, but this is a Black Quartet piece, and I need to leave space for my colleagues' responses.

The short of it is, that Trump was and is an uneducated, daddy-spoiled, narcissistic, racist, sexist, xenophobic, liar, and flimflam man as transparent as a filtered glass of water. He says what he means, he never admits a mistake, he never apologizes and will throw friends, supporters, and I suspect family, under a bus at the first sign of trouble. According to what I read in Mary J. Trump's book about her uncle, *Too Much and Never Enough*, Trump only truly cared about one person in this world other than himself—his father, who realized Trump's one great strength early on: he's a pitchman, able to sell shit to a hog farmer, able to convince people willing to listen of damn near anything including that his "university" can teach them to be real estate experts, his steak is the best, his Vodka is the best, his water is the best, and, most important, his name is gold, and putting it on anything increases the value of whatever it is tenfold. He's also an expert at using and manipulating folks through social media with both skewed information (fact + lie) and disinformation (lie + bald-faced lie).

I've always known that Black people do not represent a monolith. We differ in the ways most racial/ethnic groups of people do including gender, class, religion, sexual orientation, positions on social issues like abortion, and political party. I also understand that since Black people finally achieved the right to vote in 1965, we've voted for actually and/or potentially racist, white presidents almost exclusively including the twenty-eighth president, Democrat Woodrow

Wilson (1913–1921), who, as John McWhorter points out in "The Black People who Voted for Trump Know He's Racist" (11–16–2021):

> In 1912, W.E.B. DuBois espoused voting for none other than the nakedly racist Woodrow Wilson [who did nothing about Convict Leasing despite repeated letters from friends and family asking for help] fully aware that Wilson did not "admire," as he put it, Black people, but seeing his policies as better for Black people than Theodore Roosevelt's.
>
> (www.theatlantic.com, Accessed 6–5–2021)

And I acknowledge that I probably (I write probably because I can't recall another choice who was so transparently and racist) have faced this same dilemma several times since I was first old enough to vote. Unfortunately, for the United States, when Trump ran the first time, we had unpopular Hillary Clinton as his democratic opponent. Many of the people I know felt like DuBois did in 1912, not that they believed Hillary was racist—they just didn't like her—but considered her policies better.

Later in the same article McWhorter writes:

> To Psychologically healthy individuals. . . [who] have fulfilling lives . . . and are quite sure they're as good as him anyway . . . Trump's policies, or even just some of them . . . may seem more important than what Trump would say about them privately or in public.
>
> (www.theatlantic.com, Accessed 6–5–2021)

His statement leaves me with my mouth hanging open in disbelief, because even accounting for the fact that we aren't a monolith, McWhorter writes as if for Trump supporters, race is irrelevant, as if the only thing other than race Black Trump supporters consider are a political candidate's policies. And even though I don't know and have never spoken to any Black Trump supporters and acknowledge this might be true, I don't buy it and think it's more likely a combination of internalized racism (as members of an historically hated group, Black folks hate their Blackness, believe that white is right, that whites are superior, that they will benefit socially and financially by distancing themselves from Black people and embracing Trump), diehard Republicans, and/or the influence of Trump's mis/disinformation machine, including news outlets like Fox News and a plethora of targeted programming on various forms of social media.

What follows are a series of selected quotes from an article titled "Trump Made Gains with Black Voters in Some States. Here's Why," by Sean Collins (emphasis is added):

> With **disinformation and economic promises**, Trump lobbied hard for the Black vote in the final days of the campaign.

Ationza Smith, A Biden supporter and co-founder of the activist group "Revolutionaries Demanding Justice," told me that in her experiences, **Black Trump supporters "like how he's improved employment** . . . they're kind of basically looking at things on a business level and not necessarily an ethics level."

"[B]efore President Trump became president, the Black community loved President Trump," comedian and Black Trump supporter Terrence K. Williams told the *Washington Post*. **"Everybody wanted to be like President Trump because he was a successful businessman."**

Reinforced by Trump's prominent Black surrogates, including rapper Lil Wayne, who [posted] after meeting with Trump **"The Platinum Plan is going to give the community real ownership."**

Trump's Platinum Plan promises to **". . . uplift Black communities across the country through a $500 billion investment.** That money the . . . campaign promised, would fund 3 million new Black jobs, 500,000 new Black business, increase Black homeownership, and [provide] new opportunities for Black churches to receive federal dollars."

Note: Given Trump's lifelong record of lying and scamming how could anybody Black believe this?

"We've been voting for Democrats for 50 and 60 years and no progress," Marco Bisbee, a [B]lack man the *New York Times* spoke with at a Trump rally in Michigan said, "Y'all had eight years of a Black man as president, he ain't give you what you need."

Kevin Jones, the first vice chair of North Carolina's Nash County Democratic Party, said Trump's promise to give Black Americans the tools they need to build . . . a better life, speaks to something deeply ingrained in many **Black Americans—particularly those who live in the South . . . Nobody believes in bootstrapping [myth!] more than Black people in the South**, Jones said. **REALLY? #WTF?**

(www.vox.com Accessed 6–5–2021)

I share the preceding because out of all the online articles I read, this was one only two that went beyond Blacks caring more about policy or honor culture (notion that "men" have to be strong and never show signs of weakness) than racism or anything else.

In "'I made Juneteenth very Famous': The Inside Story of Trump's Post-George Floyd Month," for *Politico* magazine, Michael C. Bender, author of the book "*Frankly, We Did Win This Election: The Inside Story of How Trump Lost*, states:

> Trump had staked nearly his entire campaign in 2016 around a law-and-order image, and now groaned that the criminal justice reform that Kushner had persuaded him to support made him look weak and—even worse—hadn't earned him any goodwill among Black voters.

"I've done all this stuff for the Blacks—it's always Jared telling me to do this," Trump said to one confidante on Father's Day. "And they all f— hate me, and none of them are going to vote for me."

(www.politico.com Accessed 6–23–2021)

If only what Trump lamented in the preceding quote "and none of them are going to vote for me" were true. I end with a poem I wrote toward the end of Trump's first four years.

The T-rump is Done

★With apologies to Longfellow

Trump's president and the dark
covers the face of light,
as the alt-right pulls us downward,
no eagles are in sight.

I see the blight of the cities
scream through the rain and the shit,
as a feeling of sadness controls me,
that my spirit cannot resist.

It's a feeling of outrage and wrong
that's a different kind of pain,
and is as steeped in sorrow,
as grief resembles the rain.

Come, let's create some poems
the sounds shot from our hearts,
that will help us fight the hatred,
as tears from our eyelids start.

We'll write long days for labor
our nights the only ease,
we'll dream of the soul's music,
such wonderful melodies.

Our words have the power to riot
as well as express *Take Care*,
and flow like the forgiveness,
that follows after prayer.

> Though alt-right will not hear our music
> more people will begin to stare,
> and put-up blocks of resistance,
> refusing not to care.

Bryant: At first, I was baffled by the question "*Why did [so many] Black people vote for Trump?*"[1] I was not baffled by the question but baffled by the pained reality of the answer.

Then I thought about it again:

Was the vote an attempt at transcending race, as to ideologically embody the notion that race is merely a social construction created to mark difference and social hierarchies—so to vote for Donald Trump, the then personification of a far-leftist faction of the Republican Party, was to somehow ideologically transcend the politics of race for some political puritanism of the Republican Party—in which, after his election, their vote would translate into a "get out of Black" card in America? [Maybe that's not fair: Maybe it is the investment in the power of the Republican Party ticket, to which one must surely be invested to vote for Trump.]

Was their vote a commitment to the social values of the Republican party? Was it an attempt to transcend the material realities of raced bodies linked with political ideologies and political parties? The Republican/Democrat binary mapped to a White/BIPOC binary has always been a tenuous analogy, maybe a reductive division of political ideologies. But can all the Black people who voted for Trump transcend the historical legacies of their racial realties in the rhetorics of his actual campaign, in his actual presidency, and indeed in this country suffering from a reignited racial war and Trump's overt association with white supremacist groups?

Could a vote for Trump by Black people work toward transcending race (a post-race decision)? Can this be achieved while they reside in the raced bodies that they live in if, in fact, the materiality of their bodies is raced? Maybe by the virtuality and visualicity of their bodies they can pass as not raced—at least in the ways that Black people in America have traditionally been raced—via family lineage, one-drop rules (as a contamination of white blood), pigmentation, and features, barring the brown paper-bag tests that were created to establish intra-racial group hierarchies of beauty and value and nearer-to-Godness/goodness than the embodied existence of others, of darkies.

I do know that whiteness is performative and can be performed outside of white bodies, so maybe those voting practices were a performance of whiteness that did not transcend the materialities of their Black bodies. And to reference a performance of whiteness is not to say that Black people were trying to be white, such ideological values that have been traditionally associated with being white, which, of course, we should all continue to challenge relative to the volition of our own desires—within and outside of race.

I wonder if they read Trump's slogan of "Make America Great Again" as some return to a pre-slavery utopia that relocated their positionality as nonwhite raced beings. And what would that mean? And was that ever true? And where would that relocation land them, pre-slavery, when America was presumably great—or is that a timeline issue or a Black history problem or a return to when America was great for white people? It was for our Native American/Indigenous brethren. Trump was involved in a great number of regulations on the minoritized other—like his policies on immigration and DACA and building a wall to prevent Brown bodies from crossing the border or entering the country by any means possible (necessary). Was that one of their logics in voting for him, one of those "Mexican are taking our jobs" defenses that somehow better positions Black people for those same jobs?[2] Really?

Was their vote linked with class and the desire for the rich to stay rich?

Was their vote and assumed Republican party affiliation stressed on the "the ideology of governing a nation as a republic with an emphasis on liberty and the civic virtue practiced by citizens. . . . More broadly, it refers to a political system that protects liberty, especially by incorporating a rule of law that cannot be arbitrarily ignored by the government"? If so, where is the performative investment of these values as it relates to all Black people in this country?

Okay—maybe I am struggling to respond to this prompt. And while I believe in democracy and the power and potential for all people to vote their conscious—I am baffled that in a country where Black people still must march and argue and defend that Black Lives Matter, voting Republican, especially under Donald Trump—seems counterintuitive to our own survival—unless you have the privilege of living in a bubble somewhere. I am taken with the notion that some people were shocked that Katlyn Jenner is Republican; maybe they were shocked that a member of the LGBTQ+ community would be Republican. I was not; her transition from male to female did not transcend her being white or being of a certain privilege or class.

But getting back to the prompt, like Mary, who turns the brilliance of Dave Chapelle, I am reminded of one of my favorite Black comedians, Lavell Crawford, who offered a comparison between Barack Obama and Donald Trump. In his bit, he comments on Obama's lack of performative blackness and his lack of performativity as a nigga (in his words, "not a real nigga.") Then he suggests that with Trump in office, America has a "real nigga" in office.[3] He offers a series of outrageous acts of unveiled bravado and boldness in Trump, ultimately describing him as "a tangerino nigga"—that made him a viable candidate for "real niggas" to be attracted to Trump and his brandishing boldness. Hence, separate from his politics, they were attracted to his swagger. The comedy sketch is hilarious and sobering—as it talks about the representational politics of Trump's unadorned boldness that served as an appeal to diverse constituencies—and particularly some Black people. Crawford's quintessential reference to Trump's performativity ends in his reference to "grabbing a pussy from time to time."[4] He suggests that this was a turning point for "real niggas" to sign the ballot for Trump. And of course, I am not sanctioning the validity of his claims or the acts of racism/sexism and misogyny that he outlines and attributes as value to a collective Black community—only that group that he seems to claim as "real niggas"—which, of course, teases and taunts at politics of authenticity within the "African American" community at large—to which we must continue to struggle in the quest of our own solidarity.

Trapped between those Black folks who believe that their Republican vote transcends racial politics relative to class (either that they maintain or aspire to)—and—those Black folks who appreciated Trump's boldness (separate from his affiliation with white supremacist groups)—lies a series of conflicted logics to support what has become the most conflicted performances of presidential authority in the history of the United States of America. I don't know why they voted for Trump, but I do, despite it all, want to validate their right to practice volition, even with the fact that I did not vote the same.

Dominique: Because (some) Black people are more wed to freedom iconography than its actual smell, look, and spaciousness period—my gut response to the prompt. Truth be told, if Mary hadn't posed the question, I am quite certain, not more than one minute would've been given to the idea. Hell, maybe one minute is generous. Why? Black folk who voted for 45 fell outside of my scope, and upon reflection, I already surmised factors contributing to such a phenomenon.

There is this insistence on living and acting against one's self-interest. Like how poor people in the United States of North America voted for a so-called business mogul with no investments in things outside himself, his interest. Or like how Tina Campbell of the gospel group Mary Mary, insist it was 45's "Christian views"[5] that led her to vote for him over Hillary. Decisions are being made from a surface perspective, a position that often forecloses possibilities for our best living. Like how *of God* (if that's even the deciding factor) was 45's actions, tweets, character, spirit? And while Christianity emphasizes nonjudgment, the decision to vote or not vote based on mere rhetoric indicates a desire to major in the minor as well as a commitment to waging war against our actual needs. I imagine, Black folk who voted for 45 had many reasons, none of which get us collectively closer to a pleasure-filled, violence-no-more state of living.

I don't personally know any Black folk who voted for him and talked about it. I'd like to think it's the company I keep. Then again, you neva know what happens behind drawn curtains and mailed in ballots. Black folk voted for 45 because they could. They voted for him because they have money. They voted for him because they want money. Black folk voted for 45 because he's a "tangerino nigga." Because they believe in capitalism. They voted for him because they're xenophobic. Black folk voted for 45 because they had some ideas, meant well, but got shit mixed up.

Similar to Bryant, I too may be wrestling with taking up the question. I've asked myself it with slightly different phrasing, wording that does some other work. Like why wouldn't Black folk vote for 45? What kind of dish do Blackness and MAGA make? And what's the seasoning? What stands in between us and the Black folk we are reflecting upon?

At the end of the day, none of these questions grabbed me. None of them yoked me up like a Black momma does a child caught being too big for their bridges (britches). I guess that's the point. No new taste was added to the rue that is the United States of North America by Black folk voting for 45. And no new opportunities were afforded us. Black folk who felt compelled voted for him, watched to see the outcome, voted for Biden, and some prayed for Stacey Abrams to somehow save the day. They voted for him, and collectively, we continue to have to remind 46 and his administration that recognizing white supremacy and creating the conditions for a pleasure-filled, violence-no-more state of living ain't close to the same.

Black folk who voted for 45 *still* feel outside of my scope. I feel for them and wonder what type of seasonings they thought to be adding to the rue, what type of seasonings they have in their cabinets.

Durell: So first I guess I am seeking a bit more clarity. Which time are we referring to? The first time when the now twice-impeached former president actually won, with what we now know was Russian interference? Or the closer than close call, where we learned that early Election Day voter polls signaled that more Black men voted for the orange menace this time than in his first election? But in both elections, what is shocking are the depths of the smoke and mirrors involved. I mean, did you know that the Russian bots were creating Black(ish) avatars, faking our *funk* to spread disinformation. I rather like Mary's definition of disinformation a "lie + bald-faced-lie." Because not only were they spreading bald-faced lies about the scopes and aims of Black Lives Matter, Black activism, and other political matters, but also they were lying about who they actually were, lying about being Black. This happened twice (that we know of), reported once in 2017[6] that

> [a] social media campaign calling itself "Blacktivist" and linked to the Russian government used both Facebook and Twitter in an apparent attempt to amplify racial tensions during the U.S. presidential election,
>
> (O'Sullivan & Byers 2017)

and then again in 2020[7] it was noted,

> Facebook removed hundreds of accounts on Thursday from a foreign troll farm posing as African-Americans in support of Donald Trump and QAnon supporters. It also removed hundreds of fake accounts linked to conservative media outlet The Epoch Times that pushed pro-Trump conspiracy theories about coronavirus and protests in the U.S. . . . The foreign pro-Trump troll farm was based in Romania and pushed content on Instagram under names like 'BlackPeopleVoteForTrump' and on Facebook under 'We Love Our President.'
>
> (Collins & Collier 2020)

One headline even reading, "Bots in Blackface."[8] I mean, can you believe it? What an interesting revitalization and modernization of Blackface, when the minstrel show goes digital? However, none of these points actually answers the question at hand, whether we are talking about the 2016 or the 2020 election, but they feel important for the record. Important for some of what we are say-ing and wrestling with in this question. So as not to foreclose the possibilities of blackness and Black agency as Bryant denotes earlier, but rather, my seeking clarity is to illuminate the various actors influencing voting patterns in recent elections, and how race is implicated beyond the racial identity of who votes and how, but rather how are racial dog whistles being operationalized, even digitally?

Circling back to the question, I don't really have an answer but a different speculation. In another piece of writing that Dominique and I are working on in the edited collection, *Queer Kids, School Violence, and the Limits of 'Bullying,'* we returned to Pat Parker's poem, "Jonestown" (1985). I am reminded again of that poem in answer to the question, Why did Black people vote for Trump? and in Parker's words, there seems to be another possibility. She pens,

> and the pictures
> continue to flow
> images of a man
> a church man
> he cures disease
> NO
> he's a fake
> hired people
> treated liver
> he loves God
> NO
> he's a communist
> he talks many messages
> revolution to the young
> God to the old
> he believes in the family
> NO
> he destroys the family
> fucks the women
> fucks the men
> and the media continues
> to tell the tale

One of the many tragedies of Jonestown was the mass murder-suicide that took place at the People Temple Agricultural Project in Guyana in 1978, orchestrated by cult leader Jim Jones. Described to be many things, hope, someone who showed a level of "care" for people often discarded by society, a narcissist, charismatic, friendly, controlling, Jones's persona and allure as a cult leader share traits with Donald J. Trump. The phenomenon that is any dictator, any swindler, whether politician or jack-boot preacher is that they convince enough people to believe, fully, in their lie. They also keenly garner people's trust and loyalty. Well beyond my own expertise, I believe the pundits, the psychologists, those who study cults, when they say that the Republican Party and those in QAnon and those who supported and continue to support the twice-impeached ex-president of the United States, that that is a cult. Perhaps, Black folks voted for Trump because they too, unknowingly have become a part of a cult, have believed the Big Lie, have trusted a charlatan who spoke to some level of need they didn't find elsewhere. Perhaps they were also seduced by the grift, the false promise of a greater America that they could build, they could be a part of, that they would this time be entitled to away from those other forces, peoples, who have come to steal something from them. Doesn't membership to a cult require the sort of working against your own self-interest as Dominique suggests, your own desires for self-preservation because a larger-than-life virtue is the mission, and the leader, your messiah, the cozener, has led you down a path of self-destruction? Whatever the reasons, we know Black people did vote for Trump. Not enough thankfully, (but one too many) and I suppose this reality is cause for a deep sigh of relief.

★★★★★★

The question is asked. Speculations not answers are offered. **But maybe. Just maybe.** We have opened space for potential conversation about and for our collective Black futures. The conversation may not be pretty, but worth having as both a communal and a pedagogical endeavor.

Notes

1 See McWhorter, J. (2020, November 16). "The black people who voted for Trump know he's racist." *The Atlantic*. www.theatlantic.com/ideas/archive/2020/11/racism-isnt-everyones-priority/617108/.

2 Here I am thinking about Jimmy Santiago Baca's powerful piece titled, "So Mexicans Are Taking Jobs from Americans." Included in Beaty, J. & Hunter, J. P. (1994). *New worlds of literatures: Writings from America's many cultures*, 2nd edition. New York: W.W. Norton & Company, 774–775.

3 Crawford, L. "Barak Obama versus Donald Trump." www.youtube.com/watch?v=4B53rpLPxUs; www.youtube.com/watch?v=lS0YVP5XGB

4 See the Donald Trump Hollywood Access Tape story: Https://en.wikipedia.org/wiki/Donald _ Trump_Access_Hollywood_tape.>

5 www.ebony.com/entertainment/tina-campbell-donald-trump-2/.

6 O'Sullivan, D. & Byers, D. (2017, September 28). "Exclusive: Fake black activist social media accounts linked to Russian government." *CNNMoney*. https://money.cnn.com/2017/09/28/media/blacktivist-russia-facebook-twitter/index.html.

7 Collins, B. & Collier, K. (2020, August 6). "Facebook removes troll farm posing as African-American support for Donald Trump." *NBC News*. www.nbcnews.com/tech/tech-news/facebook-removes-troll-farm-posing-african-american-support-donald-trump-n1236056

8 Lynn, S. (2019, August 22). "Bots in blackface: The rise of fake Black people on social media promoting political agendas." *Black Enterprise*. www.blackenterprise.com/bots-in-blackface-the-rise-of-fake-black-people-on-social-media/.

27 Another Prayer Meeting

Bryant Keith Alexander

We come together in *a prayer meeting*.

Each of us with our own sense of religiosity and spirituality—all people of faith in ways that connect ourselves to spirits of creation, of family, of community, culture, and church.

We come together in *a prayer meeting*.

A communion to promote brotherly and sisterly love for each other, and not forestalling the love for our brethren as they exist in their twin-spiritedness, in their in-betweenness, in their/our existence, in our joint commitment to our being and becoming bravery to contribute to do the work that matters.

We come together in *a prayer meeting*.

In our act and actions like apostles, in Apostles, speaking in tongues and yet understanding each other as we profess and maybe confess our yearnings.

We come together in *a prayer meeting*.

Asking for blessings, forgiveness, and help in our unity and survival, as we summon the forces of spirit, wisdom, hope, and the possible for what is to come in our collective futures, beyond the foursome and for the many.

*We **pray** for guidance in the matters at hand and ask that you would clearly show us how to conduct our work with a spirit of joy and enthusiasm. Give us the desire to find ways to excel in our work,*[1] to make our work matter. To take the materiality of our bodies and *the materiality of our language* as signifiers and signals to pathways of social and political relations that open new spaces of knowing and showing aspects of our human experiences in blackness and beyond, unbound by the academic strictures of scholarly writing—yet rebounding to speak in critical and creative ways that are truly academic, accessible, and approachable.[2] This to reach the ones we are most interested in reaching in our preaching and our protest.

We come together in *a prayer meeting*.

Knowing that our work is vital. *Vital to the well-being of the church*, which is our Black community. Vital because articulate voices raised in *prayer and protest are essential* to the activist work we must do as we imagine a Black futurity. And vital because the Black communities we speak from and to, and the queer/quare communities we in part represent, evidence the prayer of our

DOI: 10.4324/9781003274315-34

protestations as an incite-filled *way for us to love one another.*[3] And to become a generational bridge for those who are to follow.

We come together in *a prayer meeting*.

As a volitional act for the possible as we *march and demand justice or raise hell.*[4] So let the church, the church of your religion or the church of your communion with nature, or the church of your cosmological ways of knowing, say, "Amen."

Notes

1 Prayer to Open a Meeting, Catholic Principals Council: https://cpco.on.ca/files/6915/1820/8486/6._Prayer_to_Open_a_Meeting.pdf. Accessed August 1, 2021.
2 Bleich, D. (2013). *The materiality of language: Gender, politics, and the university*. Bloomington: Indiana University Press.
3 Why Prayer Meetings Are Vital to the Well Being of the Church (2019, August 6). https://chmce.org/2019/08/prayer-meetings/. Accessed August 1, 2021
4 This is an allusion to the Caldwell, Ben play (1970). "Prayer meeting or, the first militant minister." In B. Caldwell, R. Milner, E. Bullins, & L. Jones (Eds.), *A black quartet*. New York: Mentor Book, 28–36.

28 We Are the People (*July 4, 2021*)

The Black Quartet

We the People of the United States, in Order to form a more perfect Union, establish Justice, ensure domestic Tranquility, provide for the common defense, promote the general Welfare, and secure the Blessings of Liberty to ourselves and our Posterity, do ordain and establish this Constitution for the United States of America.

Preamble to the United States Constitution

We Are. . . . . .the Black people

We are the Black people, who are often present and/or presented.

We are the Black people, who are called upon in our material presence and in our critical creative labor to represent.

We are the Black people, who show up as evidence of talent and intellectual heft— representing diversity in our academic communities.

We are the Black people, who serve on multiple committees as the evidence of institutional commitment to diversity, equity, inclusion, and antiracism; a redistribution and reconfiguration of the same faithful and overworked Black people who show up again and again and again and again in an abusive *scandal of particularity*, presenting an optical allusion to the public that there are more Black people in a contorting and multiplying room of mirrors. But it is just us in our *thisness* who run astray from public concern.[1] The same Black PhDs engaging the race labor of our institutions, of our interdisciplinary engagements, and of our scholarly and creative arenas, paying the Black tax of diversity initiatives that is very seldom reimbursed, sometimes leaving us bereft and in deficit.

We are four Black PhDs, who stand as synecdoche for many Black PhDs in higher education.

We are the Black people and the rainbow people, who stand strong for students who seek us out for our support, and our understanding as they negotiate their own particularity in homogenized spaces of their educational experience.

We are the Black people, who show up in the promotional materials of our institutions or discipline or not—when there is a new (seldom) Black

DOI: 10.4324/9781003274315-35

face or brown face as other faces of acceptable difference/diversity who arrives—to be presented as a tally of progress.

We are the Black people, who are referred to as the Black Dean, the Black Professor, the Black Scholar, the Black Writer/Artist—knowing that we are always and already Black but negotiating the use of the identifier not as a signifier but as a racist differentiator from the Dean, the Professor, the Scholar, the Writer/Artist—wondering if there is a value judgment being made; evaluation and not just description. Other differentiators are used as well. . .

We are the Black people who do the work, we do the heavy lifting—not as pawns but for our own investments, our investments in our talent and intellect, our investment in standing in front of the class to be seen and heard and to narrate cultural theories and liberatory pedagogies of hope; our investment is in sitting at the table and actually making a difference. Our investment is in the possibility; the possibility of sitting on those search committees and giving the people-of-color applicants a fair chance before the implicit bias of the system takes over—because they don't look like the norm of the department or the institution.

We Are Tired. . . . . of. . . . . . .Waiting

We are tired of the fear that drives racism and results in something not right, unjust, wrong, and fucked up happening to one or more of us every day, day in day out, a lot of it unreported in the news media but felt by all of us as stories get passed.

We are not tired of the struggle for what we should have always been getting once the Civil War was over . . . we do not accept still being on the bottom of society.

We are not tired of the struggle . . . Black people have the lowest average income of any major racial/ethnic group at a little over $18,000 per year.

We are not tired of voting . . . we will vote . . . we are going to vote. We are aware now that white politicians will do anything they can to make it hard for us to vote. We were aware from the time we got the right to vote. This will only make more of us vote, protest, pitch a bitch, write, take water, take food, go to jail.

We are tired of living in food deserts, dumps in our neighborhoods, lead paint issues, zero to no recreational possibilities in too many of our communities.

We are already tired of the current efforts to stifle critical race theory by people who didn't bother to do a quick Google search, read Derek Bell, and learn its definition.

We are tired of white folks pretending racism does not exist while proclaiming their whiteness.

We are tired of white folks stating they are "not" a racist, when no one has asked them.

We are tired of knowing that white folks who embrace the myth of **color-blindness** never mention that they'd like people "not" to see that they are white.

We are tired of being worthy based on our talent, effort, and accomplishments and being treated like we're not.

We Are Going. . . . . .Nowhere

We are the Black people from the future.

We are the Black people whose ancestors may or may not throw hands but definitely know how to fight, resist, and refuse mediocrity.

We are the Black people ushering in a new day with our dancing, humming, swaying, writing, and loving. Our yearnings stitched together become glow in the dark trapeze visible only to melaninated spirits.

We are the Black people who know our power and choose how, when, and where we want it exercised.

We are the Black people unfooled by the rhetoric of national holidays, the ones who know the difference between structural transformation and wooden nickels.

We are the Black people who like Thee Stallion, value the beauty of our posteriors and know that posterity is built also through memory.

We. . . . . .Are

We are the Black people.

We are tired.

Tired of knowing you better than you know yourselves.

Tired of being shocked, but never surprised,

We are grace and we know we extend more than deserved, knowing we could burn it all down but choosing mercy, love, and our lives instead.

We are going, going, gonna lay down these heaven burdens. 'Cause ain't you tired, Karen? Tired of these constructs with real consequences, these walls you keep building to box yourself in?

We are the Black people, preamble and postscript

We form a more perfect Union

We establish Justice

We ensure Tranquility

We provide

We the general Welfare

We secure the Blessings of Liberty to ourselves

We secure the Blessings of Liberty to ourselves

We secure the Blessings of Liberty to ourselves

We secure our Posterity

We establish this
We the Black People of whenever and wherever we be
We Black
We. . . . .
. . . . are
That's it. That's the sentence.
We are.

★★★★★★

We are the Black people, like so many considered "others," who work towards the *formation of a more perfect Union, to en/act and stage Justice,* and *pray for the Blessings of Liberty to ourselves and our posterity,* to make real the promise of the *Constitution for these United States of America* to all peoples—knowing that *justice delayed is justice denied.*

   We are tired, but we are going nowhere.
   We are.

Note

1 See Scandal of the Particular: https://cac.org/the-scandal-of-the-particular-2018–03–19/.

29 What's the Matter? (A Play)

Mary E. Weems

Cast:

> Jack: 40s, Black bartender, Iraq War Veteran
> Maygee: Black, 40s, Iraq War Veteran, Hair Salon owner and beautician

Setting: After work at local, Black bar, January 6, 2021, date of Insurrection on Capitol Hill, carried out by white rioters revolting against the US Government and democracy

(Maygee enters Jukee's Bar and Lounge after a long day of doing hair. This is her hangout spot to relax and get caught up on what's going on in the community as well as discuss current events of the day.)

Maygee:	Evening, Jack. How you doing?
Jack:	I'm good, Maygee, you?
Maygee*:*	Hanging in there. Had a busy day at the shop. Diane called off sick and asked me do a couple of her regulars. And of course, I didn't do what they wanted exactly like Diane does, so they didn't tip me like to do her.
Jack:	There's always some mess when you're working with the public.
Maygee:	No lie, Jack. Luckily, she'll be back tomorrow, 'cause I have a full day of my own clients to do. And at least one sister, needs her weave tightened, always a pain in the ass.
Jack:	I know that's right? Can I get you your usual?

(Maygee takes a seat in front of one of two televisions at the bar.)

Maygee:	Yep, a double of Jack, straight.
Jack:	You got it.

(Jack brings her a drink with a red plastic straw in it and a bar napkin.)

Jack:	Here you are. You want me to run a tab, or you running this evening?

DOI: 10.4324/9781003274315-36

Maygee:	Tab, please. I'll be here a while. Nothing to rush home to, James is out of town on business, and our cat Lucy can damn near take care of herself. As long as I make sure she has food and water. Sometimes I think we're the pets and she's keeping us.
Jack:	Maygee, you know you funny. Okay, I got you.
Maygee:	Have you been to a support group meeting recently?
Jack:	Nope. Not even sure why. Unlike the drugs the VA always wants to give us for PTSD and the therapists they recommend so we can "talk" about things they tell us not to talk about when we're debriefed back in the states, being around some of *us* is the only thing that seems to help.
Maygee:	True that. If only it would stop the nightmares.
Jack:	And always feeling like I'm on alert.
Maygee:	Yeah, I think that might be the hardest part. I don't care where I'm at. I'm never relaxed. Closest I get to it is when take the time to join a meeting.
Jack:	Me too. Always feels so good to just be around other people who went through it with us.
Maygee:	How are you and Della doing?
Jack:	Not good. I'm still sleeping on the couch.
Maygee:	Sorry, Jack. What's the matter now?
Jack:	Same thing it always is, Maygee. She's still waiting for me to come home.
Maygee:	Damn. Other than the war, that's one thing we all have in common.
Jack:	Yep, and the problem is, there's not a damn thing any of us can really do about it.
Maygee:	Except try to fake it.
Jack:	No lie. I tried that when I first got back. Forced myself to pretend like I was listening to what Diane and anybody else in my family was saying when they were talking about normal problems like not being able to pay a bill, or problems with a boss at the job or—
Maygee:	What Miss So-and-So said about them at church on Sunday.
Jack:	Exactly. At family dinners I'd act like I was enjoying my food, trying to smile or laugh in the right places as folks were talking, all the time my insides were shaking, I was waiting for something to go

	down, an ambush by a mother walking with her child, a sudden explosion—
Maygee:	An attack first thing in the morning, when you haven't slept all night, haven't had anything but them shitty-ass cans of whatever to eat.
Jack:	When you have sand in the crack of your behind, you can't do anything about but walk carefully trying not to rub the skin off. Last week we were in bed and she wanted some TLC from me. She reached over to caress the back of my neck, not realizing I'd dropped off the sleep for a moment. I smashed her in the face with my elbow, jumped up, and went straight into combat mode.
Maygee:	Lord have mercy, Jack. I've been there. What did she do?
Jack:	Nothing. I'd have felt better if she'd hit me back, started cussing me out like I deserved, but she just laid there with her face bleeding on the pillow—terrified.
Maygee:	What you do?
Jack:	At first, I ran out of the room because I was still hyped up, trembling, ready to kill. I went into the bathroom to get myself together, and I heard her rush past the bathroom, open the front door, and peel off in her car, like she was running away from somebody trying to hurt her.
Maygee:	Sorry, Jack. That's cold. Did she come back?
Jack:	Not yet. She's staying with her mother.
Maygee:	Have you talked to her?
Jack:	Every day. We Duo on our phones. I try to convince her that it won't happen again, that I love her more than life, that I want to do better but just don't know how.
Maygee:	Have ya'll talked about what to do to stay in your marriage?
Jack:	Absolutely, but we have drastically different ideas on how to do it. I want her to come and meet some of the brothers and sisters in my group.
Maygee:	Really? The one I belong to is anonymous and guests aren't allowed. Is yours different?
Jack:	Nope. I think all of them work about the same. They're modeled after Alcoholics Anonymous, and anonymity is one of the main reasons it works. Naw, I wanted her to come here for one of our monthly, get togethers. When we just sit

	around, drink, talk about everything but the war and just be together.
Maygee:	What's her idea?
Jack:	Therapy, period. No matter how many times I tell her it doesn't work, she insists it will if I stop resisting, if I can actually connect with a therapist I can open up to, if she and I can even do couples counseling with the same person or someone else.
Maygee:	Well, I know that's not going to happen. Does she?
Jack:	Again, she knows how many years I spent "going" to one therapist after another, but she doesn't believe I've ever actually tried to give it a chance and that's the whole problem. Anyway, let me freshen your drink, we have about another hour before it will get busy in here. Tonight's Karaoke night.
Maygee:	Alright, Jack, but keep me posted, okay?
Jack:	Definitely.
Maygee:	I'll be praying you and Diane find a way to work through it. Nothing easy about it, but I know how much you love each other and that makes finding a way to stay together worth it.
Jack:	Thanks, sister.
Maygee:	Let me hit the ladies' room.
Jack:	I'll have your refill ready when you get back.

(Maygee gets up to use the restroom as Jack makes her drink, puts it in front of her chair with a fresh napkin, and then uses the remote to turn on the television closest to them. The news is live on scene at the Capitol building, and he can see the thousands of white folks waving flags, pushing past unarmed police officers, several of them climbing the walls of the Capitol and attacking the police, a cameraman, and a reporter. As Maygee reenters several of them can be seen breaking out the glass in the doors of the Senate, bursting inside to interrupt the confirmation of Joe Biden as president.)

Jack:	You see this mothafuckin' shit?
Maygee:	What's the matter, Jack?

(He points his hand to the screen.)

Jack:	You see all these white folks rushing the Capitol? Climbing the walls like it's a mountain, and nobody's stopping them?
Maygee:	Is this for real? What in the world is going on?
Jack:	I feel you. There's so much bullshit in the media nowadays, you can't just trust what your eyes see, but this is being shown live on MSNBC. You trust them?

Maygee:	Yep. Well, I'll just be damned. There's got to be at least a hundred thousand white folks. What do they think they're doing?
Jack:	They goin' crazy. More important, what are the police doing?
Maygee:	Brother, I can't believe this, these mostly white men are rushing the Capitol without even a push-back. I don't even see a cop with a weapon.
Jack:	Worse, they're just standing there like this is a game and they don't know what to do.
Maygee:	Aren't these men and women who protect the Capitol supposed to be the best of the best, or am I crazy?

(Maygee pauses to drink her drink down in one gulp; she sets the glass down hard.)

| Jack: | Let me get you a refill. I'll have one with you. |

(They continue talking as he gets their drinks ready. The coverage on the screen shifts to a white woman complaining that she's just been hit with tear gas. A reporter off camera has just asked her what she's doing there.)

Maygee:	No, she didn't say, "We're here because this is a revolution, man." You hear this? Trump has driven these white folks crazy. You seen any Black folks yet?
Jack:	Not with these fools. There are plenty of Black men and women officers on duty, but so far not one of the rioters are.
Maygee:	Thank God for that, but you know Trump got more of the Black vote this time than he did four years ago.
Jack:	Sorry, to say I do know that. Matter of fact, some fools on my street "still" have their Vote for Trump sign up and the election's been over two months.
Maygee:	Wish I could say I'm surprised, but my grand-mother used to say white folks will always get a few of us to bend their way. She said it was because some of us bought into the hype that white is right and are just trying to make it in this country the best way they know how.
Jack:	I know that's right. It pisses me off, but on the other hand, after all the shit we've been through in this racist ass country, I'm not judging. I just know that's never going to be me—ever. My

grandmother used to say she'd rather "pick shit with the birds" than kiss a white person's ass, God bless her soul.

(As they talk, they keep their eyes peeled on a screen that's regularly changing to show more and more of the riot. The screen shifts to the inside where thousands are filling the Capitol floor, some putting MAGA hats on statues and taking selfies standing beside them, others breaking the glass in the doors of the Senate and rushing in to interrupt the people working to officially acknowledge the electoral vote count necessary for the peaceful transfer of power.)

Maygee:	Jack, are you thinking what I'm thinking?
Jack:	Right about now, my mind's racing through every presidential election I've ever witnessed, including Obama's. What on your mind?
Maygee:	Charlottesville. I have family down there and they were right in the thick of it, trying to peacefully protest against the white supremacists raising hell in the streets, the Klan marching unhooded carrying tiki torches like they knew Trump had their backs. After that white man ran that white woman over with his car, my family broke camp and headed home 'cause they knew all hell was about to break loose and it did, but what didn't happen was—
Jack:	What happens every time Black people have the audacity to peacefully protest against innocent Black men and women being shot and killed by cops.
Maygee:	You damn right. Remember what happened after George Floyd was killed?
Jack:	The list is long, but there was something about the way they took that brother out, like he was worthless, like his life meant so little that cop could stand there with his knee on his neck while that Black man pleaded for his life and the other cops stood around with their hands in their pockets, not even trying to stop him.
Maygee:	Did you hear Floyd keep saying "Please, sir. I can't breathe sir?"
Jack:	Yes (Beat) I did.

(He stops to turn the sound down on the TV but leaves it on the same station, where the riot continues, and then takes a rag and begins wiping down the top of the bar, lost in thought. Maygee watches.)

Maygee: What's the matter, Jack? You got quiet.

(Jack stops rubbing down the bar and sits on a stool across from Maygee.)

Jack: I'm tired, sister. (Beat) You ever have weary wash over you all of a sudden like a wave of water you can't ride out?

Maygee: Take your time, brother. Tell it.

Jack: Our people have been giving and serving and sacrificing and dying in the fields, at the ends of ropes, during war, after war, and from bullets in the back, ever since the slave ship *Jesus* landed. We've marched peacefully, we've rioted in the streets, we've worked with white allies to get the laws changed. Some of us have taken shit from white folks on our jobs, just so we could feed our children and keep a roof over our heads, but it seems like no matter what we do, work against, try to assimilate, stay away from them. No matter what we do, we always smelling the shit end of the stick. We always at the bottom of the bottom. Yeah, they let a few of us get enough ahead, so we can pretend like things have gotten better—

Maygee: But haven't they though, Jack? I mean, didn't Dr. King, and Malcolm and SNCC and the Black Panthers and the Kennedys make a difference?

Jack: Of course, they did as far as it went, but like Mandela once said, he underestimated the extent racist white folks would go to, to maintain power and that's what I'm talking about. Seems like for every step forward we've been able to make, the white people in power have been pulling us back as much as they can, like they have our necks tied with an endless white rope. Yeah, the law says our schools are desegregated, but are they? The law says we can live wherever we want to, that red lining is illegal, but look around you. How many majority Black and majority white neighborhoods continue to exist?

Maygee: What about affirmative action?

Jack: Sis, let's not even go there. Maybe some other time, right now, I just want to deal with this insurrection going on right in front of our eyes. White

folks with weapons, bombs, all kind of signs, trying to destroy a democracy created for them.

(They pause for a few moments to drink their drinks, watching the rioters shout for the lynching of Vice President Pence and the killing of Nancy Pelosi. Jack grabs the remote and hits the pause button when a gallows can be seen with a lynch rope hanging from it. Suddenly Maygee's cell phone receives a text. She reads it and slams her phone down on the bar.)

Jack: What's the matter now, Maygee?

Maygee: That was my niece on my husband's side. Remember, what I told you happened to her son last June?

Jack; I'll never forget it. He met a longtime friend of his right after work, a white girl, right?

Maygee: Yes. He only stopped at the Rocky River part of the Metro Park for a few minutes so they could touch base. He hadn't seen her for a while, and he was on his way to see his grandmother for dinner.

Jack: I remember, I'm sorry, Maygee. Some of the worst shit I've ever heard of.

Maygee: They were just sitting by the water on a park bench, minding they own business. Later, two white folks in a kayak reported seeing them at about 5 o'clock in the afternoon. According to the police, by 5:15 they were both dead. Killed our nephew, walked up behind him in broad daylight, during rush hour right off the road. Shot him in the back of his head. Apparently, his friend tried to run because they shot her in the head too, but she was found a few feet from the water under a tree. (Beat) It's been over a year, the FBI raised the reward to a hundred thousand dollars, once it was determined to be a hate crime, but I just talked to my niece, and they still don't have a single suspect. Told her what they tell her every time she calls. "Don't give up, we're working on it."

Jack: I don't have words for you, Maygee. I hope you know me and everybody who cares about you and your family, are continuing to do our best to keep this in the public eye, we're praying for you and your family and won't stop until somebody pays for what happened to your great nephew.

Maygee: Thank you brother, I know, I know. It's just hard, that's all. People always talk about how it'll get easier with time, but that's a lie. It gets harder every day because whoever killed them is still breathing and eating and walking around free, but our nephew and his friend are gone.

(Jack, comes from behind the bar to give her a long hug. Their attention shifts back to the image of the gallows frozen on the screen.)

Jack: One thing I know that's true today and will be true a hundred years after we're gone, if these white mothafuckas were Black—these police would have opened fire immediately, soon as they saw the first one of us try to set foot on the Capitol, let alone climb a wall or rush them. They would have shot our asses so fast heads would be swimming, the handcuffs would have come out like magic and so many of us would have been arrested and beat down, we never would have made it to the front door—case closed.

(Maygee, gives him a high five and Jack turns up the sound on the TV. As the lights fade, a reporter on the screen can be heard saying)

Reporter's Voice-Over: In addition to pipe bombs found inside the Capitol building, rioters have left feces and urine in various areas all over the building. Several officers were seen taking selfies with the rioters and giving them high fives. (Beat) Four people are dead, and one officer has been seriously wounded.

The End

30 The Will to Love

Dialogues on Loving Blackness in an Anti-Black World

Dominique C. Hill and Durell M. Callier

A pinky swear. Back in 2010, while in graduate school—redefining our relationships with religion and bodies and accepting the challenge of unlearning ideas we knew so well about money and love—we made a covenant. Growing up in Saving Our Lives, Hear Our Truths (SOLHOT) and the International Congress of Qualitative Inquiry as our Black queer selves, we started having conversations about the interpersonal accountability we were willing to embrace and the cultural responsibility dodged and/or elided between Black men and women in the Black queer code of ethics. In these conversations, we historicized and theorized why outside of the heterosexual desire, potential or materialized, Black men rarely are having honest dialogue with, advocating for, or paying reverence to Black women and girls. We recognized this as a funky and inconvenient truth but one that if altered could shift the nature of Black collectivity. We vowed to love each other and mean it.

This agreement to intentionally build a sustained relationship was a queer move. Straddling and transcending its demarcation as a sexual orientation, it was and remains queer because of how we have "articulated and practiced politics as well as queer in [our] intimate relationships and sense of sexual identity."[1] Such a queer connection sprouted into a long-standing collective artist-scholar practice, one that implants the heart—those fleshy, pulsating, life-sustaining matters—into methodology, scholarship, and against the calcified, life-suffocating walls and floors of the academy. In 2010, we chose to love each other, and today we choose to share the words that like tattoos have been written into our approach to showing up in and beyond academe. It is because we know as Alexis Pauline Gumbs states,[2] about our current profession. "The university does not intend to love me. The university does not know how to love me. The university, in fact, does not love me. But the universe does."[3] And we have decidedly chosen each other. What follows is a curated dialogue about love and its potential to shift the feel of places as well as how business as usual is contested. To create this conversation, we respond to each quote in italicized text sometimes as a unified voice, while at other times in dialogue with one another and the quote. The quotes within this conversation are important both

DOI: 10.4324/9781003274315-37

to our personal and academic journey and differentially mark boundaries of love and being loving that we individually and collectively mind and transgress.

> The energies that flow from hatred, from negative and hateful habits and attitudes and dogma do not promise something good, something I would choose to cherish, to honor with my own life. It is always the love, whether we look to the spirit of Fannie Lou Hamer, or the spirit of Agostinho Neto, it is always the love that carry action into positive new places, that will carry your own nights and days beyond demoralization and away from suicide.[4]

As I reflect on nearly ten-plus years of a friendship, writing collaboration, and intentional choice to choose one another, I am reminded about how I've made it here, this far. What they don't often tell you about graduate school is that the cure to your problem is in the problem. The isolation that abounds as a student and now as a faculty member is palpable and because of graduate school, I know that friends, a village, coconspirators, being present to and showing up to a collective alleviates the pain of loneliness. None of us truly make it on our own. To say otherwise is a lie. To say otherwise is to deny what your hands and heart know, that it is always love, always love, always love "that will carry your own nights and days beyond demoralization and away from suicide."[5]

Thank you for holding me. For the moments my wounds smelled of charred disappointment and overcooked expectations and still, you sat close, asked what was needed, and moved on that, thank you. "Such a love is indeed a transgression, because it flies in the face of the social order that asks us to diminish ourselves, to keep boundaries, to be dreamless for the sake of familiarity and predictability,"[6] and it lives here in us, covering us, guiding us to remember concomitant and sometimes discarded truths—love is the answer, isolation is a paradigm, we be homegirls, and yes, we can skateboard on clouds.

Beneatha: Love him? There is nothing left to love.[7]

And still, there was a piece of me left to offer, to gift; but I knew better. So instead, I negotiated the best package possible, accepted the one-year offer, and chose to walk away. Love is not a reason to stay nor a requirement for love to be. I packed some up with me and left some sprinkled in my apartment, on my office floor, and blew it into the air in preparation for the next windstorm. Love is seeded.

Offered your same office, I passed. Choosing instead to take the smaller office across from your old one. I wanted a consistent reminder that you were here. Your scent, nag champa, and oil still lingered long after you left the space. We both left to make sense of what was done to you, what that meant for us, deciding to let love continue to grow.

Mama: There is *always* something left to love. And if you ain't learned that, you ain't learned nothing. (*Looking at her*) Have you cried for that boy today? I don't mean for yourself and for the family 'cause we lost the money. I mean for him: what he been through and what it done to him. Child, when do you think is the time to love somebody the most? When they done good and made things easy for everybody? Well then, you ain't through learning—because that ain't the time at all. It's when he's at his lowest and can't believe in hisself 'cause the world done whipped him so! When you start measuring somebody, measure him right, child, measure him right. Make sure you done taken into account what hills and valleys he come through before he got to wherever he is.[8]

Considering don't mean tolerating, and tolerating don't mean a lack of self-love. This is a lesson it took me quite some time to learn. Just because I love doesn't mean I stay. My name is crystal clear, and I'm for certain that love is also about my ability to move in right relationship to my survival, my needs, my dreams. And moving on doesn't mean there wasn't some goodness, some something left to love.

"This means that as a Black feminist, I cannot be expected to respect what somebody else calls self-love if that concept of self-love requires my suicide to any degree."[9]

Wooden nickels just won't do. In an age of cancel culture, and ghosting, and flat out giving up on folks making them disposable, there has got to be some line between you are valued, loved, seen, and I won't kill myself to love you. How do we choose each other when one of us isn't well? If you aren't well does that mean that I am not? What do we do if what makes us unwell is in the air around us?

"Love him," said Jacques, with vehemence, "love him" and let him love you. Do you think anything else under heaven really matters?[10]

What I mean to say is being loving is a necessary practice to building anew. Being loving is a practice that must show up in your bones. It is an essence, a feeling, a way of moving through the world that says, I'm willing to accept the cost of being me and in the process I'm willing, compelled to let you be you. And it means sitting with the weight of the question, Does "anything else under heaven really" matter? That choosing and being chosen, reciprocating, growing, expanding, risking it all to be loved and to love?

Yea, all you think being gay is about is men switching—but you're wrong. I'm a faggot because I love *me* enough to be who I am. If your son becomes a faggot it won't be because of the way you or his mother raise him. It won't be because of television, movies, books, and education. It will be because he learns to trust the natural expression of his sexuality without fear or shame. If he learns anything about courage from you or his mother, then he'll grow up to be himself. You can't blame being straight or gay on a woman or education. The education that's needed should be for the purpose of bringing us all out of sexual ignorance. Our diverse sexuality is determined by the will of nature, and nature *is* the will of God.[11]

I love me enough. That's it. And what do we love ourselves enough to do, to be, to say, to not accept.

Lately, my being has sent me down a path of reflection, of lovemaking, of creativity, and yearning to make magic off the page. The more I be, the more I want to do, and sit, and move differently. The more I be, the more I want to be in my daily life, in my lovership. Sometimes I forget the magic of existing.

> If you can't love yourself, how in the hell can you love somebody else. Can I get an Amen up in here?[12]

Aaaaaaaaa-men! And yet a still quiet voice asks, because I know that journey, what happens in between. In-between, I love myself, so I can love you? How do you practice a thing, until you really know it. Is self-love, actually truly the prerequisite? And surely, until you find your own "greatest love of all" as Whitney use to sing to me in the '90s, the one inside of you, you are still worthy of love, of being loved up on, of experiencing someone loving you. Yes, you, even the you that hasn't come to love themselves.

Loving yourself is a journey. We ain't all been taught. And true friends like good mirrors help you along that journey. Can I get an Amen up in here?

Amen and ase'. Truth be told, I been working on the practice of loving on myself because I know too much about energy now. Know too much about the lies they told us about how love works. And since I knew tew much and want my cup of sassy, sensual, healthy love, I been busy rehearsing this thing called dating myself, called valuing my time, called

> Black men loving Black men is the revolutionary act.[13]

Black man, I love you. Not because it's revolutionary but because I know my free is connected to yours, which means my heart is connected to yours, which means my living is connected to yours. Can't you see? I could choose to insist on our difference and inability to relate, but instead, I choose to love you. Maybe that is revolutionary.

We need multiple revolutions. Isn't it that we have to make revolution irresistible, and what better way to do so than to start with a small yet grand idea and action, us loving each other at the edges of our tomorrows, in the knowingness that we are all we got and need?

"When we understand love as the will to nurture our own and another's spiritual growth, it becomes clear that we cannot claim to love if we are hurtful and abusive. Love and abuse cannot coexist. Abuse and neglect are, by definition, the opposites of nurturance and care."[14]

I cannot overstate how profoundly hooks changed my worldview about love. It was not just worldview altering but world-making altering, perhaps even more like a new galaxy was made possible. What was this thing called loving that she was telling me about, why did she insist that we be crystal clear about what love is and love is not. Telling us that we do ourselves a disservice by refusing to agree on a singular definition and ethic of love, that we had to disabuse ourselves as Black people about the rubbish we learned that love consisted of. From that moment on, I wanted to be loving, I had to stop the idea that you fall in and out of love, I didn't want to raise kids who would be confused by a so-called love that hits and yells and hurts. She made something new that day. I was new. The possibilities for what could be endless. The reality that we deserved. A first test, how to actualize that in a classroom, in a relationship with you.

"Beautiful Black Women
& I am in love
with each of them
& this is important
in the loving
in the act of loving
each woman
I have learned a new lesson
I have learned
to love myself"
(Parker, 1978, p. 138)[15]

Love is not to be misnamed nor played with. Don't call something love that is cathexis, abuse, or otherwise. It does grow on trees planted in soil that is tended to, watered, and massaged. Love cannot be thrown out, away, or disappeared. It does tuck itself away in dark places. Tuck itself away in Black notes and between pinky swears, and seal the agreement in a make-believe envelope. Love knows its name, even when we act like we forgot.

i survive on intimacy & tomorrow / that's all i've goin

& the music waz like smack & you knew abt that

& still refused my dance waz not enuf / & it waz all i had

but bein alive & bein a woman & bein colored is a metaphysical dilemma /
i haven't conquered yet / do you see the point

my spirit is too ancient to understand the separation of
soul & gender / my love is too delicate to have thrown
back on my face.[16]

Our love is too magical to have it thrown back on our face, too midnight blue to have it thrown back on our face, too ancestor fortified to have it thrown back on our face too

Our love is too possible too moving too Oya too nourishing to have thrown back on our face, too intentional too forgiving too candid too upending too collective to have thrown back on our face,

Notes

1 Carbado, D., McBride, D. A. & Weise, D. (2002). *Black like us: A century of lesbian, gay, and bi-sexual African American fiction.* Jersey City, NJ: Cleis Press, xv.

2 Gumbs, A. P. (2012, October 29). "The shape of my impact." *The Feminist Wire*, 268–274. https://thefeministwire.com/2012/10/the-shape-of-my-impact. Accessed October 13, 2021; Jordan, J. (2003). "Where is the love?" In *Some of us did not die: New and selected essays.* San Jose, CA: Basic/Civitas, 268–274.

3 See Gumbs, A. P. (2012, October 29). "The shape of my impact." *The Feminist Wire.* https://thefeministwire.com/2012/10/the-shape-of-my-impact. Accessed October 13, 2021.

4 See Jordan (2003), p. 271, in Jordan, J. (2003). "Where is the love?" In *Some of us did not die: New and selected essays.* San Jose, CA: Basic/Civitas, 269.

5 See Jordan, J. (2003). "Where is the love?" In *Some of us did not die: New and selected essays.* San Jose, CA: Basic/Civitas.

6 See Jones (2004), p. xv In Jones, J. (2004). "'Making holy': Love and the novel as ritual transformation." In S. Bridgforth (Ed.), *Introduction to love conjure/blues.* New Orleans, LA: RedBone Press, xv.

7 See Hansberry (1988), p. 145 In Hansberry, L. (1988). *A raisin in the sun.* New York: Signet.

8 See Hansberry, L. (1988). *A raisin in the sun.* New York: Signet, 145.

9 See Jordan (2003), p. 271, in Jordan, J. (2003). "Where is the love?" In *Some of us did not die: New and selected essays.* Basic/Civitas.

10 See Baldwin (2013), p. 63. In Baldwin, J. (2013). *Giovanni's room.* New York: Vintage International.

11 See Hemphill (1992), p. 128 in Hemphill, E. (1992). *Ceremonies.* San Francisco, CA: Cleiss.

12 See RuPaul

13 See Marlon Riggs in *Tongues Untied* (1989).

14 See hooks (2001), p. 6 in hooks, b. (2001). *All about love: New visions.* New York, NY: William Morrow, an imprint of HarperCollins.

15 See Parker (1978), p. 138 in Parker, P. (1999). "Group." In *Movement in black.* Ithaca, NY: Firebrand Books, 138.

16 See Shange (2010), p. 59 in Shange, N. (2010). *For colored girls who have considered suicide/ when the rainbow is enuf.* Simon and Schuster.

31 A Letter to Process, Positionality, and Possibility

Bryant Keith Alexander

A variation of this letter was sent to the three other members of this Black Quartet at the initiation of the project.

To Dominique and Durell: I am taken by your wonder and your humility yet still not knowing fully your power and your brilliance to which Mary and I also gravitate. When I first encountered each of you—I was humbled. Humbled in the grounded foundations of your accomplishment, promise, and possibility—and wanted to be connected to such potentialities. I was humbled in seeing glimpses of my own yearnings back when, back when I needed a Black senior scholar to recognize me, to see me, to invest a moment of time to say, "Hey I see you." I remember when I was looking for graduate programs and had my heart set on three prominent doctoral programs with performance studies. I did all the research on what I wanted and what I needed—knowing the difference between those two. I went to so many of those school socials at national conferences; always inching my way to the professors in the programs of my desire. And the ones with Black senior scholars were at the top of the list, only paralleled in some ways with the programs that matched more closely my academic and research needs. I was willing to give up one for the other.

I will give you one example of how I ended up where I ended up in my doctoral program. At one of those department socials, I approached a Black senior scholar, who was surrounded by a series of students or maybe former students, engaged in a joy-filled conversation. Preface to the conference, I had done my research, reading as much of the scholarship of the Black Scholar. I approached the Black Scholar and introduced myself. There was a shift in what I perceived as the openness and joy that I had witnessed in the group engagement. I stated that I was interested in the graduate program of the Black Scholar's location. I asked if I could ask a few questions, either now or later in the conference. The Black scholar then said, "I won't have the time for that." The Black scholar said other things, but I don't want to further pathologize the individual, because this experience is both particular and plural with a few other Black senior scholars at the universities on my list. So, I turned my attention to the representatives from the other universities that more closely matched my academic and research needs, but without Black scholars. I entered one of those programs and proceeded to cultivate my own potential, often in isolation.

DOI: 10.4324/9781003274315-38

But the program offered me the academic challenge that I needed, and thus prepared me for what I want to be for others who looked like me, with other particularities yearning for their own possibility.

But I remembered the experience of the search, I remembered the yearning, and I vowed to be the Black senior scholar that I wanted to encounter back then. I wanted to be the Black senior scholar in the fullness of my person and passion who would embrace the possibility of Black others in their processes of being and becoming. I wanted to be the Black senior scholar who took the time to say "Hey, I see you—how can I assist—to do, or simply be—with an invitation to engage as needed; to invite possibility." I would like to think that I have become that Black senior scholar—but I now yearn to do more and be more.

To Mary: When you and I finally connected, the impact of that collision was real and still reverberates with me today. I had met a soul-sista; a no-nonsense Black woman creative-scholar who saw in me, what I needed to be seen at the time. Your presence, your voice, your work offered an invitation of collaboration long before the inklings of co-authorship were uttered. You were the type of Black Scholar that I was looking for so far back—but maybe the Gods, your God and my God, knew the timing of our encounter and how it would catapult us both into a frenzy of collaboration that has been scholarly, poetic, performative, and playfully grounded in a deep respect.

To Durell and Dominique: All of that, but also I am just taken by your wonder and your brilliance, your present/possible/potentiality to which I gravitate, to be a part of the Glory (*think, Common and John Legend*). Durell, I am also taken by your desired reference in our collaboration to being *a bridge and a path* for others—especially those like you with complex intersectional identities on the path of their being and becoming. It is so important and speaks to Dominique's reference to "what somebody didn't want, still perhaps don't want us to know"—to be, and to go—to discover ourselves, and the assistance that is needed along the way.

To all: We have voluntarily come together in this project. Voluntarily using our creative, articulate voices as acts of volition. Voting for the possible by placing our bodies and words on the line. In this intergenerational dialogue, let us continue to be a bridge and path for each other and to help others to get there, wherever *their there* should be. I strive to continue to be a Black bridge and a Black path toward a Black futurity. Our work together is building that path for self and others. Let's continue to vote and act upon being the change we want to see in the world. Let us continue to tell the young, old, Black, and marginalized others seeking their possibility—that they matter.

Your brother,

Bryant

Performative Intergenerational Dialogues

A Conclusion

The Black Quartet

The nature of this project has been based on the construct of "performative intergenerational dialogues." Grounded in an enacted doing, the project engages performative dialogue between four Black teacher–artist–scholars using thick description, evocative language, and the articulation of lived experience to both invoke and invite the reader into the worlds of the texts.

The texts do what they say—perform action, words that offer *tribute and libation*, words that not only speak but also *listen and offer lessons*, words that comprise *letters to those who mattered* with heart and passion, words that describe and become *monuments of memory and remorse*, words that articulate a form of *B(l)ack talk* that speaks of culture with histories of pain to build bridges to possibility.[1]

The texts in this volume speak to *voting rights and writing volition*—word selection and the construction of messages that take a position and occupy a positionality about Black people, blackness, and aspects of the Black experience in America from our own perspectives.

All of this is very much about rights in the struggle for social justice. The authors (we) write with volition to right the wrongs of the past as an overt act—placing their (our) Black bodies on the line as activism. In the process, we are "redefining the political and the cultural in performative and pedagogical terms,"[2] engaged in deep theorizing through performative texts without apology but with a strong invitation to the reader to come to know the politics of performative blackness as *qualitative inquiries on race, gender, sexualities, and culture,* as critical methodology at the meeting place of our complex intersectionalities.

Within this project we stage a dialogue across generations and between generations, recognizing the places in which Black lived experience (while not monolithic) bleed and blend the borders of time and place (past, present, and future).

The writing in this project seeks to interrupt generational drama to avoid intergenerational trauma with a direction toward an embolden Black futurity. The necessity of a critical performative dialogue in this project goes beyond the sharing of experiences. We are witnessing, testifying, and interrogating those experiences to dig deep into meaning to collectively plot a pathway forward.

In the following section, we bring some of those pieces into a more interanimating dialogue so that you can see/hear and witness the performative and intergenerational dialogue at play/in performance.

DOI: 10.4324/9781003274315-39

A Black Quartet II: A Performance Script[3]

Performers in order of engagement: Bryant Keith Alexander, Mary E. Weems, Dominique C. Hill, Durell M. Callier.

Figure 31 The Black Quartet—Bryant Keith Alexander, Mary E. Weems, Dominique C. Hill, Durell M. Callier

As per the style of this Black Quartet, we set the tone using sound, movement, and gestures to invite the audience into an experience not to entertain them but to inform and educate them.

The aesthetics help conjoin the individual pieces, generate the intended energy, and steward a process and experience both for the performers and the audience.

The choreography begins with Mary E. Weems soulfully humming, then a loose groove of movement by Dominique, a desirous and yet gasping breathing by Durell, then a direct line delivered by Bryant that serves as the speech activation of the performance.

All performers wear black attire, with Mary E. Weems and Dominique C. Hill wearing wraps on their heads.

Each performer has a beverage of choice in a medium-sized Mason jar. The beverage is refreshment engaged with at differing times in the performance, often at the beginning of speaking parts and transitions. The Mason jar is a black colloquialism that the performers share as aspects of practical Black experiences—in which Mason jars signify traditions of homemade preserves and jams, everyday tableware, and drinking receptacles.

Bryant: Intergenerational dialogues sometimes go without words.

Mary: Our bodies tell stories of diasporic, biological, and genealogical proportions.

Dominique: Sometimes the messaging travels in the blood and other times through music, movement, and musings.

Durell: The question is: Are we listening?

Bryant: Are we reading?

Mary: Are we recognizing?

Dominique: Are we witnessing the meaning through wisdom and *wit*?

Mary: Black Motha Wit is at the core of becoming in the Black communities of Black Girls.

Dominique: Black Motha Wit is at the core of being and becoming for Black girls becoming Black women within and across generations.

Bryant: Black Fatha Wit is at the core of being and becoming in the Black communities of our lives for Black boys.

Durell: Black Fatha Wit is at the core of being and becoming in the Black communities of our lives for Black boys becoming Black men.

Mary: Black Motha Wit speaks across genders.

Bryant: Black Father Wit with speaks across sex.

Dominique: Each builds the interstitial structures of being and become scars and lessons on the souls of possibility.

Durell: Each helps structure the interstitial ways of seeing and knowing yourself in the world—reading your body possibility into Black futurities.

[All deliver the following lines in a staggered echo.]

Mary: Establishing performative intergenerational dialogues.

Dominique:	Establishing performative intergenerational dialogues.
Bryant:	Establishing performative intergenerational dialogues.
Durell:	Establishing performative intergenerational dialogues
	[Transitional movement/moment here: Each performer takes a sip from their Mason jar]
Bryant:	From the *Oxford English Dictionary*, *wit* is defined as follows: (n) 1. Intelligence, quick understanding. 2a. Unexpected combining or contrasting of ideas or expressions.
Mary:	Mama got pregnant with me when she was just sixteen, back then a girl couldn't stay in school unless she gave up the name of the father, and since mama refused—she had to drop out in the tenth grade. She could have gone back after I was born, but instead, she married my stepfather and by the time she was twenty-one, she'd had all four of us and became a single parent a few years later.

Consequently, she was still growing up, she was still listening and not always paying attention to the "Motha Wit" shared with her by her mama and the other mothas in her life. Here, we use the word *motha* in the term instead of the more traditional *mother* for two reasons. First, because as speakers of African American English or Black English, we often use language in culturally specific ways, especially in conversation with other Black folks. Second, because in addition to our mamas, most Black women I know have grandmothers, aunties, play aunties, play mamas, and so on, who help raise us by sharing their time, talents and motha wit in an attempt to help us become strong, resilient, able-to-take-care-of-ourselves Black women, and since they've lived through what we've yet to experience, what they share is an invaluable part of our growing up.

Mama's motha, my late grandmother and namesake, Mary Isabel Lacy, one of eight sisters and three brothers, was the main woman in my life to share hers with me. Beginning when I was aged of thirteen, the five of us moved into a big, four-bedroom house my grandparents bought so we would have a stable place to live. Mama tried hard to provide for us, but with one low-wage-earning job after another, we were always moving from one tenement roach-infested apartment to the next. Granny, which was what we called her, was my best friend and confidant.

I talked to her every day several times a day during the six years I lived with her until I moved out at nineteen and she never provided any motha wit that didn't turn out to be true. In this moment, I wish to God I'd listened to her all the time but am also feeling blessed that I did sometimes and "always" remembered her advice.

. . .

Several years ago, I was in the Grand Central train station having something I can't remember, and out of nowhere the distinct smell of tangerines, her favorite fruit, filled the air. I took out a pad and pen and wrote:

[In the group staging Mary's poem, each member of the Black Quartet takes different lines to reinforce the shared sense and sensibilities of her sentiments across genders and generations.]

Mary: Tangerines

For: Granny

Bring her back, the juice
the sting of memory, her
blood, the way her hands held
together when she peeled.

Each layer careful as her love, each
section chewed and sucked through a face
I can't re-see.

Dominique: At night, I peel my own skin
the edges of my palms orange,
my fingers change to her fingers strange
at the ends of arms forming a circle,
making a space to enter.

My eyes hurt from the smell
That's never her.

[Delivered in a staggered refrain.]

Bryant: I don't know where I'd be today without the support, unconditional love and motha wit my granny, mama, step-mama, aunties,
and the other Black women I'm not remembering provided,

Durell: I don't know where I'd be today without the support, unconditional love, and motha wit my granny, mama, step-mama, aunties,
and the other Black women I'm not remembering provided,
Bryant/Durell: but I know my life would be lacking in the critical
foundation created by what each of them shared.

Mary: I remind myself of all the Black women including me, doing
our best to mentor every young'un we can—to share our motha
wit, listen to what they have to say, and offer support, love, and
encouragement.

Including When They Said

Dominique: *"Don't take no wooden nickels!"*

BJ stated sternly for the first time when I was about six years old. It would take almost two decades to return to her advice and get clear on the nature of these nickels. It would require some solid reflection to come to terms with the ones I'd unknowingly carried around and unsuccessfully tried to cash in. My great-grandma had a way with words and knew no such thing as biting her tongue. BJ was known for tellin' it like it is, and if your feelings weren't spared in the process, it was okay because that wasn't the goal. Her motha wit was sharp, unapologetic, and from the gut.

The first grandchild of the family with a grandma working multiple jobs, and a mother on a quest to find love, BJ and I spent lots of time together. She was my great-granny and friend in a way. Like when she was diagnosed with diabetes, she'd try to convince me to sneak her some *real* soda instead of the *shit* she had to drink.

And as her granfriend, I'd occasionally give her half-and-half and more often top her cup off with *real* stuff. As the first grandchild, she didn't hold her tongue with me. I surmise she wanted to teach me lessons before there was ever a potential consequence. For instance, I loveeed me some Bubbli-cious gum and every time we went to the store, I would ask for some. On this one particular day, I did my usual ask and BJ replied, "you steady asking for shit. You needta make sure there's more going in your pocketbook than goin' out."

. . .

Looking back, she, like the motha wit she served up, was spells, recipes on how to live on your own terms. And while I packed some of them away, I appreciate what she offered me/us—a pathway home to our family's garden where tough skin grows (Hill, 2021) and a plot all my own awaited my tending.

Bryant: Motha wit is necessary, honest, and far from monotone. From criti-cally reflecting on time spent with aunties, grans, and other women we concretized the sound, feel, and faith of motha wit.

Durell: To motha, as evinced in the stories and wit offered above is a skill set. It is a way of living, communicating lessons, a stylized way of attempting to save daughters (and others) from rock bottoms.

[Delivered in a staggered refrain.]

Mary: Our writing journey helped us see each other differently and afforded us the opportunity to share the wit that guides our living. With these new openings, came the possibility to again recognize the labor of mothering, of communicating lessons, and the time and difference between the two.

Dominique: Our writing journey helped us see each other differently and afforded us the opportunity to share the wit that guides our living. With these new openings, came the possibility to again

recognize the labor of mothering, of communicating
lessons, and the time and difference between the two.

Mary: Two daughters,

Dominique: two poets,

Mary/
Dominique: two hearts suturing cross generations, regions, and mothas, together.

Bryant: In the Black community of my experience there is often a reference to "Motha Wit," that lineage of cultural knowledge passed on from *maternal figures like mothers, grandmothers, multiple aunties, and other play mothers who gave us invaluable advice*— often spoken about by women of women.

Durell: Sometimes that is woman to girl-child, but boys also listened. We listened when talked to and we listened through observation. But we also listened sometimes sitting off in the distance when girl-talk or woman-talk was happening— cooking, sewing, quilting, doing hair, sitting on the porch, or at church.

Bryant: Sometimes we were admonished in our listening because of the directionality of intent when women talked to women or women talked to girls.

We listened.

We the boy-children with particular sensibilities learning about our own sexuality, sensuality, sensitivities.

We listened.

We listened because the wit passed on by those motha mouths seemed to speak to a part of our being we had not yet named; had not yet been beaten out of us by lessons of compulsory masculinity.

We listened.

We listened with the desire to know more, to hear more—not about the intimacies of certain acts but the intimacies of knowing, of sensemaking, of negotiating feels and bodies and relationships; the intimacies of talking about feelings and desires and yearnings.

We listened.

We listened in the natural way in which boys become men, different types of men; the ones we modeled ourselves on and against. The ones who taught us about strength and survival.

We listened.

Durell: We listened.

Mary/ We listened

Dominique: We listened

Bryant: We listened to their words and deeds. We listened to what they said to us and what they did to us; the heavy hand, the not-so-soft touch; the inappropriate touch; no touch. We listened and learned, then made choices regarding our own being and becoming.

Durell: The men in my family—grow things.

Cousin Chicken and his container garden. A country oasis of tomatoes, cucumbers, peppers, and green beans could be found in his modest 6-feet by 3-feet concrete slab backyard. Fenced off from the alleyway, over East (Baltimore). A row home of love, from cinnamon-touched yeast rolls—soft, high, just sweeeeeet enough—to handcrafted wooden items with inspiration scriptures, engraved hearts, and sitting/stepping stools.

Cousin Tony knows how to grow locs. A converted Jehovah witness now Rastafari. His crown now hanging on by thin threads, as long as his days.

Uncle Arthur, his father, also knew how to grow a garden. My country cousins. Not because they lived in the country but because they lived, not in the city like us. Land. Land they owned, tended to, tilled, made beautiful around them. His garden unlike Cousin Chicken's; straight from the soil sprouted string beans and strawberries, watermelon, and peppers, and cucumbers.

The men in my family know how to grow things.

Uncle Mikey could cuss a curse word out! Invented grammar rules on how to cuss a motha★ucka out, show a motha★ucka how much you care, encourage a motha★ucka to be their best self, leave a (sorry-a★★) motha★ucka alone, and love the hell out of em. He taught me that sometimes you used curse words like punctuation and at other times as the subject to communicate with others. He grew in us a fanciful language and an imagination to know our history.

More than anything he knew how to grow a laugh. The punchline, the setup, the crazy cross-eyed comical face, that started in your belly and radiated out in seismic thunder.

. . . .

Joy.

The men in my family know how to grow things. And I find myself, a man. Me, a brotha, uncle, partner, lover, friend, homegirl, great grandson of Florence and Herman, who begat Silvine, who begat Silvine, who begat me.

. . .

I come from people who are cultivators of soil and soul.

Mary: I come from people who are cultivators of soil and soul.
Dominique: I come from people who are cultivators of soil and soul.

[A Black Chorus]

Bryant: *Every generation has its own dramas.* The challenges of everyday life, in which the answers to the who, what, where, by what

	means, why, and how establish conflict in a confluence of circumstances that leaves a residue of effect in living.[4]
Mary:	*Generational dramas travel.* They travel on the tongue in "the telling of the told" as people narrate their experience as processes of healing or keeping the old wounds open.[5]
Dominique:	They tell of experience sometimes as a curse to those who would not heed their warning. They also tell and retell the story as an object lesson to be learned from, not for the drama per se but the flight of living that energized the telling of the told.
Durell:	In such cases, we listened to and acted upon, generational dramas, the repetition of patterns that are shame and challenge filled, with each generation bartering between the voices of mothers and fathers, between powerful cultural institutions, and collective identity formations that become fomented "between the telling and the told."[6]

[Delivered is staggered repetition]

Bryant:	**We are Black people.**
Mary:	**We are tired of waiting.**
Dominique:	**We are not going nowhere.**
Durell:	**We are not going nowhere.**
Bryant:	We are the Black people, who are often present and/or presented.
Mary:	We are tired of the fear that drives racism and results in something not right, unjust, wrong, and fucked up happening to one or more of us every day, day in day out, a lot of it unreported in the news media.
Dominique:	We are the Black people from the future.
Durell:	We are the Black people. We are tired.

Tired of knowing you better than you know yourselves.
Tired of being shocked, but never surprised.

Bryant:	We are four Black PhDs who stand as synecdoche for many Black PhDs in higher education.
Mary:	We are tired of living in food deserts, dumps in our neighborhoods, lead paint issues, zero to no recreational possibilities in too many of our communities.
Dominique:	We are Black people ushering in a new day with our dancing, humming, swaying, writing, and loving.
Durell:	We are the Black people, preamble, and postscript
Bryant:	We are the Black people and the rainbow people who stand strong for students who seek us out for support and understanding as they negotiate their own particularity in homogenized spaces.

Mary: We are tired of knowing that white folks who embrace the myth of **colorblindness** never mention that they'd like people "not" to see that they are white.

Dominique: We are the Black people who know our power and choose how, when, and where we want it exercised.

Durell: We the Black People of whenever and wherever we be. "*We are.*" That's the sentence.

★★★★★★

All: We are . . . the Black quartet: singing, dancing, writing, and professing toward the future.

The End.

Notes

1 See Austin, J. L. (1962). *How to do things with words.* Cambridge, MA: Harvard University Press.

2 Denzin, N. K. (2006). "The politics and ethics of performance pedagogy." In D. S. Madison & J. Hamera (Eds.), *The Sage handbook of performance studies.* Thousand Oaks: SAGE, 332.

3 Black Quartet I script appears in the introduction of this volume and was performed at the International Congress of Qualitative Inquiry (ICQI) 2021, serving as the foundational impulse of this volume. Black Quartet II is slated for performance at ICQI 2022.

4 See the Dramatistic Pentad: < https://en.wikipedia.org/wiki/Dramatistic_pentad>.

5 Pollock, D. (1990). "Telling the told: Performing 'Like a family.'" *The Oral History Review,* 18.2, 1–36. www.jstor.org/stable/4495291. Accessed May 30, 2021.

6 See Villenas, S. (2005). "Between the telling and the told: Latina mothers negotiating education in new borderlands." In J. Phillion, M. F. He, & F. M. Connelly (Eds.), *Narrative & experience in multicultural education.* SAGE Publications, Inc., 71–92. www.doi.org/10.4135/9781452204376.n5.